Virginia at War, 1865

VIRGINIA AT WAR 1865

Edited by William C. Davis
and James I. Robertson Jr.
for the Virginia Center for Civil War Studies

THE UNIVERSITY PRESS OF KENTUCKY

Editorial and Sales Offices: The University Press of Kentucky
663 South Limestone Street, Lexington, Kentucky 40508-4008

ISBN 978-0-8131-3468-0

Manufactured in the United States of America.

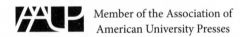 Member of the Association of
American University Presses

Book Club Edition

Contents

Preface

The war had to end eventually, and by the time 1865 dawned, there were few in the Old Dominion who could continue to ignore the stark realities before them that the end was not going to be a happy one for Virginians. After more than three and one-half years of conflict, the state was reeling. Most of northern Virginia was lost to the Yankees, most of the Shenandoah Valley was gone, the far western part of the state was now West Virginia and completely lost, and the Tidewater was largely in enemy hands. For all practical purposes, Confederate Virginia was little more than Richmond and Petersburg, and a scattering of supply depots and bases on the Southside at Danville and Lynchburg. More to the point, by January 1865 Confederate Virginia—like the Confederacy itself—resided chiefly in Robert E. Lee's army.

The state was exhausted. Almost all of its railroad mileage lay in enemy hands or had been torn up. Even though commissary wagons still managed to collect considerable amounts of grain and meat, the government no longer had the ability to deliver it to the places that needed it most. Fields in the Valley were close to exhaustion, while barns and pastures were depopulated as the army swallowed most of the livestock. Communications were all but restricted to courier as most telegraph lines went silent. Most newspapers had ceased publication, and most schools had closed. Business stagnated and currency was inflated to the point of worthlessness. With the rest of the Confederacy in even worse shape, little help was available to alleviate the state's shortages.

Most of all, the exhaustion of the war told on the faces of the people, both soldiers and civilians at home. Children had lost their childhood. Too many parents had lost sons, and too many wives husbands. Three years of relentless bad news from west of the Appalachians sapped the optimism from people who had seen most of the Confederacy's successes on their doorsteps. For the first time desertion became an epidemic problem for Lee's army as thousands of men finally decided that their first loyalty was to their hard-pressed families at home, and others simply lost heart and gave up. Words like *hope* and *victory* had simply faded from their vocabularies, and January 1865 gave little promise of their return.

Indeed, as Chris Calkins demonstrates in his opening essay on the military operations in the state in 1865, there were few, if any, reasons for optimism. General Lee himself almost certainly felt it was futile to continue after the reelection of Abraham Lincoln in November 1864 demonstrated that the North had the will to continue the war another four years if necessary. After a long career with the National Park Service at Petersburg National Battlefield Park, Calkins spearheaded the development of Sailor's Creek Battlefield State Park in Virginia, and in 2009 became its first manager. He is the author of *Thirty-Six Hours Before Appomattox, the only modern history of Sailor's Creek, and also of The Appomattox Campaign, From Petersburg to Appomattox—A Tour Guide to the Routes of Lee's Withdrawal and Grant's Pursuit, April 2-9, 1865,* and *Lee's Retreat: A History and Field Guide.*

Any work on the Confederacy has to confront the ravages to society and family life on the home front, and Virginia suffered more than any other state thanks to its hosting the war on its hearth for four years. Examining the life of women and children on the home front is Ginette Aley, assistant professor of history at Washburn University at Topeka, Kansas. A contributor to the 1864 volume in this series, she specializes in agricultural history.

Jaime Amanda Martinez, who did her doctoral dissertation at the University of North Carolina at Pembroke on the conscription of slaves in the Confederacy, contributes an essay on wartime economy to this volume. At the University of Virginia she worked on the acclaimed Valley of the Shadow digital archive, a path-breaking endeavor comparing the wartime experiences of a Virginia county and a Pennsylvania county.

Though Virginians may not have had much to sing about in 1865, song and music were vital elements in maintaining patriotism and morale during the war for civilians and soldiers alike. E. Lawrence Abel is an authority on Civil War–era music in addition to being a professor of psychology at Wayne State University in Detroit. His book *Singing the New Nation: How Music Shaped the Confederacy, 1861–1865* appeared in 2000 and is still the finest work on the subject.

Appropriately, the story of Danville's few days as capital of the Confederacy is written by a fifth-generation son of Danville, F. Lawrence McFall Jr. He is the author of *Danville in the Civil War* and *The Fortification of Danville,*

Virginia, during the War between the States, 1861–1865. For many years he has been active with the Danville Museum of Fine Arts and History and the Danville Historical Society in studying and preserving the story of the last capital of the Confederacy.

Little or no work has been done for many years on the story of the demobilization of the Civil War armies on either side. Kevin Levin rectifies that omission with his contribution on the demobilization of Lee's army. He has published numerous articles on the Civil War experience in scholarly journals and is the author of a forthcoming book on the battle of the Crater and its role in Civil War memory. He is currently a high school teacher at St. Anne's–Belfield School in Charlottesville.

As Dr. Ervin L. Jordan Jr. ably demonstrates, emancipation and the end of the war offered promise for Virginia's slaves and free blacks, but it was a promise that went mostly unfulfilled for generations. Research archivist at the University of Virginia Library in Charlottesville, Dr. Jordan is the author of the widely acclaimed *Black Confederates and Afro-Yankees in Civil War Virginia,* a groundbreaking work on the black experience during the war, and has written essays dealing with the controversial topic of Negroes serving with the Confederate army.

The final original essay comes from John M. McClure, who earned his master's degree in history from Virginia Commonwealth University and previously managed the reference department in the library of the Virginia Historical Society in Richmond. He has written essays for the *Encyclopedia Virginia, Virginia's Civil War,* and the *Dictionary of Virginia Biography.* He is currently completing doctoral studies at the College of William and Mary.

As was the case with our previous volumes, there is one Virginian we cannot thank in person. Judith Brockenbrough McGuire kept her diary faithfully through both the best and the worst of the wartime experience, and the final portion is presented here, edited as before by James I. Robertson Jr., whose extensive annotations illuminate the diary and make it even more useful to general readers and scholars alike. We have broken up the diary into relatively equal segments in these five volumes, meaning that the chronology does not always match the year in the volume's title. Here we present her entries from August 1864 to May 1865.

As throughout this series of books, *Virginia at War, 1865* is deeply indebted to the generosity of the William E. Jamerson family of Appomattox for sustained and generous support of this series. The Virginia Center for

Civil War Studies has had no finer friends in its twelve-year history to date. This volume's appearance in 2012 is a fitting close to the series, coming as it does during the sesquicentennial of the Civil War. Virginia has been a leader whose commemoration to date has served as a template for the efforts of other states and offering eloquent testimony to the continuing interest and stewardship of Virginians like the Jamersons, who embrace their past. We must also thank the University Press of Kentucky for its years-long commitment to this project, from director Stephen M. Wrinn to editors Ann Malcolm and Ila McEntire. It has been a great pleasure to work with them.

Virginia at War, 1865

Land Operations in Virginia in 1865

Time Catches Up with Lee at Last

Chris Calkins

In Richmond on January 16, by a vote of 14–2, the Confederate Senate passed a resolution that Gen. Robert E. Lee should be appointed general in chief of the armies of the Confederacy and Gen. P. G. T. Beauregard should command the army in South Carolina, Georgia, and Florida, while Gen. Joseph E. Johnston returned to command of the Army of Tennessee. On February 6 Lee assumed the duties of his new position but remarked that even with the expansion of his authority, "I do not think I could accomplish any good," adding, "If I had the ability I would not have the time."[1]

It became more apparent that Jefferson Davis must do something to buy a little time, and on January 28 he agreed to send three commissioners to hold informal talks about an armistice with Federal authorities. He chose Vice President Alexander Stephens, former Confederate secretary of state R. M. T. Hunter of Virginia, and assistant secretary of war and former U.S. Supreme Court justice John A. Campbell. The commissioners passed through military lines near the Crater battlefield at Petersburg and then went on to City Point and by vessel to Fort Monroe at Hampton Roads to meet with Abraham Lincoln. President Lincoln had already discussed with Gen. U. S. Grant his forthcoming meeting at the fort, concluding, "Let nothing which is transpiring, change, hinder, or delay your military movements, or plans."[2] Already, on January 6, Grant had removed Maj. Gen. Benjamin Butler from command of the Army of the James, replacing him with Maj. Gen. Edward O. C. Ord, and Grant intended to lose no time in pressing Lee on all fronts with Ord's army and Maj. Gen. George G. Meade's Army of the Potomac.

Lincoln left Washington on February 2 with Secretary of State William H. Seward aboard the *River Queen,* bound for Hampton Roads. Meeting with

1

Davis's emissaries, he affirmed foremost "that the national authority of the United States must be recognized."[3] They discussed an armistice, but found it impossible to agree to one before the reestablishment of the United States. Concerning the question of reconstruction, Lincoln told the Confederate commissioners that their armies must be disbanded first and national authority resumed before anything else could be discussed. Therefore, it was a standoff between Lincoln's insistence on restoration of the Union and Davis's demand to negotiate terms between two independent nations.[4] In such a situation, compromise was impossible, and a final solution would have to be left to the armies in the field.

The initiative was always with Grant, for Lee, penned up in the Richmond-Petersburg fortifications, could not move without risk to the capital. Generally the armies did not actively campaign during the winter months but Grant, wanting to keep unrelenting pressure on Lee's army, broke with common practice and sent his troops out of their winter quarters on the siege lines on February 5 to launch an offensive movement, despite the winter of 1864–1865 being what many regarded as "one of unusual severity."[5] The objective was for Federal cavalry under Maj. Gen. David McM. Gregg to ride to the Boydton Plank Road near Dinwiddie Court House and attempt to intercept a line of supply trains known to be on their way to Lee's army. Elements of Maj. Gen. A. A. Humphreys's II Corps and G. K. Warren's V Corps would support the operation. As the two Union corps moved out toward Hatcher's Run, Humphreys established a bridgehead on the north side of the stream facing the main Confederate defenses that extended as far south as the run. During the day Southern forces under Lt. Gen. John B. Gordon and Maj. Gen. Henry Heth both unsuccessfully assailed Humphreys's position.

The next day, with the V Corps now south of Hatcher's Run, Gordon moved his Second Corps, supported by Confederate cavalry under Maj. Gen. W. H. F. Lee, against two thrusts made by Gregg's cavalry and two of Warren's division commanders, major generals Samuel Crawford and Romeyn B. Ayres. The Rebels repulsed the Federal push, but at the cost of Brig. Gen. John Pegram, killed near a local landmark known as Dabney's Steam Sawmill. Fighting on the following day was relatively minor, with the Federals unsuccessfully attempting one more push. A Confederate remembered the three-day action as "preliminary skirmishing on the 5th, sanguinary action on the 6th, followed up by the enemy feebly on the 7th." However, a Union soldier thought the operation important. "It put our army in a position to attack the Southside railroad and cut off the avenue of Rebel supplies when we pleased," he wrote, "and at the same time it opened up to us an ample supply of fuel which had become scarce." It also put the Yankees about three miles closer to Richmond.[6]

Lee, reading Grant's intent in the Hatcher's Run movement, warned Secretary of War John Breckinridge on February 21, "Grant, I think, is now preparing to draw out his left, with the intent of enveloping me. He may wait till his other columns approach nearer [meaning Maj. Gen. Philip H. Sheridan's cavalry] or he may be preparing to anticipate my withdrawal. I cannot tell yet. I am endeavoring to collect supplies convenient to Burkeville [Junction]." The same day he communicated with his First Corps commander, Lt. Gen. James Longstreet:

> With the army concentrated at or near Burkeville, our communications north and south would be by that railroad [Richmond & Danville] and west by the Southside Railroad. We might also seize the opportunity of striking at Grant, should he pursue us rapidly, or Sherman, before they could unite. . . . I desire you also to make every preparation to take the field at a moment's notice, and to accumulate all the supplies you can. General Grant seems to be preparing to move out by his left flank. He is accumulating near Hatcher's Run depots of supplies, and apparently concentrating a strong course in that quarter.[7]

By this time operations in the Shenandoah Valley were all but over, as the last soldiers of Lt. Gen. Jubal A. Early's beaten Army of the Valley moved out of their scattered winter camps. Sheridan's Federal cavalry expedition skirmished with Early from Winchester up to Staunton, finally pressing Early across the mountains toward Charlottesville. At this point the Confederate commander had only two remnants of brigades of infantry, under Brig. Gen. Gabriel Wharton, and Maj. Gen. Tom Rosser's cavalry with which to make a stand in the village of Waynesboro on March 2. Attacked by Maj. Gen. George A. Custer's division of Union horsemen, the remainder of Early's army all but evaporated, though Early and Wharton managed to escape, as did Rosser, who headed back for the Valley.[8] Upon hearing of the disaster, Lee relieved Early of his command, while Sheridan, after resting his command in Charlottesville for a couple of days, put his troopers on the road to

Grant's army around Petersburg. At first he planned to move on Lynchburg but, finding it heavily fortified, then decided to press on as far as Amherst Court House, with Custer tearing up the Orange & Alexandria Railroad track while Brig. Gen. Thomas Devin marched along the James River, destroying locks, dams, and boats. By March 8 Sheridan's cavalry reached White House Landing on the Pamunkey River, close enough now to cooperate with Grant against Lee.

A week later, on March 14, General Lee wrote to President Davis: "The greatest calamity that can befall us is the destruction of our armies. If they can be maintained, we may recover from our reverses, but if lost we have no resource."[9] Fearing the worst, Lee realized that somehow he must take the offensive with a bold but desperate plan if he were to stop Grant's inexorable encirclement. After Lee conferred with his Second Corps commander, John B. Gordon, they scouted the Federal line east of Petersburg for a possible target for penetration by a Confederate assault. They chose the area between Union Fort Stedman and Colquitt's Salient along the Southern defenses, where just 150 yards separated the opposing picket lines.

Lee planned to attack the Union line east of Petersburg, hoping that a successful breakthrough would result in that line of defense being evacuated, giving him an opening to press on into Grant's rear. With this advantage, he hoped to cut the United States Military Railroad supply route near Meade's Station and possibly allow Confederate cavalry to ride on to Grant's logistic and supply base at City Point to disrupt communications there. Such a movement might cause the Federals to withdraw troops from the lines west of Petersburg to stem the assault, allowing Lee to shorten his own lines in that sector and possibly send troops farther south to reinforce Johnston's army in North Carolina, where he faced the armies of Maj. Gen. William T. Sherman. It was an enormous gamble with little hope for success, but by now Lee's desperate situation called for desperate risks.

Lee set March 25 for the predawn attack on Fort Stedman and the adjoining batteries. Initially Gordon surprised and took the fort and its surroundings, but his assault soon stalled as defenders on either side of the breakthrough rushed in to stem the attack. By noon the operation was over, leaving Lee with more than 1,500 casualties for his effort. Later that afternoon, thinking that Lee might have weakened his line on Hatcher's Run to build up Gordon's attack, Grant ordered the II and V Corps to make an attack west of the city. Though the counterattack failed, the VI Corps captured a section of the Confederate picket line near Union Fort Fisher, which put the Federals much closer to the main Southern line than they had been before.[10] That gave Grant a position from which to launch what he hoped would be the final push for Richmond, Petersburg, and Lee's army.

General Lee now wrote to his daughter that "General Grant is evidently preparing for something & is marshalling & preparing his troops for some movement, which is not yet disclosed." At the same time he informed President Davis that "I fear now it will be impossible to prevent a junction between Grant and Sherman, nor do I deem it prudent that this army should maintain its position until the latter shall approach too near."[11] In the meantime, Sheridan's cavalry now arrived on the Petersburg front and circled around to the west of the city. Some 50,000 men of the II Corps and V Corps as well as the cavalry corps worked in conjunction with Sheridan's movement, their objective to cut Lee's final supply routes via the Boydton Plank Road and the South Side Railroad.

The first day of what was to become known as the Appomattox campaign began on March 29 as the V Corps moved up the Quaker Road and encountered Confederate forces around the Lewis farm. These proved to be elements of Lt. Gen. Richard H. Anderson's small Fourth Corps, comprised of only Maj. Gen. Bushrod R. Johnson's division, which held the trenches along nearby White Oak Road. By that evening, Johnson's troops had been forced back into their defenses, and the V Corps held a foothold across the Boydton Plank Road. While both armies jockeyed for positions on the 30th, the next day Sheridan's cavalry reached Dinwiddie Court House as Warren's corps pressed against the White Oak Road trenches.

At this point in the Federal advance, the main objective was a local road intersection known as Five Forks, one of whose roadways led directly to the South Side Railroad. Lee realized the importance of controlling this junction and sent division commander Maj. Gen. George E. Pickett to defend it. Upon reaching Five Forks, Pickett decided to move southward to attempt to stop Sheridan just north of Dinwiddie Court House. While he gained a tactical victory over the Federals when he temporarily stopped Sheridan on the 31st, Pickett was eventually forced to withdraw from the field when elements of Warren's corps, after fighting all day to gain possession of White Oak Road, moved upon Pickett's left and rear, thus threatening his position. Lee immediately admonished him to "hold Five Forks at all hazards."[12] Pickett must prevent Union forces from striking the South Side Railroad.

By the morning of April 1, Pickett had his men dig in along the White Oak Road at the Five Forks intersection, spreading out along a mile and three-quarters front. There they waited until around 4:15 in the afternoon, when Sheridan's cavalry attacked along the Confederate front while Warren's corps swung around and hit Pickett's exposed left flank, virtually rolling up the Confederate line. By nightfall Five Forks was in Federal hands. A Southern general later remarked that this battle was the "Waterloo of the Confederacy."[13]

When Grant heard of this victory at his field headquarters near Dabney's Mill, he gave instructions for an all-out assault upon the Confederate lines defending Petersburg. Two Union corps would make the initial attacks. The IX Corps, under Maj. Gen. John Parke, would move up the Jerusalem Plank Road and assail the Confederate works surrounding Fort Mahone. At the same time, Maj. Gen. Horatio Wright's VI Corps would storm the Hatcher's Run line protecting the Boydton Plank Road. As they could use their previously won position along the old Confederate picket line and had half the ground to cover, their attack was swift and complete. Lee's defenses southwest of Petersburg were literally cut in half. Shortly thereafter, Lt. Gen. A. P. Hill, while riding to the front, was killed by a Union skirmisher. As the VI Corps swept down the pierced Confederate line to Hatcher's Run, a portion of General Ord's Army of the James, which had previously moved down from Richmond, passed through the captured lines and swung around to take the city from the west.

They ran into two outposts, Forts Gregg and Whitworth. The garrisons of these earthen works had been previously told by General Lee to hold at all costs until reinforcements could arrive from Richmond. These proved to be a division under Maj. Gen. Charles W. Field, which took its position within the inner defenses protecting the western environs of Petersburg. The Army of the James XXIV Corps, commanded by Maj. Gen. John Gibbon, began its assault on the two forts, centering on Fort Gregg. After some of the most desperate fighting to be seen in these final days of the war, sometimes referred to as a "Homeric Defense," the Confederate command finally surrendered after suffering tremendous casualties.[14] The Federals pressed no further against the city this day. About six to eight miles farther to the west from Petersburg, at Sutherland Tavern, a division of Union infantry of the II Corps under Brig. Gen. Nelson Miles assailed a Confederate force defending the nearby South Side Railroad. After three attempts to break the line, the

Southerners finally gave ground and the Federals severed Lee's last supply line. That night the Confederate commander gave the orders for Richmond and Petersburg to be evacuated.

By 11:00 p.m. President Davis and most of the cabinet departed on a special train headed for Danville. Richmond itself began the evacuation. Government records were sent away or burned. Cotton, tobacco, and military stores were set afire, and soon the fire raged out of control. Businesses, factories, residences, and hotels would soon be victims of the ensuing conflagration. Soon loud explosions were heard to the southeast as the James River Squadron was blown up. That evening Lee gave orders for Petersburg to be abandoned. His point of concentration would be about thirty miles west of both cities at Amelia Court House along the Richmond & Danville Railroad. Here, it was reported, would be supplies awaiting his army. At this point, Lee hoped to replenish his men with rations as he continued his movement to Danville, where he hoped he could link with General Johnston's army, then being pursued by Maj. Gen. William T. Sherman in North Carolina.

As the Confederate army began its retreat, four major columns withdrew from the Richmond-Petersburg front. Lt. Gen. Richard S. Ewell's troops departed from Richmond after crossing the James River. Maj. Gen. William Mahone's division pulled out of the Howlett Line in Bermuda Hundred (between Richmond and Petersburg) while passing through Chesterfield Court House. Lt. Gen. James Longstreet, now commanding both his First Corps and A. P. Hill's Third Corps, passed over to the north side of the Appomattox River near the village of Ettrick, eventually having to recross it farther up the road. Gordon's Second Corps generally followed Longstreet's on routes north of the river. South of the river, remnants of Hill's corps, the Confederate cavalry, and Anderson's Corps soon found themselves pursued by the Federal army.

While three of the four columns moved relatively unscathed in their journey to Amelia, the last one's rearguard would be in almost constant contact with the enemy. On April 3 Confederate cavalry under Brig. Gen. Rufus Barringer made a stand at Namozine Church, only to be overrun by General Custer's troops. Later Barringer would be captured and sent back to City Point, where he would dine with President Lincoln. Meanwhile, Union cavalry, determining that Lee and his army were headed for Amelia, swung around to the south and west of the county seat village, reaching Jetersville along the Richmond & Danville Railroad. Here Sheridan's cavalry, supported by the V Corps, began entrenching across Lee's intended path of retreat.

Back in Amelia, as his troops began arriving for the supposedly waiting subsistence, they found empty boxcars at the station. In desperation, Lee issued a proclamation to the local inhabitants to provide any surplus food items they might have, but to no avail. The extra day spent in awaiting supplies and the arrival of the balance of his army eventually proved disastrous, as he lost the one-day lead he had over Grant. Lee later wrote to Jefferson Davis that "this delay was fatal and could not be retrieved."[15]

Meanwhile, down at Jetersville, the II and VI Corps now arrived on the scene and began digging in. On the afternoon of April 5 Lee sent his scouts forward only to find the Federals entrenched across his path. Rather than attempt to break through their defenses, he decided to make a night march around and to the north of the Army of the Potomac. For the time being, Lee would have to make a detour to his original plans. He would now head due west to Farmville where, he was informed, another shipment of rations awaited his men. From that point he could then strike south to Keysville and regain his path along the Richmond & Danville Railroad and continue with his journey to Danville.

While the Confederate column began to follow this change in plans, Union cavalry members went out on a reconnaissance heading north from Jetersville. Reaching a crossroads village known as Painesville, they encountered a wagon train sent from Richmond with supplies for Maj. Gen. G. W. C. Lee's division. Overtaking it, they soon destroyed the wagons, capturing its guard along with some artillery. Shortly thereafter Confederate cavalry arrived on the scene and began a running engagement back to Amelia Springs near the Federal left flank. Under cover of darkness the main Southern column continued to move undetected around Grant's.[16]

In the early morning hours of April 6 members of the Union II Corps awoke and realized that the Confederate army was passing around their flank and spread out along a single road. Setting out in pursuit, they soon encountered the rearguard under General Gordon. Leading the march to Farmville was Longstreet's combined First-Third Corps accompanied by General Lee and its wagon trains, then Anderson's Corps (Bushrod Johnson and George Pickett), Ewell's Reserve Corps, the main army wagon train and, bringing up the rear, Gordon's Corps. As Humphreys's II Corps skirmished with Gordon, the latter made a determined stand at a crossroads called Deatonsville until finally swept away.

In the meantime, Sheridan's cavalry and Horatio Wright's VI Corps followed the Confederate line of march on parallel roads, waiting for the chance to carry on hit-and-run tactics whenever they could. Closer to Farmville, where the South Side Railroad crossed the Appomattox River, sat a large structure known as High Bridge. Built in 1853, it was 2,400–2,500 feet long and 126 feet high, built on twenty-one brick piers over the river valley. The railroad crossed over the bridge to the north side of the river then returned to the South Side at Farmville, four miles away. Below High Bridge stood a small wagon bridge over the 75-foot-wide river. Back at Burkeville Junction, now in the possession of Ord's Army of the James, it became apparent that Lee' army would try to use the bridge as an avenue of escape. To thwart this, Ord sent out three companies of the Fourth Massachusetts Cavalry, along with two infantry regiments, the Fifty-fourth Pennsylvania and 123d Ohio, to destroy the structure before Lee's column arrived at Rice's Depot.

Sometime during the morning Longstreet received news of this bridge-burning party and sent Maj. Gen. Fitzhugh Lee's cavalry after it. Word also filtered back to Ord about this situation and he sent his assistant adjutant general, Brig. Gen. Theodore Read, to warn those on the mission. Just as he arrived so did Fitz Lee's cavalry. First Union and Confederate horsemen clashed, with heavy casualties. Confederate brigadier general James Dearing was mortally wounded and General Read killed outright. The Southerners then pressed on, eventually capturing the two infantry regiments. For the time being the bridge was saved for Lee's men to escape across.

As the afternoon wore on, Lee, along with Longstreet at Rice's Depot, wondered why the rest of his army had not come along. Returning down the road he had come, he saw his men in retreat across Big Sailor's Creek. Astonished, he remarked, "My God! Has the army dissolved?"[17] What Lee did not know was the extent of the calamity that had fallen upon his troops this day. The battle of Little Sailor's Creek was actually three separate engagements fought in the vicinity of the creek. One was along the creek itself between Ewell's Corps and Wright's VI Corps, fought on what was known as the Hillsman farm. The second, between Sheridan's cavalry and Anderson's Corps, occurred a mile farther on at Marshall's Crossroads. The third, two miles north along the creek at the double bridge crossing, was the final rear-guard action of the day between Gordon and Humphreys at Lockett's farm. Among all these engagements Lee lost close to one-quarter of his effective force, with a casualty figure of 7,700 men including eight generals captured.[18]

Once again Lee decided to proceed with a night march, and his men headed for Farmville, a town of 1,500 inhabitants. Some crossed High Bridge (it also had a pedestrian walkway along the tracks) while others used the lower wagon bridge. To the south the remainder of the army took the direct road into town. Arriving early the next morning, those lucky enough to reach the freight depot of the South Side Railroad found rations awaiting them and began their distribution. Nonetheless, quickly pursuing Union cavalry rode into Farmville from the east, forcing the Confederates to close up the trains and send them farther west. Now Lee faced a dilemma. With Grant's forces swinging around to the south of town, his avenue to Keysville was closed off. If he could burn all the bridges over the Appomattox River before the Federals got there, he could possibly open a gap between his army and Grant's. With orders to destroy the crossings, the Confederate engineers went to their tasks, successfully burning the two bridges at Farmville and firing High Bridge and the wagon bridge four miles downriver. However, members of Humphreys's II Corps reached High Bridge and extinguished the fire at the lower wagon bridge, allowing them to cross the Appomattox and threaten Lee's army north of the river.

At this point Lee made the decision to send his men westward to their next destination at Appomattox Station on the South Side Railroad. Supplies had been ordered there beforehand and possibly he could reach them before Grant's men did. Unfortunately, as a staff member pointed out to Lee, by following the road north of the river, it was approximately thirty-eight miles to the station. Had he stayed south of the river, it would have been only thirty. In short, the Federals south of the stream had the shorter roadway. But it was too late to make any changes.

To the north of Farmville, around Cumberland Church, Lee's men were forced to protect their wagon train from the advancing Federal troops coming from High Bridge. The Confederates successfully warded off numerous attacks, and by nightfall they began their third night march in a row as they headed to Appomattox Station. That evening the first communication between Grant and Lee took place, with the former bringing up the possibility of surrender. Lee handed the note to Longstreet, who replied, "Not yet."

April 8 was a day of relative calm for both armies. Longstreet and Gordon switched their positions in the column (Gordon in the lead, Longstreet now the rearguard) while being pursued by the Federal II and VI Corps north of the river. South of the Appomattox, Sheridan's cavalry, followed by the Army of the James and the V Corps, moved to get within reach of the station first since scouts made them aware of the trains waiting at Appomattox Station. As the day came to a close, Lee's column reached the village of Appomattox Court House just three miles from the Appomattox Station. Leading the line of march was his surplus artillery and wagon train, commanded by Gen. Reuben L. Walker, who went into camp about a mile from the station. Soon the sound of gunfire was heard down by the waiting trains at the station, signaling that General Custer's cavalry had reached them first and captured the Confederate's supplies. The Federals then turned toward the county seat village and ran into Walker's encampment. After a brief engagement, Walker's men were scattered and the Federal cavalry pushed forward to the high ground overlooking Appomattox. They were now directly across Lee's avenue of escape toward Lynchburg.

Realizing he was being pressed in his rear by the II and VI Corps, the Confederate commander decided on the early morning of April 9 that he would use Gordon's infantry and Fitzhugh Lee's cavalry in an attempt to break through the Federal roadblock. After first successfully pushing back Sheridan's cavalry, the Confederates saw Ord's Army of the James blocking their path of retreat. Realizing his situation, Lee sent out flags of truce while dispatches were conveyed to General Grant requesting a meeting to discuss terms of surrender.

While one of Lee's officers procured a site in Appomattox Court House for the conference, Grant and his staff rode from the rear of his army cross-country to reach the village. At about 1:30 p.m. they arrived and were instructed to go to the home of Wilmer McLean. Upon entering the house, the two opposing commanders faced each other—not now to fight again but to make a peace. After brief introductions, the two generals sat down as Grant wrote out his terms:

1. Officers and men would be paroled and agree not to take up arms against the government of the United States until properly exchanged.
2. The arms, artillery, and public property were to be parked and stacked, and turned over to the appointed officers.
3. The men were allowed to keep their private horses and baggage while the officers could retain their swords and sidearms.
4. Free government transportation home (where available) would be provided to paroled prisoners.

Both generals signed their respective documents and, on this Palm Sunday virtually the only fighting in Virginia in 1865 came to an end.[19]

Notes

1. In his new role Lee proposed a pardon to deserters who reported for duty within thirty days. After the fall of Wilmington, Gen. Joseph E. Johnston was restored to command the Department of South Carolina, Georgia, and Florida (because Lee was not certain of General Beauregard's health), and the Department of Tennessee and Georgia on February 25. Christopher Calkins, "The Final Months of the Civil War in Virginia, January–April 1865" (speech, Smithsonian Institution Civil War Series, n.d.), located in the research files of Sailor's Creek Battlefield Historical State Park.

2. Ibid.

3. Ibid.

4. For discussions of the Hampton Roads Conference, see Alexander H. Stephens, *Recollections of Alexander H. Stephens*, ed. Myrta Lockett Avary (New York: Doubleday, 1910); Jefferson Davis, *The Rise and Fall of the Confederate Government* (New York: Appleton, 1881), 2; William C. Davis, *Jefferson Davis: The Man and His Hour* (New York: HarperCollins, 1991); Bruce Catton, *Never Call Retreat* (New York: Doubleday, 1965); Sidney W. Thaxter, "The Peace Conference of 1865," in *War Papers Read Before the Commandery of the State of Maine, Military Order of the Loyal Legion of the United States* (Portland, Maine: Lefavor-Tower, 1902), 3:201–19; R. M. T. Hunter, "The Peace Commission of 1865," *Southern Historical Society Papers* 3 (April 1877): 168–76.

5. Calkins, "The Final Months of the Civil War in Virginia."

6. The Battle of Hatcher's Run, also known as Armstrong's Mill or Dabney's Mill, amounted to 171 killed, 1,181 wounded, and 187 missing for the Federal side; Confederate losses are estimated at 1,000. For a study on this battle, with maps, see Christopher M. Calkins, *History and Tour Guide of Five Forks, Hatcher's Run and Namozine Church* (Columbus, Ohio: Blue and Gray, 2005), 8–28.

7. For full texts, see *The Wartime Papers of Robert E. Lee*, ed. Clifford Dowdey (New York: Da Capo, 1987), 906–9.

8. Along with Early and Wharton, Gen. Robert D. Lilley also escaped, with about fifteen or twenty men, across the Blue Ridge. Sheridan's cavalry claimed that at Waynesboro they captured seventeen battle flags, 1,600 officers and men, and eleven pieces of artillery. See P. H. Sheridan, *Personal Memoirs of P. H. Sheridan* (New York: Charles L. Webster, 1888), 2:115–23.

9. Douglas Southall Freeman, ed., *Lee's Dispatches: Unpublished Letters of*

General Robert E. Lee, C.S.A., to Jefferson Davis and the War Department of the Confederate States of America, 1862–65 (New York: G. P. Putnam's Sons, 1915); Dowdey, *Wartime Papers.*

10. For various accounts of the battle of Fort Stedman, see Douglas Southall Freeman, *R. E. Lee: A Biography,* vol. 4 (New York: Scribner's, 1935); John B. Gordon, *Reminiscences of the Civil War* (New York: Scribner's, 1903); A. Wilson Greene, *Breaking the Backbone of the Rebellion—The Final Battles of the Petersburg Campaign* (Mason City, Iowa: Savas, 2000); William H. Hodgkins, *Battle of Fort Stedman, March 25, 1865* (Boston: Privately published, 1889).

11. Calkins, "The Final Months of the Civil War in Virginia."

12. Ibid.

13. U.S. War Department, *War of the Rebellion: A Compilation of the Official Records of the Union and Confederate Armies* (Washington, D.C.: Government Printing Office, 1880–1901), series 1, vol. 46, pt. 1 (hereafter cited as *OR*; all references are to series 1 unless otherwise noted). See also Edwin Bearss and Christopher M. Calkins, *Battle of Five Forks* (Lynchburg, Va.: H. E. Howard, 1985); Calkins, *Five Forks, Hatcher's Run and Namozine Church*; Christopher M. Calkins, *The Appomattox Campaign* (New York: Da Capo, 2001); F. C. Newhall, *With General Sheridan in Lee's Last Campaign* (Philadelphia: Lippincott, 1866); Burke Davis, *To Appomattox: Nine April Days, 1865* (New York: Rinehart, 1959); Henry Edwin Tremain, *Last Hours of Sheridan's Cavalry* (New York: Bonnell, Silvers and Bowers, 1904); Philip Van Doren Stern, *An End to Valor: The Last Days of the Civil War* (Boston: Houghton Mifflin, 1958).

14. Calkins, "The Final Months of the Civil War in Virginia."

15. *OR,* vol. 46, pt. 1, 1265–67. For the most plausible explanation as to what happened to the supplies, see Freeman, *R. E. Lee,* 4, appendix 4, p. 2. See also Douglas Southall Freeman, *Lee's Lieutenants: A Study in Command* (New York: Scribner's, 1946), 3. For a current and controversial interpretation of the final campaign, see William Marvel, *Lee's Last Retreat: The Flight to Appomattox* (Chapel Hill: University of North Carolina Press, 2006).

16. For a brief description of events transpiring during the Appomattox campaign, along with the marking of all routes followed by the armies, refer to Christopher M. Calkins, *From Petersburg to Appomattox—A Tour Guide to the Routes of Lee's Withdrawal and Grant's Pursuit, April 2–9, 1865* (Farmville, Va.: Farmville Herald, 1983).

17. Calkins, "The Final Months of the Civil War in Virginia."

18. For varying accounts of the battle of (Little) Sailor's Creek, which is the correct contemporary spelling, see Greg Eanes, *Black Day of the Army, April 6, 1865: The Battles of Sailor's Creek* (Burkeville, Va.: E and H, 2001); Derek Smith,

Lee's Last Stand: Sailor's Creek Virginia, 1865 (Shippensburg, Pa.: White Mane, 2002); Christopher M. Calkins, *Thirty-six Hours Before Appomattox: The Battles of Sailor's Creek, High Bridge, Farmville and Cumberland Church* (Farmville, Va.: Farmville Herald, 1980). The eight generals were Richard S. Ewell, G. W. C. Lee, Seth Barton, James Simms, Joseph Kershaw, Dudley Dubose, Eppa Hunton, and Montgomery Corse. Earlier in the day, the newly appointed (March 28, 1865) general of the Florida Brigade, Theodore Brevard, was captured near Sailor's Creek.

19. For a detailed account of the final battles around Appomattox, see Christopher M. Calkins, *The Battles of Appomattox Station and Appomattox Court House, April 8–9, 1865* (Lynchburg, Va.: H. E. Howard, 1987). For details of the meeting between Lee and Grant and events leading up to the surrender, see Frank P. Cauble, *The Proceedings Connected with the Surrender of the Army of Northern Virginia, April 1865* (Lynchburg, Va.: H. E. Howard, 1987).

"Uncertainties and alarms"

Women and Families on Virginia's Home Front

Ginette Aley

De war comes ter de great house an' ter de slave cabins jist alike.
—Former North Carolina slave woman

As he had done with so much constancy and concern throughout the war, twenty-five-year-old Confederate officer and now prisoner of war Green Berry Samuels took up his pen on March 7, 1865, to resume his connection to his wife, Kathleen, and the family hearth. He had been captured, an experience shared by more than one-quarter of all Virginia soldiers. Samuels was hopeful of a speedy exchange. In the meantime, the dullness of prison life afforded him little respite from thoughts and worries about home. In truth, he wrote Kathleen, "I sometimes foolishly make myself miserable by imagining all sorts of misfortunes befalling you." Samuels's earlier letters reveal this ongoing awareness of the frequent and threatening merging of Virginia's home front and battle maneuverings. His February 1864 letter to Kathleen at their Front Royal home, for example, expressed his fear that Gen. Jubal Early's recent raiding in the Valley might "bring the enemy down upon you again." He was troubled by the "helpless condition at home." The war had been hard on his young bride, who was now in 1865 mother to their toddler, Lucy. Samuels knew his wife's situation had been trying, "living as you do in the midst of uncertainties and alarms, deprived of many things once so essential to your comfort." This was an observation that easily could have been applied to homes and families, white and black, across the Virginia home front. About three months later, in June 1865, weakened and discouraged by lack of food but still hopeful of a speedy release now that the war was over, Samuels doubted that "the Govmt will keep much longer this large body of men from their needy families."[1]

By this time, Kathleen—like countless Virginia women—was weary of war, deprivation, sacrifice, and fear. "I have become so used to trials," she wrote back, "I feel that I can endure any thing now but final separation from you." She was impatient to have her husband home. The daily appearance of former soldiers and prisoners passing through on their way to rejoin their families was frustrating because Green was still not among them. She came to believe that her husband might be refusing to take the requisite oath of allegiance to the U.S. government, thus hindering his release. She scolded him: "You can do our unhappy country no good by lying in prison and now I think you owe your life to your family at home." It was time to leave the war behind and look forward: "The soldiers have all come home and gone to work." Kathleen urged Green, "Consider this matter well my dear husband." In reality, the releasing of prisoners was not that simple, as he had explained to her, but she appears not to have received his letters in which he pledged to be seeking all avenues to come home. He assured her that he was not being "witheld by a false sense of honor from returning to your support." Honor and duty were home with her and Lucy, and shortly thereafter he was discharged.[2]

The Samuels family members were among the fortunate ones who had their family circle restored after the war. Many of their kin and neighbors could not say the same, nor could many of their fellow Virginians, as the Samuels's and so many other Civil War–era letters attest. The war and the state's strategic location for military operations, Union and Confederate, imposed a serious crisis upon Virginia families and communities, regardless of race and class. Communal, racial, and family dynamics changed further in light of men's prolonged (frequently permanent) absences from homes and communities, the new orientation of women's domestic circumstances, the Union's shift in 1863 to a "hard-war" policy, the resulting destruction of much of the economic and the domestic infrastructure (for example, barns and outbuildings, homes, mills, churches, transportation), desperate shortages, especially of food, and the disruptive Yankee presence that, for black Virginians, inspired both a hope for freedom from slavery behind Union lines and fear of being forcibly taken away from family when labeled as "contraband." Along with deprivation, a war-imposed separation from loved ones and altered or broken family circles represent the most common wartime experience in Virginia. The Civil War was felt first and most profoundly in the home. From this perspective, home front women and families shouldered a tremendous burden, and the war affected and inspired them in numerous ways. Yet it can also be said that wherever possible the familiar rhythms of the family life cycle went on, even if altered by war.[3]

It is well established that enlisted men initially believed that the war would be of short duration and that the separation from families and home would be brief. Green Samuels characterized the war as simply an interruption to the rest of their lives in letters to Kathleen. As the war went on, though, these assertions rang hollow and were less convincing. The Samuels letters are significant because they also include the period of the couple's courtship as they planned to marry despite the inevitable approach of war and the difficulties they would endure as a result. Kathleen and Green had both enjoyed a privileged Old South upbringing. Kathleen was born in 1842 to Abraham Rockingham Van Nort and Eliza Ann Boone Van Nort. The Van Norts were a prominent Shenandoah Valley family who employed three generations of slaves on their place. Kathleen recalled later in life the deep impression that her grandparents' world made upon her of the interdependence of white and black lives. Noting the discussions provoked by the publication of *Uncle Tom's Cabin,* she explained that there was little that the slaves (called servants by Kathleen) "did not get an inkling of sooner or later for they were part and parcel of our lives from the time we were born until we died." And since all were raised to be industrious, the footsteps one heard throughout the day were as likely to belong to a white person as a servant. They even shared the family cemetery. Clearly, though, slave labor served the Van Norts and the Boones, and the power dynamic was resolute. It is also interesting that proper Virginia women did not involve themselves in certain kinds of labor, as is apparent from Kathleen's remarks when, during a rail trip between Dayton, Ohio, and Indianapolis, Indiana, visiting relatives as a teen, she observed to her apparent surprise white Northern women toiling in the fields. "That was a sight to me," she said.[4]

It certainly would have appeared strange to Kathleen given that her adolescence had less to do with labor and more with visiting, parties and balls, dancing, music lessons, the pursuit of fashion trends, even chivalric tournaments. When she was sixteen her father sent her to Alexander Powell's Boarding School in Winchester and later to the Woodstock Female Academy. Kathleen's family and educational background made her and Green well suited for each other on several levels. Green was born in 1839 in Woodstock to Judge Green Berry Samuels and Maria Gore Coffman Samuels, both from well-established Valley of Virginia families. In fact, upon the death of the elder Samuels in 1859—he had been a member of Congress, U.S. Circuit Court judge, and a justice of the Supreme Court of Appeals of Virginia—Governor Henry A. Wise is said to have asked that his body be brought to the Senate Chamber out of respect until family members could come to take it back to Woodstock. As with the Van Norts and the Boones, the Samuels were likewise intimately involved with slavery and accustomed to servants. Young Green was a law student at the University of Virginia when his father died. He completed his studies and was just beginning to practice law in Woodstock when the war broke out. The exact circumstances under which Kathleen and Green met are unclear, except that it is known they met during the fall of 1860 and were secretly engaged by December 5.[5]

Their courtship letters reflect a tacit acknowledgment of the companionate marriage ideal with their expressions of deep affection, the centrality of making each other happy, and references to their expected family roles. Shortly after their engagement, Green wrote, "I can scarcely realize the thought that you have promised to *love* me *through life,* to share my joys and to partake of my sorrows." By the end of March 1861, they had made their engagement public. The next month, April, they were making wedding plans, but war news had now intruded upon them, imposing the first serious challenge the two faced as a couple. Green told Kathleen that he would be unworthy of her love if he did not heed "the voice of honour," yet his youthful optimism prevailed in his hope that "the dangers that now threaten our unhappy country may soon disappear and the sunshine of peace smile again on this land." He concluded by asking her to look for him on Wednesday and to "have your *sweet mouth* prepared for a *dozen kisses.*" Green and Kathleen could not fail to connect the symbolism behind talk of dissolving the Union with their own marital union: "Though the *disunion* of these States may be Eternal, I hope *our Union* may be forever." For much of the remainder of their engagement, Green mostly addressed his letters to Kathleen as "Dear Sister" or left the salutation blank. This, he said, was to protect their privacy since he lived in such close quarters in the military. While his letters are articulate about a range of topics, especially military life, he lamented his inadequacy in expressing his love as Kathleen could. "A man cannot write a *love letter*[;] his nature is too severe and stern, his love may be as strong and enduring as the mountain but still he cannot express it in words like a woman." The war also imposed an organizational dilemma on their wedding in that Green would need to secure a thirty-day furlough, which he ultimately did, effective February 12, 1862. The ceremony took place a week later on February 19, officiated by a Presbyterian minister. It was "a very quiet affair," given the circumstances, and yet the bride and groom were serenaded by a group of soldiers.[6]

The enormous number of published and unpublished Civil War–era letters serves as ample and poignant testimony to the degree to which families sought to stay connected during a time of great upheaval. Along with providing virtual companionship, letter writing enabled the communication of family and community news, personal expression and private concerns, hope and inspiration, questions, especially from wives, regarding household or financial matters, and safety issues. This last provoked considerable anxiety among Virginians, as seen, for example, in Green Samuels's letters during the spring of 1863 when he repeatedly implored Kathleen, who was pregnant, to return home to Front Royal from visiting. He begged her not to delay a single day because an impending military campaign would cut her off from the kin and community she needed. Proximity to family and community often meant a lesser degree of hardship and deprivation and a greater chance for survival and safety (even if this meant "refugeeing" with or to kin elsewhere). Indeed, the central importance of interdependent kinship ties in the nineteenth-century South, rural and urban, cannot be overstated; nor can it be divorced from the construction of Southern identity. Letters, with their references to visiting as well as their constant inquiries about the welfare and location of kin, bear this out. This pattern of kinship ties was not limited to the white community. Southern blacks developed a parallel network of kin ties that they could draw upon for "assistance and security." However, given the extent of dislocation they experienced (whether Union raiders took them, Southern masters moved them, or they decided to run away), black Virginians were seriously hindered in making these networks work for their families with as much success.[7]

In the same way that Virginia families and the home front were linked to (and sometimes merged with) the battlefield, so, too, was the local community, be it rural, town, or urban. Here, too, a range of interdependent networks newly actuated by wartime conditions is evident. White women and families were at both ends of these networks, as recipients of the increasingly futile efforts to protect soldiers' families from want and also as acutely determined and purposed providers of assistance at numerous levels for the Confederate cause. Either way, the war almost instantly changed the dynamics of everyday life. As early as the first month of war, Mary Smiley of Augusta County remarked to her soldier brother, "It appears like there has been a stop put to business of every kind [and] there is very little doing except what is obliged to be done[, and] that is farming." Indeed, food production, coupled with transportation and distribution issues, would turn out to be perhaps the most crucial crisis facing the Confederate home front. Smiley noted that their father was struggling with the plowing, presumably due to the loss of help from male relatives and laborers who were now enlisted in the army. To farm people, the implications were obvious. "Great fears are entertained," she continued, "that you will suffer for food[:] so many soldiers and where will the bread come from to feed them."[8]

When it came to supplies, Virginia counties made good use of home front families, especially harnessing women's patriotism. The women of Rockbridge County exemplified this in their tireless action. One woman recalled the forming of "sewing bands" to sew shirts for soldiers and supplies for the hospital. According to the *Lexington Gazette,* in a little more than a week in 1861 the women of Brownsburg and vicinity "made 80 coats, 80 pants, about 140 fatigue shirts, 80 knapsacks, 80 haversacks, 80 cloth caps, and covered 80 canteens with cloth, and ten tents" for the local Rockbridge Guards. From the outset of war, some seventy women and children were involved in the work of the county's Soldiers Aid Society. The Ladies Aid Society made repeated selfless offers to oversee the convalescence of one hundred wounded men in their own homes. The women's group at Natural Bridge set out to maintain the connection between fallen soldiers and home community in their efforts to raise money to build a monument memorializing Rockbridge County soldiers who fell at First Manassas. At the same time, soldiers' families disadvantaged by the loss of male members also became the object of relief efforts. Counties across the state appropriated monies to be distributed to these families. For example, in 1863 the Rockbridge County Court set aside $15,000 to be disbursed in this way in weekly amounts: women, $1.25; daughters twelve years and older, 75¢; children under twelve years, 50¢. The problem was, however, that financial assistance could not overcome either skyrocketing food prices or food shortages. In 1863 it would take a soldier's wife one month's assistance to purchase one bushel of potatoes, which was going for $5—and rising. Records indicate that the families of black men forced to work on fortifications were awarded the same levels of assistance.[9]

Before long, the war's disrupting circumstances spread weariness among home front families. Margaret Junkin Preston, wife of Col. J. T. L. Preston, came to loathe the word *war*. "It is destroying and paralyzing all before it," she lamented; "all the able-bodied men gone—stores shut up, or only here and there one open; goods not to be bought, or so exorbitant that we are obliged to do without." A common regret was the disappearance of staple household items such as coffee. "We have some on hand," Preston noted, "and for eight months have drunk a poor mixture, half wheat, half coffee. Many persons have nothing but wheat and rye" to use for their coffee. Confederate shortages and increasing deprivation were widespread, affecting home front and battlefield alike. They were the result of a combination of wartime government and military policies (including Confederate impressments, the Union blockade, and the Union's hard-war strategy, which was particularly destructive to Virginians) and a long history of importing foodstuffs from outside the region, sources that were cut off from the Confederacy at the outset of the war. Managing shortages with substitutes so as to be able to feed their families became women's greatest challenge and preoccupation. They were faced with serious shortages in meat (largely due to the scarcity of salt for preservation); sugar; flour; fats, including butter and lard; milk; fresh fruits and vegetables; and additives like spices. Fish, eggs, and even mule meat served as meat substitutes when available. The same was true of sorghum for sugar, but desserts were offered less and less. Flour substitutes ranged from white potatoes to cornmeal to rice. Bread or cake made from the latter was often labeled as "Secession bread" or "Secession cake," which was an indicator of the rising "cult of sacrifice" for the Cause. Given the deteriorating circumstances, there would be plenty of opportunity to sacrifice, willingly or not. Another indicator is seen in the regularity with which many newspapers published shortage- and substitute-oriented recipes. Indeed, women diarists often detailed with pride the success of their new recipes in pleasing family and friends. Yet it was serious business, for women had to be ever vigilant and inventive in finding new dishes and new ways to make them.[10]

Food was only one of the so-called necessaries of life in short supply. Clothing shortages and substitutes became critical home front issues during the last half of the war, by which time Southerners could be easily characterized as "ill-clad." Shoes represented the most dire problem due to the scarcity of leather. Reportedly, War Department agents and civilians could be seen on battlegrounds after the fighting, carting dead horses away in hopes of using the skins for shoe leather. Wood and cloth were more typically used as substitutes. For other essential daily-wear garments, Confederate women turned, or rather returned, to the basics of domestic manufacturing such as knitting, carding, spinning, and weaving. Rural women were still generally familiar with these modes of household production; but many other women were not, and they often looked to a skilled house slave to either oversee this activity or to train the white women of the household. Existing clothing items were constantly reworked to remain wearable, to the eventual point of becoming threadbare. The essential hat—be it straw or bonnet style—also fell into this category. In reality the straw might be wheat, rye, or oats, and the trimmings consisted of whatever was at hand to pass for fashionable. Women's efforts to keep their families clothed were hampered by shortages of cards, looms, sewing needles, pins, dyes, wool, and linen; however, they were assisted by cooperative spinning bees among kin, neighbors, or both, as well as the incorporation of children's help in domestic productions. The newfound old way of spinning and weaving produced the highly visible and symbolic Confederate homespun. As with women's recipes for food substitutes, the production and wearing of homespun engendered pride in both the achievement and the sacrifice. Homespun was characterized by a variety of woven checks, stripes, and plain fabric, and because of shortages in linen and silk, it was often used to make undergarments. These were less popular among women. Patriotic though it may have been, urban women nevertheless apparently were less inclined toward anything homespun. A higher standard of fashion, however, was elusive, with prized items such as hoops and corset stays scarce.[11]

Homespun, of course, was not particularly new to Virginia slave families. Depending upon the circumstances of the slave owner, slave clothing was typically made by designated slave women, occasionally from store-bought material but more often—certainly during wartime—through spinning and weaving. "We wore home spun clo'es made [on] de loom," recalled one former slave. Clothes were handed out by slave owners seasonally, usually twice a year, and included shoes, hats, and undergarments that were sometimes made out of "sacks an' bags," according to another former slave. A third ex-slave from Virginia, George White, described their shirts as being made from stiff flax. "An' we didn' have to scratch our backs; just wiggle an' our back was scratched." But clothing wore out, and materials to make new or patch old items were scarce during the war. This led to slave owners taking drastic measures to keep their slaves clothed, such as ripping up carpets and mattresses in hopes that they might yield workable fabric. Slaves kept in the more urban areas appear to have experienced less of a crisis in clothing. Prior to the war it had been customary among some slave owners to hand down clothing that was no longer worn by them to their slaves, but that practice essentially ceased due to the effectiveness of the Union blockade, which made clothing materials (along with numerous other items) unavailable to whites. This produced an unusual dynamic whereby some urban slave women in particular appeared to be more adequately, even somewhat more stylishly, dressed than their white counterparts, who no doubt regretted having earlier given away their store of old clothing.[12]

Along with food and clothing shortages, Virginia women and families contended with depleted supplies of basic household necessities, a situation that would also have repercussions at the community level in several important ways. The daily and weekly routines of the household were altered and made more difficult, often distressing, to families by a lack of such things as heating, lighting, linens, matches, and cleaning items. The scarcity of fuel in the form of wood and coal for home consumption, for example, had serious repercussions on a family's health and well-being. Candles for lighting were extremely hard to come by, as they had been largely imported from the North before the war. Homemade candles were said to burn too fast, and the tallow molds were difficult to find. Cornelia McDonald was praised for the "Confederate candles" she made by repeatedly dunking a cord through melted beeswax. Oil lamps proved to be another challenge to continue using given the lack of kerosene and wicks. In place of kerosene, Southerners tried to make do with sunflower and cottonseed oils, but the weak substitutes for wicks could not be effectively overcome. In a preelectric world, diminished access to lighting naturally would have a limiting effect in many areas of family and community life, including churchgoing. Rockbridge County resident and diarist Margaret Preston complained in 1862, "For months we have had no service at night in any church in town, owing to the scarcity of candles, or rather to save lights and fuel." Bedding and blankets all but disappeared because so many such items had been donated, either for hospital supplies or the troops, and could not easily be replaced. In addition to all of this, Massey observes, long before the war's end, cleaning items were virtually "unobtainable," with soap particularly elusive. Newspaper editors exhorted housewives and their slaves to make homemade soap, but limited access to fats and potash greatly hampered the endeavor. Periodically, factory-made soap was available for purchase, but spiraling inflation and the dire circumstances of war made it prohibitively costly. Being required to forgo the accustomed routines of personal cleanliness and clean clothes was a constant reminder of home front sacrifices.[13]

As with households, the war disrupted routines and created distractions for the local community's services and institutions as well. More typical than not was a Sunday church service in May 1863. Just as it was beginning, the mail arrived; "so great was the excitement," Preston related, "and so intense the desire for news, that [the minister] was obliged to dismiss the congregation." From the outset of the war, churchgoing had been undergoing significant outward changes as a result of the large numbers of male congregants, heads of households, and ministers who had left to enlist in the Cause. Funding was evaporating as well. Occasionally the physical destruction of the buildings or Yankee interference in occupied areas such as Winchester amounted to the same thing. Interference could include requiring that prayers be said for President Lincoln or even merely Union soldiers in attendance, either of which caused some Virginia women and families to forgo public church services for private ones. For a variety of reasons many Confederate churches closed their doors, leading to a tapering off of formal worship and, frequently, women's assumption of religious leadership to fill the breach. Virginia military hospital nurse Kate Rowland remarked: "We have had no Chaplain all winter so we had to make up the deficiency as far as possible ourselves." This trend can also be observed on many plantations, where women oversaw religious instruction and observances.[14]

School attendance likewise took a hit within a portion of the white Virginia population during this period. In 1862 Washington College was described as having only five students, and these were younger than military age; male students of military age attending classes would have been considered unacceptable. The student body remained low at the college throughout the war. On the other hand, Ann Smith Academy and other schools that girls attended actively continued their academic mission. Indeed, enrollment at many Confederate girls' boarding schools increased because parents believed these to be safer places for their daughters than many parts of the home front. The story concerning Virginia blacks and education was manifestly different. The war and Yankee intrusion into Virginia created new and lasting educational opportunities for freed or refugee blacks and their children; in fact, the origins of the Federal push to establish schools for Southern blacks lie in actions taken in Virginia. The American Missionary Association (AMA), in conjunction with Gen. Benjamin Butler, made a significant effort to set up schools for blacks in the South. Of particular note was the one the AMA established in Norfolk, which was managed by a free black woman named Mary Smith Peake. This school would later become Hampton Institute. Contraband children could also find informal schools set up for them in camps. The profound impact that new and unfettered access to schools and education had upon the former slaves is evident in their narratives and cannot be overstated.[15]

Of all the hardships endured on the home front by Virginia families, the most terrifying, wrenching, and deeply offensive (especially for white Virginians) were the attacks on civilian households and communities. The scope of the war changed in April 1863 with the Union War Department's publication of "Instructions for the Government of Armies . . . in the Field," otherwise known as General Order No. 100 (or Lieber's Code), the basis for a new hard-war policy. Essentially, this was a field manual of sorts for soldiers that outlined a range of appropriate wartime behavior toward the enemy, including civilians. The overarching theme was the encouragement of the Confederacy's destruction by eliminating all means it still had to sustain itself—thus literally carrying the war to the homes and barnyards of Confederate families. Union soldiers were admonished to remember that "war is not carried on by arms alone. It is lawful to starve the hostile belligerent, armed or unarmed, so that it leads to the speedier subjection of the enemy." Nancy Emerson's description of the actions taken by Union soldiers during the summer of 1864 in Augusta County is just one of a host of similar accounts. At one neighbor's place, the Yankees "took every thing they had to eat, all the pillow cases & sheets . . . [and] then poured out their molasses, scattered their preserves & sugar & other things about the floor, & mixed them all together & destroyed things generally." At another, "they took all of their meat (some 30 pieces of bacon) & nearly everything else they had to eat, all their horses (4) & persuaded off their two negro men." Yankee confiscation of horses and servants was particularly injurious to the agrarian-oriented Virginians, and many complained about the potential for disaster, especially when Confederate officials "drafted" the use of slave labor as well. "People here do their farming with horses instead of oxen," Emerson explained, "[and] it is an immense loss to have them & the servants swept off to such an extent, just as harvest is about to begin too." A final point she made concerned a frustrating sense of war-imposed gender vulnerability that was widely expressed. Apparently, upon hearing the approach of Union soldiers, some Confederate men and boys tended to keep themselves out of the way for fear of retaliatory treatment or violence; "thus the women were left to shift for themselves as best they could."[16]

Union-occupied (or, as in the case of Winchester, reoccupied) areas created a different though no less trying set of circumstances for home front families; uncertainties and alarms came to characterize their daily lives. It is hard to judge from their writings which provoked more contempt on the part of Rebel women—Union raiding or Union occupation. Yet one thing stands out: while Union raiding and burning of homes and farms succeeded in causing great hardships and deeply bruising Virginia women's spirits, the prolonged and often interpersonal contact with Yankees that came via occupation, instead of intimidation, actually encouraged boldness and barely disguised, unrestrained detestation. This was also extended to Unionist civilians residing within the occupied areas and even more so toward the wives of Union officers. To some extent, Confederate Winchester women accommodated themselves to a highly fluid situation. Mary Greenhow Lee recorded, "The first sound I heard this morning was the clanking of sabers & dash of Cavalry; so accustomed have I become to border warfare that I did not get up to see whether they were Confederates or Yankees." But the latter could expect rough treatment at the hands of these women, ranging from verbal insults to slammed doors and shutters to refusals to take loyalty oaths, walk under the U.S. flag, or assist willingly in any way. Lee wondered how the Yankees could find such ill treatment surprising, considering that they were "the murderers of our friends & the enemies of our liberty." It pleased the women to learn that their behavior annoyed Union leaders like Secretary of State William Seward, who famously declared that in Winchester "the men had all gone with the enemy and the women were all she devils."[17]

Rebel boldness came with a price, however. Some of the more brash or rebellious Winchester women and families were forced to remove behind Union lines, thus leaving their homes and possessions unguarded. Others, not sent away, were subjected to having their homes repeatedly searched for supposed contraband items, or their kitchens suddenly "invaded" for food—and such was considered a very personal invasion. In their determination to impose order, Union occupying forces issued various rules and regulations, some more odious to Confederate women than others. Cornelia McDonald complained in April 1863 of being "more severely dealt with by our tyrants every day. Today every shop and place of business was closed to those who would not take the Federal oath." As the family's food supplies dwindled, women in these areas faced what was to them an unacceptable choice: either take the loyalty oath to the Union or be denied access to shops and thus the ability to feed their families. Even more galling were Union officials' indiscriminate harassments of women guilty only of having a comfortable home. When the Union commander of the division of Winchester, Maj. Gen. Robert Milroy, eyed the residence of successful tobacco merchant Lloyd Logan, he proceeded to commandeer it for his headquarters, ordering Logan's wife and family to leave. The town was further incensed to learn that the Lloyd women, including one who was ill, were loaded into a wagon "and driven six miles out of town, where they were set down by the roadside, destitute of everything." A son was detained in the guardhouse for safekeeping. Thus the Union presence darkened the Virginia landscape in numerous ways.[18]

If the wide-ranging interviews of Virginia's ex-slaves (and some identified as free blacks) conducted during the mid-1930s are any indication, Union incursions and the war's unfolding on the home front intensified the already precarious slave conditions, especially as they related to families and kin. As was the case with white Virginians, Confederate and Union actions and policies reverberated across the black population, but usually with sharper consequences. Even ex-slaves who claimed to have had good masters or mistresses described a chaotic, confusing, and often racially charged home front that, because of its constant proximity to military actions, imperiled slave families. Although aimed at crushing the Confederacy and its white civilians, the Union's shift to a "hard-war" policy of destroying the enemy's sustenance ironically ensured that Virginia's black families would also suffer. Many if not most ex-slaves remembered hunger so extreme that children and the elderly died as a result. Indeed, slave food rations were hardly sufficient for the strenuous labor demands before the war. Then, the general slave diet included rations of cornmeal and pork along with game, syrup, and a range of vegetables. But wartime circumstances prompted significant dietary changes among the enslaved. For example, salt shortages, compounded by the food demands of the Confederate military, created widespread shortages in meat, generating public discussions about how to make substitutions and reductions in the slave diet. One result was the elimination of meat rations from the diets of female and children slaves. Overall, however, black families could be optimistic. Unlike white Southerners, slaves and free blacks could actually hope to improve their families' status at the war's end with emancipation; that is, they could finally make real the most fundamentally important element of freedom—protection for the sanctity of their family circle. Former slave Elizabeth Sparks was awed by her first encounter with that possibility. When a small group of Yankees rode up to her and her baby, one of them dismounted to "snap off his hat an' bow low to me" before asking directions. After some polite small talk, he thanked her and said, "Goodbye, Mrs. Sparks." She told an interviewer years later, "Now what you think of dat? Dey call me 'Mrs. Sparks.'"[19]

While some former Virginia slaves maintained that they did know why the whites were fighting or when Lincoln had proclaimed them "free," the waging of war and attendant consequences were evident everywhere and thus inescapable. Ex-slave Horace Muse said, "When de war came, de news spread like [a] whirlwin! We heard it whispered 'roun' dat a war come fer to set de niggers free." Increasingly, many field and house slaves found their daily lives and routines drastically altered and threatened. When allowed by overseers, Virginia's field hands worked in family groups to produce the state's major crops—tobacco, wheat, and corn. "In dat way," explained ex-slave Frank Bell, "one could help de other when dey got behind." These same fields could be suddenly overrun by soldiers, several or many; and in Virginia, they were Confederate nearly as often as Union. Occasionally, the slaves' warning of soldiers approaching was the sudden piercing of a stray bullet. A common frightening result, as Mollie Booker expressed, was that the "Yankees took all de animuls, de golds, an' everything of value. What dey didn' take, dey burned." On the other hand, in oft-repeated scenes on the rural and urban home front, some Yankee soldiers encouraged slaves to assert control over the food and material goods they had produced. Yankees opened Danville ex-slave George White's master's smokehouse and offered the slaves hams; they did the same with the mistress's fine dresses, saying, as White recalled, "Dis is your labor an' not theres." In urban areas Union soldiers broke into shops and offered their goods to slaves and free blacks, although they could not rationalize such actions in the same way. Seemingly generous gestures aside, the military always took from the farm, plantation, or town and urban shops what provisions they needed first, leaving only residual behind.[20]

As house servants, slave women, children, and some men who performed domestic labor (for example, churning, spinning, sewing, cooking, washing, dusting, child care, personal servant, coachman) in the master's house were no less vulnerable to intrusion or manipulation. The performance of daily chores was constrained by increasingly drastic shortages of necessary items, especially raw materials. Tension was high, and the days were unpredictable. At a moment's notice, slaves could be told to help hide the valuables from approaching Yankees. In this scenario, mistresses without husbands present often fled, temporarily entrusting the property's safety to a servant. Former Culpeper County slave Annie Wallace remembered that she and her mother had been left behind to meet the Yankees at the gate. Ex-slave William I. Johnson Jr. was left in charge of a plantation house in Albemarle County when his master, followed by four sons, enlisted. Others were compelled to prepare food for soldiers and sometimes were paid for their trouble. Likewise, Eliza Brown, an ex-slave from Charlottesville, described the day that the house was surrounded by "de blue coats." The commanding officer ordered that a "great big barrel of whisky" be rolled up to the house. Brown's mother was put in charge of doling out the rations to the men because she could read enough to verify their passes. Some slaveholders took overtly destructive measures when Yankees approached, such as setting furniture and other property afire to keep it out of Yankee hands, some even threatening to do the same to their slaves.[21]

In all of this, a common feature of the interviews of Virginia's ex-slaves about their wartime experiences is the references to their mothers as being remarkably strong and committed to survival, as they mediated the range of home front disruptions and crises suddenly confronting them. Matilda Carter's mother exemplified this resourceful, even opportunistic, spirit in the midst of Yankees. Carter remembered that she "uster cook things an' sell em in de camps. Deed my mother could go mos' anywhere in de lines [and] I uster go wid her." The interviewees were themselves quite young during the war, ranging in age from childhood to young adulthood. As such, they encountered the war on somewhat different terms. True, whether slave or free black, the child's world largely revolved around labor expectations. But the war caused their routines to change as well; for example, they now could be hired out to meet the needs of either the master, whose adult slaves may have emancipated themselves, or of the Cause. In another sense, proximity to Union soldiers enticed some children, like free black Octavia Featherstone of Petersburg, to go to the camps in search of edibles like hard tack, which she fondly recalled the soldiers sprinkling with brown sugar. Child's play, too, was colored by the harsh realities of war. A common game among a plantation's black and white children, "Injuns an' Soldiers," became "Yankees an' Federates." "'Course," noted a former slave, "de whites was always de 'Federates. Take us black boys prisoners an' make b'lieve dey was gonna cut our necks off. Guess dey got dat idea f'om dere fathers." A more troubling game, one that reveals the merging of home front and battlefield in what can only be described as an obscene way, was leapfrog in winter in Norfolk. Ex-slave Virginia Hayes Shepherd related that conditions were such that the ground was so hard and white people died so frequently that bodies were stacked high near the sidewalks, awaiting burial. She and her young friends looked at this through uncritical children's eyes and saw an opportunity for a game of dare, jumping over the bodies, and they played it over and over.[22]

Clearly, Virginia slave women and families endured a multitude of serious challenges on the home front. It could even be argued that they felt their slave status most keenly during the war, given that both Confederates and Unionists seemed intent upon their whereabouts, actions, and ultimate status. The whispers among slaves or the deliberate talk by Union soldiers that "Marsa Lincoln" was going to set them free threatened to upset the social structure of power, and this led to a kind of hypervigilance over black activities by whites. "White folks watched you all de time," said one free black Virginian. Similarly, white accounts contain references to closely observing changes in slaves' attitudes and recorded instances of marked insolence, disobedience, or worse—running off.[23]

Given that a number of the ex-slaves matter-of-factly recounted that their parents had belonged to masters at separate plantations or that a sibling had been sold away, Virginia's black population certainly understood the dynamics of being wrenched from loved ones and the fact of broken family circles long before the war. Separation and loss were pervasive themes in the lives of both white and black home front families during the war, and it would get worse for black families before it got better. Reflecting the complex interdependence of the master-slave relationship, some of the ex-slave narratives include remarks about the confusion and anxiety slave children felt at being separated from their mistresses, or at seeing their masters ride off to join the military. The war also imposed a separation of slave fathers (or other male relations) from children, although for different reasons, such as being forced to go build fortifications, to accompany the enlisting master, or being taken as contraband by Union forces, often to cook and do menial labor for them. At times, approaching Union forces symbolized a chance for the enslaved to escape their bondage; for many other slaves, however, it meant a grim probability of losing track of loved ones due to the chaos of war and an unknown future. Virginia's home front had indeed become a landscape in disarray and of various peoples, white and black, in motion.[24]

Virginia slaves became aware of the dilemma posed by Union forces promising freedom to those willing to follow them. Fannie Berry recalled "dem niggers who left wid de Yankees and were sot free but, poor things, dey had no place to go after dey got freed. Baby, all us wuz helpless an' ain't had nothing." Archie Booker, who permanently lost track of his brother during the war, observed, "A great numbuh o'slaves follered de army roun." Similarly, Mollie Booker (and numerous others) said that when Union soldiers appeared "mos' of de slaves wen' wid 'em." Other narratives recount hiding from the Yankees in the woods out of fear. More commonly, however, family and kin became dislocated and disconnected from each other. "Lord, Lord, honey," lamented Minnie Folkes, "dem times too over sad, 'cause Yankees took lots of slaves away an' dey made homes. An' whole heap of families lost sight of each other." Folkes claimed to know of a case representative of many in which a brother and sister separated by war had afterwards lived next to each other for ten years before learning that "dey wuz blood kin." Attempts to reunite slave families during the war were also chronicled, such as Martha Harper Robinson's well-planned childhood escape, in the company of her uncle, from a farm in Saluda to her parents in Richmond. They traveled by night, usually without food, until they reached a certain Hanover County farm where her father had stashed a wagon for them. Martha lay on the bottom of the wagon and was covered by a load of provisions (vegetables)—her uncle was ostensibly headed for market. The ruse allowed them to proceed without trouble into Richmond, a city hungry for food. "When my mother saw us coming," Martha related, "she screamed so loud that they must have heard her all over Richmond." Nevertheless, such success stories were rare; the separation of families and kin seems to have been the dominant reality.

According to Sister Harrison, "After the war wuz over, they came back home, but lots of people wuz separated that way."[25]

As it was for Martha Harper Robinson's family, Richmond turned out to be a safe haven of sorts for a new social class produced by home front uncertainties and alarms—the refugees. While large numbers of blacks ran toward Union lines and camps anticipating freedom, scores of white Virginians fled to kin in the opposite direction, seeking safety. Judith McGuire of Alexandria chronicled the breaking up of her community with the outbreak of war, which hit most profoundly at home—family members were sent out of harm's way and people were faced with the sad realization that the happier life they knew might never return. It soon became clear that she, too, would have to leave, and that meant leaving home and possessions at the mercy of the servants' faithfulness and invading armies. "It was a sorrowful thought;" she wrote, "but we have kind relatives and friends whose doors are open to us, and we hope to get home again before very long." Yet she conceded that the war had made them "homeless." Refugees' hopes of returning home soon typically went unrealized. More commonly, once civilians overcame their understandable reluctance to flee as refugees, they were likely to continue on in this way, due to circumstances beyond their control, for the remainder of the war. Urban rather than rural areas tended to be viewed as safe havens; additional popular destinations chosen by Virginia refugees included Staunton, Lynchburg, and the southwestern communities of Bristol and Abingdon. Sometimes, however, the military situation in Virginia dictated that nearly the entire populations of urban areas be evacuated to fend for themselves, like the civilians of Fredericksburg in late 1862 and those in Petersburg at the time of the siege beginning in 1864. Families who had no place to flee to could be seen seeking shelter in outlying areas—in tents, already crowded farmhouses, and other outbuildings.[26]

Throughout the war, refugees flocked to Richmond hoping to find safety and sustenance in the state and Confederate capital. What they found instead was a city teeming with war-related problems of scarcities and shortages, crime, discontent, and more, made many times worse by a streaming influx of refugees. "Tales of suffering," recounted Richmond resident Sallie Brock Putnam, were "the theme of thousands of tongues, as the homeless and destitute crowded into our city for safety and support." The ability to house, supply, and feed the refugees simply wasn't there, and many were compelled to gradually sell off whatever possessions they had with them in order to buy food; their situation, Putman observed, "was often painful in the extreme." Those who were not refugees but Richmond residents suffered as well. One father's diary entries for 1864 reveal the effects of deprivation and starvation upon his family. In March he recorded that his daughter's cat was staggering about for lack of food. He then wondered if he was likewise staggering. Some months later he noted the cat's death. In August he bought a bushel of red peas that was labeled to feed "*horses.*" "Such," he continued, "is the food that my family is forced to subsist on." By November, his family was subsisting alternatively on shin soup and bean soup, and he had noticed that their fireside conversations had taken on a certain pattern; "They mostly relate to the savory dishes we once enjoyed." Clearly the war had stripped home front families of everything but the ties, affections, and spirit that held them together.[27]

Just like Green Berry Samuels, Confederate captain George Washington Nelson Jr. was also captured at Winchester (in 1863) and remained a prisoner of war until Lee's surrender. Nelson, whose nickname was Wash, ended up at the same prison, Fort Delaware, and from there he exchanged contemplative and loving letters with his fiancée, Mollie Scollay, at home in Middleway. Their letters reveal what the war meant to them and their communities, and provide as well as a glimpse of post-Confederate life. Mollie remarked that the area, "tho terribly devastated is still beautiful." In town many of the houses now had bullet holes on them. Her thinking also had been profoundly changed by the war; by this point, upon hearing of a battle she immediately wondered "which of our friends have been killed." Wash, who called Mollie "quite a veteran," took Lee's surrender hard, but Mollie would have none of it. "We have acted as we believed to be right;" she encouraged him. "We were inspired by the noble principles of duty, then why should we feel humiliated?" She continued: "Though we have ceased to strike for success, and bright hopes for the future have ceased to animate us, still it is very comforting to have the approval of a quiet conscience, and to feel we have always followed in the path of duty." Now duty must guide Wash home. "Nearly all the soldiers from this place and vicinity have returned," Mollie pointedly said. "It looks quite like old times to see them."[28]

Notes

Epigraph quoted in Leon F. Litwack, *Been in the Storm So Long: The Aftermath of Slavery* (New York: Vintage Books, 1980), 106.

1. G. B. Samuels to My Dear Wife, Fort Del[aware], March 7, May 19, June 4, 1865, G. B. S. to My Dear Wife, Camp Pisgah, February 1, 1864, in Carrie Esther Spencer, Bernard Samuels, and Walter Berry Samuels, eds., *A Civil War Marriage in Virginia: Reminiscences and Letters* (Boyce, Va.: Carr, 1956), 221, 224, 226, 205; see also Aaron Sheehan-Dean, *Why Confederates Fought: Family and Nation in Civil War Virginia* (Chapel Hill: University of North Carolina Press, 2007), especially chapter 5.

2. Kathleen Samuels to My dear husband, Front Royal, May 19 and June 6, 1865, and G. B. Samuels to My Dear Wife, Fort Del[aware], May 19, 1865, in Spencer, Samuels, and Samuels, *A Civil War Marriage*, 252, 253, 224.

3. Many published and unpublished collections of Civil War letters and correspondences exist. One that represents the timelessness of soldiers' personal perspectives is James I. Robertson Jr., *Soldiers Blue and Gray* (Columbia: University of South Carolina Press, 1988). Home front women's experiences have also been published as excerpts and in full. Ones consulted for this study include Marilyn Mayer Culpepper, ed., *Women of the Civil War South: Personal Accounts from Diaries, Letters and Postwar Reminiscences* (Jefferson, N.C.: McFarland, 2004); John G. Selby, *Virginians at War: The Civil War Experiences of Seven Young Confederates* (Wilmington, Del.: Scholarly Resources, 2002); Andrew J. Torget and Edward L. Ayers, *Two Communities in the Civil War* (New York: Norton, 2007); Charles G. Waugh and Martin H. Greenberg, eds., *The Women's War in the South: Recollections and Reflections of the American Civil War* (Nashville: Cumberland House, 1999); Judith White McGuire, *Diary of a Southern Refugee during the War, by a Lady of Virginia,* 3rd ed. (Richmond: J. W. Randolph and English, 1889); Cornelia Peake McDonald, *A Woman's Civil War: A Diary, with Reminiscences of the War, from March 1862,* ed. Minrose C. Gwin (Madison: University of Wisconsin Press, 1992); and Sallie Brock Putnam, *Richmond during the War: Four Years of Personal Observations* (Lincoln: University of Nebraska Press, 1996). Consulted scholarly works include George C. Rable, *Civil Wars: Women and the Crisis of Southern Nationalism* (Urbana: University of Illinois Press, 1991); Drew Gilpin Faust, *Mothers of Invention: Women of the Slaveholding South in the American Civil War* (Chapel Hill: University of North Carolina Press, 1996); Sally G. McMillen, *Southern Women: Black and White in the Old South* (Arlington Heights, Ill.: Harlan Davidson, 1992); Edward D. C. Campbell Jr. and Kym S. Rice, eds., *A Woman's War: Southern Women, Civil War, and the Confederate Legacy* (Charlottesville: University of Virginia Press, 1996); Richard R. Duncan, *Beleaguered Winchester: A Virginia Community at War, 1861–1865* (Baton Rouge: Louisiana State University Press, 2007); Brian Steel Wills, *The War Hits Home: The Civil War in Southeastern Virginia* (Charlottesville: University

of Virginia Press, 2001); Daniel E. Sutherland, *Seasons of War: The Ordeal of a Confederate Community, 1861–1865* (Baton Rouge: Louisiana State University Press, 1995); and William C. Davis, *Look Away! A History of the Confederate States of America* (New York: Free Press, 2002). I also perused the *Journal of Women's Civil War History.*

4. Kathleen Boone Samuels, "Reminiscences of Kathleen Boone Samuels," in Spencer, Samuels, and Samuels, *A Civil War Marriage*, 1–28 (quotes are on 27 and 17 respectively).

5. Ibid., 13–28; Bernard Samuels, "The Love and War Letters," in Spencer, Samuels, and Samuels, *A Civil War Marriage*, 63–70.

6. On companionate marriage, see Anya Jabour, *Marriage in the Early Republic: Elizabeth and William Wirt and the Companionate Ideal* (Baltimore: Johns Hopkins University Press, 1998). For a useful related analysis of courtship letters in the postwar era, see Leroy S. Carpenter, *Love in an Envelope: A Courtship in the American West,* ed. Daniel Tyler (Albuquerque: University of New Mexico Press, 2008). G. B. Samuels to Kattie, Woodstock, December 30, 1860, and March 26, 1861, G. B. Samuels to Kattie, Strasburg, April 15, 1861, G. B. Samuels to My Dear Sister, Harper's Ferry, April 24 and 30, 1861, in Spencer, Samuels, and Samuels, *A Civil War Marriage,* 71, 77, 81, 82, 87; see also the note on 129 for the reference to the Samuelses' wedding.

7. G. B. Samuels to My Dear Wife, Camp Skinker, March 19 and April 3, 1863, in Spencer, Samuels, and Samuels, *A Civil War Marriage,* 170, 175; Jean E. Friedman, *The Enclosed Garden: Women and Community in the Evangelical South, 1830–1900* (Chapel Hill: University of North Carolina Press, 1985); Robert C. Kenzer, "Family, Kinship, and Neighborhood in an Antebellum Southern Community," in William J. Cooper Jr., Michael F. Holt, and John McCardell, eds., *A Master's Due: Essays in Honor of David Herbert Donald* (Baton Rouge: Louisiana State University Press, 1985): 138–60; Brenda E. Stevenson, *Life in Black and White: Family and Community in the Slave South* (New York: Oxford University Press, 1996).

8. Mary A. Smiley to Thomas M. Smiley, Augusta County, April 26, 1861, in Torget and Ayers, *Two Communities,* 146–47.

9. Robert J. Driver Jr., *Lexington and Rockbridge County in the Civil War* (Lynchburg, Va.: H. E. Howard, 1989), 22, 23, 25, 27, 28–29, 34, 35, 40. Driver's book is a compilation of primary source accounts with some added narration, all of which is rooted in the place under study; see also James H. Bailey, *Henrico Home Front, 1861–1865: A Picture of Life in Henrico County, Virginia* (Richmond: n.p., 1963); and Charles V. Mauro, *The Civil War in Fairfax County: Civilians and Soldiers* (Charleston: History Press, 2006).

10. Driver, *Lexington and Rockbridge County,* 32–33. Virtually every Virginia Civil War diary, letter, and newspaper gives testimony about the food shortages and the need for developing substitutes. For analyses of Confederate food shortages, including their prewar origins, see Paul W. Gates, *Agriculture and the Civil War* (New York: Knopf, 1965), chapters 1–5; Sam Bowers Hilliard, *Atlas of Antebellum Southern Agriculture* (Baton Rouge: Louisiana State University Press, 1984); Davis, *Look Away!* chapters 7–10; and Ginette Aley, "'We are all good scavengers now': The Crisis in Virginia Agriculture during the Civil War," in William C. Davis and James I. Robertson Jr., eds., *Virginia at War, 1864* (Lexington: University Press of Kentucky, 2009); Mary Elizabeth Massey, *Ersatz in the Confederacy: Shortages and Substitutes on the Southern Homefront* (Columbia: University of South Carolina Press, 1993), chapters 1–4 (quote is on 77).

11. Massey, *Ersatz,* chapter 4.

12. Of recollections concerning the slave (and sometimes the free black) experiences during the Civil War era, particularly insightful and frequently cited is Charles L. Perdue Jr., Thomas E. Barden, and Robert K. Phillips, eds., *Weevils in the Wheat: Interviews with Virginia Ex-Slaves* (Charlottesville: University of Virginia Press, 1976): in this collection, see Samuel Walter Chilton, interview by Susie R. C. Byrd, 71; Charles Crawley, interview by Susie R. C. Byrd, 80; George White, interview by William T. Lee, 309. See also Bell Irvin Wiley, *Southern Negroes, 1861–1865* (New Haven, Conn.: Yale University Press, 1965), chapter 2; Claude H. Nolen, *African American Southerners in Slavery, Civil War and Reconstruction* (Jefferson, N.C.: McFarland, 2005), chapter 1.

13. Massey, *Ersatz,* chapters 6 and 9; Driver, *Lexington and Rockbridge County,* 79, 33, respectively.

14. Driver, *Lexington and Rockbridge County,* 43. Home front letters often express a diminution of religious faith; for what this meant to white women, see Drew Gilpin Faust, "'Without Pilot or Compass': Elite Women and Religion in the Civil War South," in Randall M. Miller, Harry S. Stout, and Charles Reagan Wilson, eds., *Religion and the American Civil War* (New York: Oxford University Press, 1998), 250–60 (Kate Rowland quote is on 254); Faust, *Mothers of Invention,* chapter 8; Culpepper, "Life in a Divided City—Perspectives from Winchester, Virginia," in *Women of the Civil War South,* 188–94. On religion among the wartime black population, see Wiley, *Southern Negroes,* chapter 6.

15. Davis, *Look Away!* 204–6; Driver, *Lexington and Rockbridge County,* 33, 82; James Marten, *The Children's Civil War* (Chapel Hill: University of North Carolina Press, 1998), 52–61, 132–36; Wiley, *Southern Negroes,* chapter 14; Ervin L. Jordan Jr., *Black Confederates and Afro-Yankees in Civil War Virginia* (Charlottesville: University of Virginia Press, 1995), chapter 4.

16. Mark Grimsley, *The Hard Hand of War: Union Military Policy toward Southern Civilians, 1861–1865* (Cambridge: Cambridge University Press, 1995), chapter 7; Francis Lieber, *Instructions for the Government of Armies of the United States, in the Field* (New York: D. Van Nostrand, 1863), 7; Nancy Emerson, diary, July 13, 1864, in Torget and Ayers, *Two Communities*, 156, 157. For an example of the complaints made by civilians to Confederate officials about the effects of the loss of slave labor on food production, see L. H. Minor to Sir, May 2, [1862], reprinted in Ira Berlin, Barbara J. Fields, Thavolia Glymph, Joseph P. Reidy, and Leslie S. Rowland., eds., *Freedom: A Documentary History of Emancipation, 1861–1867*, series 1, vol. 1, *The Destruction of Slavery* (Cambridge: Cambridge University Press, 1987), 698–99.

17. Culpepper, "Life in a Divided City," 180–81, 182; see also Stephen V. Ash, *When the Yankees Came: Conflict and Chaos in the Occupied South, 1861–1865* (Chapel Hill: University of North Carolina Press, 1995), chapter 7.

18. Culpepper, "Life in a Divided City," 185, 182 respectively.

19. Perdue et al., *Weevils in the Wheat*; Litwack, *Been in the Storm So Long*, especially chapters 1 and 3; Wiley, *Southern Negroes*, chapter 2; Nolen, *African American Southerners*, especially chapters 6 and 7. Major papers such as the *Southern Cultivator* contain discussions of ways to deal with shortages and substitutes, including making changes to the slave diet. Elizabeth Sparks, interview by Claude W. Anderson, in Perdue et al., *Weevils in the Wheat*, 277.

20. Horace Muse, interview by Claude W. Anderson and Marietta Silver; Frank Bell, interview by Claude W. Anderson; Mollie Booker, interview by Claude W. Anderson; George White, interview by William T. Lee, all in Perdue et al., *Weevils in the Wheat*, 216, 26, 55, 311.

21. Annie Wallace, interview by Margaret Jeffries; William I. Johnson Jr., interview by Milton L. Randolph; Eliza Brown, interview by unknown; Fannie Nicholson, interview by Thelma Dunston, all in Perdue et al., *Weevils in the Wheat*, 294, 167, 59, 218.

22. Matilda Carter, interview by Claude W. Anderson; Octavia Featherstone, interview by Susie R. C. Byrd; Candis Goodwin, interview by Claude W. Anderson; Virginia Hayes Shepherd, interview by Emmy Wilson and Claude W. Anderson, all in Perdue et al., *Weevils in the Wheat*, 69, 90, 109, 262–63; Marten, *Children's Civil War*, chapter 5.

23. Mollie Booker, interview by Claude W. Anderson, in Perdue et al., *Weevils in the Wheat*, 55.

24. John Brown, interview by Susie R. C. Byrd; Mollie Booker, interview by Claude W. Anderson; Fannie Berry, interview by Susie R. C. Byrd; Robert Ellett, interview by Claude W. Anderson; Liza Brown, interview by Susie R. C. Byrd,

all in Perdue et al., *Weevils in the Wheat,* 62, 54, 39–42, 86, 63–64. Examples of complaints about the large numbers of Virginia slaves being pulled away to work on Confederate fortifications and slave men's aversion to being taken away from their families like this are, respectively, Wm. F. Thompson to Hon Geo. Randolph, April [8], 1862, and Wyndham Robertson to Hon James A. Seddon, January 13, 1864, in Berlin et al., *Freedom,* 692–93, 778–79.

25. Fannie Berry, interview by Susie R. C. Byrd; Archie Booker, interview by Claude W. Anderson; Mollie Booker, interview by Claude W. Anderson; Minnie Folkes, interview by Susie R. C. Byrd; Martha Harper Robinson, interview by Milton Randolph; Sister Harrison, interview by Claude W. Anderson, all in Perdue et al., *Weevils in the Wheat,* 36, 53, 55, 95, 239, 240, 135.

26. Mary Elizabeth Massey, *Refugee Life in the Confederacy* (Baton Rouge: Louisiana State University Press, 2001), chapters 1 and 5; McGuire, diary, May 4, 10, 15, and 25, 1861, in *Diary of a Southern Refugee,* 9–15, 17–20 (quoted material).

27. Massey, *Refugee Life,* chapter 5; Putnam, *Richmond during the War,* chapters 14 (first quote is on 78), 21, 48 (second quote is on 253); J. B. Jones, diary, March 18, July 31, August 25, November 20 and 22, 1864, in *A Rebel War Clerk's Diary at the Confederate States Capital,* ed. Howard Swiggett (New York: Old Hickory Bookshop, 1935), 2:173, 258, 272, 335, 337.

28. Mollie to My dear Wash, Home, March 24 and April 4, 1865; Wash to Mollie, Fort Delaware, April 12, 1865; Mollie to My dear Wash, Home, April 23, 1865, all in Waugh and Greenberg, *Women's War in the South,* 262, 263, 253.

"The question of bread is a very serious one"

Virginia's Wartime Economy

Jaime Amanda Martinez

The question of bread is a very serious one to our citizens & unless a large wheat crop is sown the present season, want must inevitably result to many of our families.

—Washington County Court to Governor John Letcher,
October 26, 1863

In April 1865, Thomas S. Bocock of Appomattox County sold twenty-two barrels of corn and seventy-four bushels of wheat to his neighbor, Col. Thomas H. Flood. Rather than accept Confederate currency, Bocock allowed Flood to purchase the grains by bartering a commodity, in this case "Lydia & nine children, Martha & four & Sarah mother of Lydia and Martha." In his memoranda book, Bocock noted that another neighbor, J. A. Carter, had "agreed to take Martha & her children & Sarah" in exchange for "fourteen barrels of corn & thirty bushels of wheat." By May, however, perhaps angry that he had traded valuable wheat and corn for ten newly freed slaves, Bocock wrote, "I do not think that the wheat is due."[1]

Bocock's story illustrates two key realities of Virginia's wartime economy, especially by the spring of 1865. First, despite unprecedented intervention in the state's economic activities by local, state, and national governments, shortages and inflation plagued all Virginians, even those in positions of relative wealth and power. For those who had possessed limited economic resources at the start of the conflict, the war years frequently brought moments of dire economic necessity, and government assistance and regula-

39

tion, while often impressive, failed to meet all of their needs. By regulating currency; impressing agricultural goods, farm animals, and laborers; and taking control of key industries, however, the state and national governments did manage to shelter most Virginians from actual starvation.

In addition, white Virginians clung to the institution of slavery until the very end of the war, and most were unprepared to grapple with the realities of emancipation. Thomas Bocock should have been better prepared than most: as Speaker of the Confederate House of Representatives, Bocock had evacuated Richmond with the rest of the Confederate government on April 2, 1865. Rather than follow President Davis to North Carolina, Bocock returned to his home in Appomattox Courthouse, from which he no doubt watched the surrender of Robert E. Lee's Army of Northern Virginia just a few days later. Yet he agreed to purchase sixteen slaves sometime *after* that surrender. As the wartime economy evolved into the postwar economy, white Virginians struggled to adapt to a new reality, one in which black Virginians were laborers but not commodities.

By almost every standard, antebellum Virginia was a wealthy state with a flourishing economy. As historian James Huston has noted, Virginia, like the other states of the Upper South, "housed a large population capable of throwing much weight around politically, and was a region that possessed impressive wealth." In 1860, the state's total wealth approached $800 million, and while most of that came from agriculture, the state also produced more than $50 million worth of manufactured goods. Among all of the states in 1860, Virginia ranked ninth in both the total value of its manufactured products and the amount of money its residents invested in manufacturing. Virginia was also the fifth-most populous state in the Union; of the slaveholding states, it contained the largest free and slave populations. Yet Virginia's robust economy faltered under the strains of prolonged conflict, and Virginians faced severe wartime shortages of manufactured goods, food, and labor as well as skyrocketing inflation. The Confederate government, meanwhile, took an active interest in the state's economic development; while Congress and President Davis ultimately failed to curb inflation, they did manage to harness most of Virginia's agricultural and industrial pursuits to the benefit of the Confederate cause.[2]

Scholars of the 1860–1861 secession crisis have always emphasized the importance of Virginia's decision to leave the Union, and indeed it is difficult to overstate the Old Dominion's potential value to the Confederacy.

Virginia had symbolic value, of course, as the home of patriot leaders like George Washington and Thomas Jefferson, but it also brought significant human, manufactured, and agricultural resources to the aid of the Confederate war effort. For example, Virginia's two key industries—iron and railroads—proved critical to the Confederacy's survival during the four years of fighting. Meanwhile, by virtue of proximity, Virginia's farms fed the largest Confederate army. Finally, it was in Virginia that the Confederate government's program of economic intervention reached its apogee. Virginia's valuable advantages at the outset of the war, however, concealed hidden liabilities, and the state's economy eventually declined over the course of a conflict far more prolonged than anyone had anticipated.

Virginia ranked sixth among the states of the Union in terms of the absolute number of railroad lines built in the 1850s, but like all Southern railroad projects, those in Virginia suffered from serious disadvantages when compared with the transportation infrastructure of the Northeast. First, much of the South's capital was tied up in land and slaves, making it difficult to finance large-scale railroad projects. Thus, many of Virginia's antebellum rail lines were extremely short, and the state had failed to build a single east-west trunk line through Richmond by 1860. Moreover, because different companies operated each line, coordinating the transportation of troops and supplies across the state proved extremely difficult. Finally, Virginia's iron manufacturers lacked the necessary supplies and knowledge to repair or rebuild train engines that deteriorated during the war.[3]

Even with these disadvantages, politicians from the Deep South recognized the potential benefits Virginia's industrial development could bring to the Confederacy. Henry Lewis Benning, a secession commissioner from Georgia, encouraged Virginians to join the Confederacy so that they could become its industrial center; the state could only benefit, he argued, by filling "the place now held by New England and New York, to furnish the South [with manufactured] goods." In particular, Benning and the other commissioners sought to bring Richmond's two most successful industrial establishments—the Tredegar Iron Works and the Gallego Flour Mills—firmly into the Confederate fold.[4]

Richmond had experienced rapid growth during the late antebellum period and thus was well equipped to become the Confederacy's industrial and commercial center. Indeed, Richmond was perhaps better suited to the role of *Confederate* industrial center than even Baltimore, despite Baltimore's more impressive size and economic power, because antebellum Richmond had constantly reaffirmed its pro-slavery Southern identity even while attracting large numbers of Northern immigrants and maintaining strong connections with Northern industrial centers. While Richmond's growth strengthened the institution of slavery in late antebellum Virginia, slaves strengthened the city's industry, providing labor for dockyards, railroads, and factories. The city's immigrant communities, meanwhile, provided an essential pool of skilled white labor for factory owners like Joseph R. Anderson of the Tredegar Iron Works.[5]

During the secession crisis, Anderson continued casting heavy cannon for the U.S. Army while also accepting orders from the State of South Carolina; once Virginia seceded, he turned his attention to Confederate production. "By January, 1863," historian Emory Thomas observed, "Joseph R. Anderson employed 2,500 men and operated a tannery, shoemaking shops, firebrick factory, sawmill, and nine canal boats in addition to his mills and furnaces." Anderson also operated several farms, the produce of which fed the enslaved factory workers he preferred to hire. The overwhelming majority of Anderson's wartime manufactured goods went into the service of the Confederacy. Countless smaller producers in Virginia—independent iron forges, tanneries, and wagon makers, for example—also filled contracts for the Confederate armies.[6]

As the war progressed, the Confederate government became more involved in Virginia's industrial work, in some cases even directly employing laborers in government workshops. Nearly 3,000 women worked as seamstresses for the Clothing Bureau of the Quartermaster's Department. Meanwhile, the Conscript Bureau spent a great deal of its time evaluating exemption requests from male industrial workers of military age, but the February 1864 Conscription Act simplified matters by enlisting and then detailing them. This gave the army more flexibility, historian William Blair noted, by turning most workers "into soldiers whose economic importance would be judged by the War Department. As an enlisted man in the Confederate army, a wheelwright or carpenter could be assigned to a quartermaster's shop and then quickly returned to a regiment when a situation warranted." Confederate and state officials also intervened regularly in railroad operations, especially to hasten key supply deliveries, but they were hampered by the deterioration of railroad lines and equipment as the war progressed.[7]

Virginia's deficiencies in rail transportation greatly exacerbated the

Old Dominion's wartime food shortages, shortages that were all the more devastating in comparison to the state's antebellum agricultural abundance. In 1860, Virginians grew a diverse array of crops, including tobacco, wheat, corn, rye, and vegetables, in addition to producing livestock. Moreover, Virginia's farmers were wealthier than those in the old Northwest. With a population relatively equivalent to Virginia's free population, Indiana's farmers grew a similar array of crops and had better access to a large urban market. Yet the 1860 value of Virginia's farms exceeded $330 per free person, while Indiana farms were valued at only $260 per capita. The wealthiest agricultural counties in Virginia primarily grew wheat, although tobacco-growing counties along the Chesapeake Bay were also among the wealthiest areas in the state.[8]

Yet Virginia's farmers found themselves facing both food and labor shortages within the first two years of the war. Important grain-growing counties like Fauquier and Loudoun quickly fell behind Union lines. Yeoman farmers and small planters left their farms to enlist in the Confederate armies. The government took enslaved men out of agricultural work to perform military labor; other slaves took advantage of their masters' absences to shirk fieldwork or even escape completely. Labor shortages at the salt mines in the southwestern portion of the state meant that farmers lacked the ability to preserve what meat they could produce. All of these shortages occurred against a backdrop of increased demand: hundreds of thousands of soldiers converged on the Old Dominion, and all needed food. "The middle & western portions of this county have almost entirely been devastated of corn by our own troops quartered upon us," officials of the Washington County Court informed Governor John Letcher in October 1863. "We have between three & four thousand cavalry upon us for the last Ten days or two weeks, besides a large number of horses belonging otherwise to the army & a large amount of stock driven from the border counties by refugees in order to save it from the enemy." Either army's presence in a community could temporarily disable every aspect of its economy.[9]

Commodity shortages combined with Confederate fiscal policy to spawn rampant inflation. The Confederate government had three ways to generate income: taxes, loans, and printing money. Congress enacted a few modest taxes, including a personal income tax, a property tax, and sales taxes on some consumer goods, none of which provided more than 5 percent of the revenue necessary to wage the war. Farmers also paid a tax-in-kind, giving

10 percent of their agricultural produce directly to government agents, but to purchase guns and ammunition, the War Department needed cash. Unable to garner significant foreign loans, the Confederacy sold bonds to its citizens, thus generating an additional 35 percent of its income. The remaining 60 percent of the Confederacy's income came through paper currency, which the government printed in voluminous quantities. Congress, however, refused to make that paper currency legal tender, thus fueling an inflation rate that exceeded 6,000 percent by April 1865.

Although the value of Confederate currency remained relatively stable throughout the first year of the war, Virginians did not silently watch as their purchasing power slowly disappeared. They first sought help from local governments, but by spring 1862 were turning to state and national officials for assistance. "Given the chance," Blair argued, "the consuming public would have instituted price controls on food, with either the state or national government regulating the procedure. Producers—typically planters and owners of large farms—succeeded in fending off these attempts, but only for a time. An important signal was sent, with the public describing the levels of support that it needed to continue fighting." Yet that support came slowly, especially at the national level. County and municipal governments worked more quickly to provide assistance to indigent families, but they lacked the resources to meet everyone's needs.[10]

"Shall we starve?" government clerk John B. Jones lamented in January 1863. "Yesterday beef was sold for 40 cts. per pound; today it is 60 cts. Lard is $1.00. Butter $2.00." Historians have charted similar trends: "In the six months from August 1862 to March 1863," Blair observed, "prices of most foodstuffs increased on average nearly threefold. Family flour that had cost $7.50 per barrel in 1860 went from a low of $10 per barrel to $30. Bacon soared from a low of 35 cents per pound to $1.10 per pound." While residents of Virginia's towns paid more for food, farmers faced increasing costs for goods they purchased in town, including farm implements, horseshoes, and seed. Yet President Davis and the Congress failed to respond to letters and petitions. By the spring of 1863, Virginians had begun to seek more obvious forums to publicize their discontent.[11]

On April 2, 1863, several hundred protesters converged on the streets of Richmond. These demonstrators were primarily white women, most of them soldiers' wives, refugees, or factory workers; they broke into stores to steal food and clothing as they marched toward the government buildings at the heart of the city. President Davis, Governor Letcher, and Mayor Joseph Mayo awaited the rioters at the capitol building, where Davis ordered the women to disperse before arresting sixty-eight protesters. Smaller public protests occurred in Lynchburg and other cities throughout the Confederacy.

The local and state relief programs that emerged in the wake of the April 1863 bread riots, though never completely successful at relieving the agricultural shortages that plagued Virginia's civilian population, at least forestalled additional violent protests. The Richmond City Council and the city's YMCA both operated supply stores for indigent residents during the winter of 1863–1864, for example. That same winter, Blair proposed, the "escalation of charitable efforts would consume increasingly substantial portions of community budgets, taxes, and resources" in Albemarle, Augusta, and Campbell counties. In Lynchburg, according to historian Steven Tripp, elected officials and wealthy residents provided assistance to the city's working men and women, but at the expense of political gains workers had made during the first two years of the war. "Economic necessity," Tripp noted, "forced [people] back to elites."[12]

Economic necessity also forced Virginians into a greater reliance on the state government, especially under the populist governor William "Extra Billy" Smith, inaugurated in 1864. Smith outfitted blockade-runners with cotton in an attempt to obtain supplies and food from England; he also commandeered a train from the York River Railroad and sent state officials south to purchase corn for distribution among the state's indigent residents. Smith also took control of Virginia's salt reserves, which state officials allocated to county governments for sale at below-market rates. Staunton resident Joseph Waddell recorded one such transaction in his diary in January 1865, noting, "The State sells *salt* to citizens at less price than the market affords, and I have secured all I am entitled to as the best investment for Confederate money."[13]

Other Virginians sought assistance from the national government, focusing in particular on draft exemptions and impressment. "It is a curious feature of the conscript & exemption laws," the Smyth County Court wrote the governor, "at a time when the question of bread & meat is so vital to the maintenance of our armies, that all the producers of bread & meat are taken as conscripts, whilst the exempts are almost exclusively consumers." Complaints like this one, whether sent directly to Congress or the secretary of war, or relayed through state officials, no doubt contributed to changes in Confederate conscription policies. According to Blair, "Orders to conscription authorities [after May 1863] specified exemption for overseers who otherwise would report to the army whenever a farm's crops went to the government or fed the indigent. Officials hoped that increasing the supply of food would alleviate discontent on the home front and, subsequently, the pressure on soldiers to desert." Conscription regulations passed in February 1864, meanwhile, ended exemptions for farmers who grew tobacco or cotton at the expense of food crops. Thanks to the bread riots, the Confederate government had become significantly more responsive to discontent and deficiencies on the home front.[14]

One method of overcoming shortages was to impress grains, livestock, firewood, and laborers for the benefit of either the army or civilians receiving assistance through local governments. In addition, impressment commissioners set government prices for agricultural products every two months, thus placing a small check on inflation. Virginians with limited resources welcomed this measure of government assistance. "Impressment became the principal irritation on the home front for the last year of the war but not among the lower classes usually blamed for this discontent," Blair argued. "The most vocal protests," he continued, "emanated from prosperous farmers and large slave owners who provided the biggest targets for government agents, while the poor and the nonproducers supported impressment so that they could acquire food at regulated prices." The vocal protests of Virginia's wealthy farmers perhaps prompted Congress to reject Treasury Secretary Trenholm's November 1864 plan to increase taxes and stop issuing paper currency. "The real difficulty" with the plan, according to War Department employee Robert Kean, "is that he proposed very heavy taxation and to lay it fairly on the agricultural and planting interest."[15]

Thus, the Confederacy entered the final six months of the war with no plan to halt the rapid depreciation of its currency. The Confederate inflation rate skyrocketed from 280 percent in November 1864 to approximately 1,000 percent in early April 1865; the fall of Richmond and the surrender of Robert E. Lee's Army of Northern Virginia pushed the rate to somewhere between 6,000 and 9,000. Joseph Waddell put these changes in practical terms in early January 1865, noting, "A dress which formerly cost $10 to $15, now costs $400 to $500—that is, my pay for four or five months." In April, hotelkeeper John Nadenbousch counseled his wife, "In using funds hold back any *coin* you may have until the last as it is the most valuable & safest." While the Confederate government utterly failed to construct a solid

financial foundation for the war effort, and while state and national leaders were unable to resolve every food shortage, many historians agree that
those leaders still deserve at least as much credit as blame. The attempts of
local, state, and national governments to respond to Virginians' economic
needs in the last two years of the war, while ultimately unsuccessful, at least
provided sufficient assistance to prevent another riot—and poor civilians
applauded those efforts rather than blaming their governments.[16]

From the perspective of many Virginians, blame for the food shortages
and other economic problems they faced during the final months of the war
fell squarely on the shoulders of Maj. Gen. David Hunter and Maj. Gen. Philip
H. Sheridan of the U.S. Army. Hunter's men were the first Union soldiers
to spend any significant time in the upper (southern) Shenandoah Valley,
easily defeating a hastily cobbled-together force of Confederate infantry and
reserves in Augusta County on June 5, 1864. Hunter's men then occupied
Staunton—a new experience for many of the town's residents. One, Nancy
Emerson, called the invading forces a "cloud of locusts from the bottomless
pit," but Hunter's visit to Staunton and Lexington in fact brought little more
destruction than many other Virginia towns had witnessed in the previous
year. The Union soldiers generally took flour, bacon, whisky, horses, shoes,
clothing, and blankets. Hunter saved his army's destructive power for targets
of clear military or symbolic importance: factories, mills, and stables that did
business with the Confederate War Department; railroad lines; and, most
famously, the Virginia Military Institute and the home of former governor
John Letcher in Lexington. Hunter then turned his sights toward Lynchburg
and its key Confederate supply depots, railroad junctions, and hospitals, but
Confederate forces under Maj. Gen. Jubal Early managed to push Hunter
back out of the Valley and into Maryland in early July.[17]

To counter Early's threat to the population of Maryland, on August
7, General Grant placed Sheridan in command of all Union forces in the
Shenandoah Valley theater. Sheridan had orders to pursue Early relentlessly,
sever all railroad connections between the Valley and Richmond, and destroy
the Valley's economy. It was very clear to Grant and Sheridan that Virginia's
military and civilian populations needed the provisions being raised in the
Shenandoah Valley, so their plan was to test what military historians have
termed a "strategy of exhaustion." They also hoped that such a campaign
would both raise Northern morale and simultaneously convince Southern
civilians that their government and army lacked the power to protect them.

Sheridan's striking victories in September and October did indeed provide clear evidence to Northern observers that Union armies could win battles, and many historians have cited those victories as crucial to Abraham Lincoln's successful reelection campaign.

The effects of Sheridan's economic campaign, what Valley residents succinctly termed "the Burning," are less conclusive. Certainly, Sheridan's men destroyed a great deal of property. According to his official reports, Federal soldiers captured or destroyed 3,772 horses, 10,918 cattle, 12,000 sheep, 15,000 hogs, 20,397 tons of hay, 435,802 bushels of wheat, 77,176 bushels of corn, 71 flour mills, and 1,200 barns. Even allowing that Sheridan exaggerated the extent of his destruction, still, this probably represented one-third of the agricultural capacity of the Shenandoah Valley—obviously a huge blow, but not necessarily one that would reduce the civilian population to starvation. A report that officials from Rockingham County sent to Governor Smith confirmed Sheridan's one-third estimation. Sheridan did not include official reports on the number of slaves who left their owners, however, and reports from Valley residents failed to give a clear picture. Certainly, the Valley counties, where slaves had comprised between 25 and 40 percent of the total antebellum workforce, lost many slaves as a result of the 1864 campaign. This reduction in the labor force would have to be added to the one-third loss in provisions in order to calculate the true economic cost of the campaign.[18]

Quite a few Valley residents were anticipating a poor crop even before "the Burning; their fears had increased exponentially by the end of the campaign. "We have had a good deal of dry weather this Summer," Thomas McGuffin of Lewisburg wrote in early September, "in consequence of which corn will be cut short." He also lamented, "Wheat crops this year were not verry good hardly an average Crop." By mid-October, Daniel Schreckhise was worried about "suffering times in the valley this winter as the yanks have burn all of the barns from hear down & all of the mills except one occasionly." The residents of the Shenandoah Valley would not be the only ones to suffer, he feared. According to Schreckhise, Sheridan's campaign had achieved its military objective, for "I dont see how our army is to live in Va this winter the valley has bin our main support & that is nearly all destroyed."[19]

Soldiers and civilians alike struggled to cope with deepening shortages in the winter of 1864–1865. In Staunton, the Waddell family adjusted both their schedule and their idea of what constituted a good meal. "For some weeks past we have been eating only two meals a day, the second one at 4 or 5 o'clock in the afternoon," Joseph Waddell wrote in January. "It is a convenient arrangement on several accounts. Having no sugar, coffee and tea as formerly, we cannot afford supper, and do not need it after a late dinner." Families in Richmond felt an even greater pinch. "Through the effect of Sheridan's raid," Kean observed, "Richmond is rapidly approaching a state of famine. Bacon is $20 a pound, flour $1200 a barrel, butter $25 a pound, beef and that the worst $10 to $12, wood $200 a cord, etc., and the supply exceedingly meager." Soldiers in the field fared worst of all, though. In early February Kean noted, "General Lee wrote that his troops beyond Petersburg had been in line of battle three days and nights in snow, hail and rain *without a mouthful* of meat; that they would be so weakened by exposure and privation as not to have the physical strength to march and fight." While these shortages reflected numerous problems, including the blockade, the deteriorating conditions of Virginia's railroads, insufficient labor supply on many farms, and a dry growing season, Virginians blamed them on just one thing—Sheridan's destruction of the Shenandoah Valley.[20]

This single-minded condemnation of the Yankees probably kept President Davis and the Confederate Congress from becoming targets of widespread discontent among white Virginians. Historians William Blair and Jacqueline Campbell have both suggested that occupation by Union army forces decreased partisanship and dissent among Confederates by giving them an external enemy to fight, rather than placing all of the blame for their economic difficulties on their own government. The frequently acerbic Kean thought the Confederate government deserved at least some of the blame, however. In January 1865, he chastised Congress for lacking the courage to face the full extent of the Confederacy's fiscal crisis. "As the real condition of the treasury comes to be known," he wrote, including "the hopeless bankruptcy in which it is plunged, the arrears of $320 million, and the proposition to tax 16% ad valorem as a means of meeting it—the Congress get more and more weak in the knees."[21]

By early 1865, countless other Virginians, though perhaps not blaming the Confederate government for all aspects of the fiscal crisis, recognized the Confederacy's dire financial straits. Nadenbousch encouraged his wife to sell her Confederate currency for Union greenbacks, regardless of the unfavorable exchange rate, "as no doubt it will be more useful than to invest in property here." Augusta County minister Francis McFarland sold four barrels of flour to the Confederate army in early April. He noted, with some bemusement, "the Govt. give $400 per B. in an order on the Treasy, where I presume there is no money." Waddell made a similar observation one week after Lee's surrender, complaining, "I have not a cent of money, and no prospect of getting any. Cant by anything to eat or wear. Confederate notes are of course, entirely worthless, so far as relates to purchase."[22]

"There is little to eat in the country," Robert Kean observed in the spring of 1865, "and less currency. Hence wages are low and subsistence dear." In the immediate aftermath of General Lee's surrender, Virginians struggled to revive their economy—to begin planting grain crops, to resume processing tobacco, and to reopen as many rail lines as possible. Often they did so with assistance from Federal authorities, who took control of the Old Dominion's politics but, in the interest of stability, left many of its economic activities in the hands of antebellum and wartime leaders. As they rebuilt their economic lives, white and black Virginians also clashed over the true meaning of free labor; some white Virginians, like Thomas Bocock, simply failed to recognize the changes that emancipation had brought. All aspects of economic revival came slowly—too slowly for many Virginians, who had already faced years of wartime deprivation and now wanted both peace *and* abundance.[23]

Many, like Kean, complained that "this overthrow of the labor system of a whole country without preparation or mitigation" had ruined Virginia's chances for long-term recovery. "As there is great scarcity," he continued, "and the crops were all immature, there was the utmost danger of a famine from a general cessation of labor. Great numbers of negroes quit work and flocked to Richmond and other garrisoned towns, where they had to be supported by the issue of rations." Waddell witnessed a similar situation in Staunton with great disgust. "It was provoking, ludicrous, and pitiful," he wrote, "to see the poor Negroes crowding the streets, some of them, especially the women, dressed in all their finery, rejoicing in their freedom." During the first few months of peace, white Virginians routinely complained that former slaves, rather than working and living as they had under slavery, publicly enjoyed their freedom and leisure time. Many, to the chagrin of their employers, simply disappeared. "This morning early," McFarland noted in late June, "Liz, being now free, left us without making it known to any of the white family. A foolish negro." McFarland apparently had an easier time retaining the services of Caroline, whom he hired for 50¢ per week.[24]

Officials of the Federal Bureau of Freedmen, Refugees, and Abandoned

Lands, charged with facilitating Virginia's transition from slave labor to free labor, often found white Virginians reluctant to make that transition, especially when it meant paying wages to their former slaves. In Staunton, Waddell complained that "a Rev. Dr. Dudly, of New Haven, agent of the 'Freedmen's Bureau,'" expected Virginia's farmers and factory owners to "adopt a schedule of prices for negro labor—Humbug!" Augusta County Freedmen's Bureau agent W. Storer How found it necessary to inform one farmer that he was "quite at liberty to hire any colored man without the consent of his former master, as he is also at liberty to engage his services without such consent," despite what some former slaveholders had charged. Some landholders, however, quickly learned the value of the bureau's advice and assistance, especially when they needed to enforce their contracts. "In those parts of the country where the farmers promptly made regular and explicit contracts with the slaves for hire there has been comparatively little trouble," Kean reported, "and the work has progressed pretty well. In the towns there is great confusion, and in the neighborhood of the towns the crops are left uncultivated by the flocking of the negroes into them." Most officers of the federal government, while seeking to protect the rights of former slaves, saw restoring the stability and profitability of Virginia's agriculture as one of their top priorities.[25]

Federal officials also sought to rebuild Virginia's industrial and commercial sectors, although this process moved very slowly. Factory owners, in particular, saw little improvement in their economic state before the end of the year. In Lynchburg, where tobacco processing was the primary form of factory work, the outlook seemed particularly bleak. "The tobacco factories that had long been the engine of Lynchburg's economy had not operated in two years and would not reopen until the fall," noted Tripp, "because few farmers had planted tobacco during the previous summer. As a result, many of the artisans and shopkeepers who catered to the tobacconists found little demand for their work during the summer of 1865." Mill operators also suffered from low crop yields, while small iron forges faced continued shortages of materials. Larger establishments like Tredegar recovered more quickly due to federal patronage.[26]

As Tripp observed in Lynchburg's case, "Federal officials worked to revive [Virginia's] war-ravaged economy—usually on terms that benefited the business community." Not only did they write and enforce labor contracts for former slaves and wage-earning whites, they also rebuilt Virginia's transportation infrastructure and funded new manufacturing projects. Agent How urged the Freedmen's Bureau to build a sawmill in Staunton, "as by so doing, Lumber that will certainly be needed can be furnished, and employment given to freedmen who will require it." Newspaper editors celebrated the potential economic benefits that rebuilding Virginia's industries—and especially its railroads—would bring. "With the improvement and extension of all her lines of trade," wrote the editor of Staunton's *Vindicator,* "the development of her resources and the advancement of her manufacturing interests, will come the golden opportunity for the poor, unfortunate Virginia of to-day to amass many times more wealth than she has lost in her devastation and her slaves."[27]

For most Virginians, however, the immediate aftermath of the war brought few economic benefits, and the challenges of rebuilding the state's industries and infrastructure seemed insurmountable. "See no prospect for making a living, yet I must do something soon, or I shall come to want," Waddell reported in September. "Have no money—cannot pay a bill of Six dollars—and can collect nothing due me. Have not carried a dollar since the war ended . . . many other people in the same dilemma." The editor of the *Richmond Republic* had a solution for unemployed clerks like Waddell: he urged them to take up farm work. "Young men who are lounging about cities and villages in quest of clerkships would do well to imitate the example of the greater number of returned soldiers," he wrote, and cultivate their families' farms. "They would, besides, secure for themselves much larger pecuniary return than any clerkship, public or commercial, affords." Waddell may have taken this advice, but it is difficult to know for sure: in mid-October, lacking the money to buy a new blank book, he ceased writing his diary. His experiences demonstrated that even as the state's farms and factories made tentative steps toward recovery, the Confederacy's inadequate fiscal policies left an enduring legacy for the postbellum Virginia economy.[28]

Notes

1. Memoranda Book of Thomas S. Bocock, May 1865, Bocock Family Papers, mss 10612, series 3, box 8, Albert and Shirley Small Special Collections Library, University of Virginia, Charlottesville.

2. James L. Huston, *Calculating the Value of Union: Slavery, Property Rights, and the Economic Origins of the Civil War* (Chapel Hill: University of North

Carolina Press, 2003), 25–27; Historical Census Browser, 1860, http://fisher.lib
.virginia.edu/collections/stats/histcensus/index.html (accessed January 3, 2009).

3. John Majewski, *A House Dividing: Economic Development in Pennsylvania and Virginia before the Civil War* (New York: Cambridge University Press, 2000), 111–14, 161–72.

4. Speech of Henry Lewis Benning, February 18, 1861, in George H. Reese, ed., *Proceedings of the Virginia Sate Convention of 1861* (Richmond: Virginia State Library, 1965), 1:70. Charles B. Dew, *Apostles of Disunion: Southern Secession Commissioners and the Causes of the Civil War* (Charlottesville: University of Virginia Press, 2001) discusses the secession commissioners who traveled from Georgia, South Carolina, and Alabama to speak at secession conventions in the Upper South. Dew, in *Ironmaker to the Confederacy: Joseph R. Anderson and the Tredegar Iron Works* (New Haven, Conn.: Yale University Press, 1966) and *Bond of Iron: Master and Slave at Buffalo Forge* (New York: Norton, 1994), charted the growth of Virginia's iron-making industry in the late antebellum period as well as its importance to the Confederacy.

5. Gregg D. Kimball, *American City, Southern Place: A Cultural History of Antebellum Richmond* (Athens: University of Georgia Press, 2000), argued that "railroads, agricultural improvements, and industrialization only made the city stronger through the reciprocal relationship between the city and the [slaveholding] countryside" (xvii). Midori Takagi, *"Rearing Wolves to Our Own Destruction": Slavery in Richmond, Virginia, 1782–1865* (Charlottesville: University of Virginia Press, 1999) also explores the role of slave laborers in Richmond's industrial development.

6. Emory M. Thomas, *The Confederate State of Richmond: A Biography of the Capital* (Baton Rouge: Louisiana State University Press, 1998), 112. See also Frank E. Vandiver, *Ploughshares into Swords: Josiah Gorgas and Confederate Ordnance* (Austin: University of Texas Press, 1952).

7. Thomas, *Confederate State of Richmond,* 112; William Blair, *Virginia's Private War: Feeding Body and Soul in the Confederacy, 1861–1865* (New York: Oxford University Press, 1998), 105.

8. Historical Census Browser, 1860.

9. Washington County Court to Governor John Letcher, October 26, 1863, John Letcher Executive Papers, Library of Virginia, Richmond.

10. Blair, *Virginia's Private War,* 56.

11. John B. Jones, *A Rebel War Clerk's Diary at the Confederate States Capital* (Philadelphia: Lippincott, 1866), 1:240; Blair, *Virginia's Private War,* 69.

12. Thomas, *Confederate State of Richmond,* 147; Blair, *Virginia's Private War,* 76; Steven Elliot Tripp, *Yankee Town, Southern City: Race and Class Relations in Civil War Lynchburg* (New York: New York University Press, 1997), 141.

13. Thomas, *Confederate State of Richmond,* 169–70; Joseph Waddell Diary, January 12, 1865, http://valley.lib.virginia.edu (accessed March 2, 2009).

14. Smyth County Court to Governor John Letcher, February 11, 1863, John Letcher Executive Papers; Blair, *Virginia's Private War,* 83.

15. Blair, *Virginia's Private War,* 111–12; Robert Kean, November 20, 1864, in *Inside the Confederate Government: The Diary of Robert Garlick Hill Kean,* ed. Edward Younger (Baton Rouge: Louisiana State University Press, 1957), 179.

16. Confederate Inflation Chart, Official Publication #13, Richmond Civil War Centennial Committee (Richmond: 1963), Broadside 1963, C664, Albert and Shirley Small Special Collections Library; Waddell Diary, January 12, 1865; John Quincy Adams Nadenbousch to Hester J. Nadenbousch, April 1, 1865, http://valley.lib.virginia.edu (accessed March 2, 2009).

17. Nancy Emerson Diary, July 21, 1864, http://valley.lib.virginia.edu (accessed February 23, 2008).

18. Philip H. Sheridan to Henry W. Halleck, November 24, 1864, in U.S. War Department, *War of the Rebellion: A Compilation of the Official Records of the Union and Confederate Armies* (Washington, D.C.: Government Printing Office, 1880–1901), series 1, vol. 43, pt. 1, 37–38; "Rockingham's Losses," *Staunton Republican Vindicator,* November 18, 1864, http://valley.lib.virginia.edu (accessed February 23, 2009).

19. Thomas McGuffin to Templeton McGuffin, September 4, 1864; Daniel K. Schreckhise to James M. Schreckhise, October 17, 1864, http://valley.lib.virginia.edu (accessed March 2, 2009).

20. Waddell Diary, January 12, 1865; Kean, March 23, 1865, and February 10, 1865, in *Inside the Confederate Government,* 204, 200.

21. Blair, *Virginia's Private War;* Jacqueline Glass Campbell, *When Sherman Marched North from the Sea: Resistance on the Confederate Home Front* (Chapel Hill: University of North Carolina Press, 2003); Kean, January 13, 1865, in *Inside the Confederate Government,* 188.

22. John Quincy Adams Nadenbousch to Hester J. Nadenbousch, January 24, 1865; Francis McFarland Diary, April 8, 1865; Waddell Diary, April 19, 1865, all at http://valley.lib.virginia.edu (accessed March 2, 2009).

23. Kean, June 1, 1865, in *Inside the Confederate Government,* 209.

24. Ibid., 208; Waddell Diary, May 1, 1865; McFarland Diary, June 27, 1865, and June 10, 1865.

25. Waddell Diary, June 29, 1865; W. Storer How to L. P. Dangerfield, August 7, 1865, http://valley.lib.virginia.edu (accessed March 2, 2009); Kean, June 27, 1865, in *Inside the Confederate Government,* 211.

26. Tripp, *Yankee Town, Southern City,* 165.

27. Ibid., 168; W. Storer How to Orlando Brown, August 7, 1865; *Staunton*

Republican Vindicator, September 1, 1865, http://valley.lib.virginia.edu (accessed March 2, 2009).

28. Waddell Diary, September 18, 1865, and October 18, 1865; "All Should Labor," *Richmond Republic,* reprinted in *Staunton Spectator,* December 26, 1865, http://valley.lib.virginia.edu (accessed March 2, 2009).

"Better to be merry than sad"

Music and Entertainment in Wartime Virginia

E. Lawrence Abel

During the Civil War, musical entertainment was considered such an essential part of the Southern war effort that well-known entertainers were exempted from conscription until late in 1864, and salaries for entertainers were among the highest in the Confederacy.[1] Every large city in America had at least one musical director, an orchestra, and singing actors, actresses, and specialty acts. Every drama was preceded by an instrumental overture, usually from some familiar opera. Intermissions always included musical interludes, and song and dance acts were inserted in every play, with no regard for plot. After the play, audiences remained in their seats for the one-act operas and various musical acts that always followed.[2]

In 1860 Richmond, located on the James River, about 150 miles from its mouth, was one of America's most elegant cities. The Richmond Theatre, located at the junction of Seventh and Broad, was the city's best-known showplace. Built in 1819, it was refurbished in 1838 and rechristened the Marshall Theatre in honor of Supreme Court Chief justice and former Richmond native John Marshall, but Richmonders still preferred the old name, affectionately calling it "the Richmond." The city was on the theater circuit for many of the world's great virtuosi when they visited the United States; the theater had hosted some of America's and Europe's best-known entertainers, among them the "Swedish Nightingale," Jenny Lind, who performed there in 1850 at ticket prices as high as $105.[3] Although Richmond had been culturally overshadowed by New Orleans in antebellum America, as the Confederacy's capital, it quickly became the South's entertainment center, especially after New Orleans was captured early in 1862.

John Hill Hewitt, the "Bard of the Confederacy," was the Richmond Theatre manager. A feisty sixty-year-old in 1861, Hewitt, had asked President

Jefferson Davis to give him a commission in the Confederate army, citing his attendance at the United States Military Academy, but Davis declined because of Hewitt's age and instead offered him a job as drill master for new recruits. Hewitt did not accept, choosing to take the job as manager of the Richmond Theatre in October 1861. On January 2, 1862, the theater burned down (as the result of arson, some thought). The fire destroyed all the company's musical instruments, stage scenery, costumes, and sheet music. Hewitt and actor Richard D'Orsey, both of whom were sleeping in the theater when the fire broke out, managed to escape, but both suffered severe burns.[4] The *Richmond Daily Dispatch* expressed deep regret over the loss of that "popular institution, the theater."[5]

The maxim of the show having to go on had not been expressed in its familiar terms yet, but it was Hewitt's musical mantra and he immediately booked his company into the nearby Franklin Hall, popularly known as the "Richmond Varieties." Formerly a church, the Varieties had been transformed into a theater in 1861. The South was deeply religious, but religion came second to entertainment. On January 6, 1862, just four days after the fire, the current show reopened. The *Richmond Daily Dispatch* applauded the performance, adding that Hewitt was entitled to no little credit for giving the public pleasure in spite of extremely difficult circumstances.[6]

Later that month at one of the Varieties performances, a Mademoiselle Boisvert sang "Home, Sweet Home," the most popular song of the war on both sides.[7] A soldier in the audience, far from his Mississippi home sobbed so loudly it attracted the attention of everyone in the house, but no one said a word. Unaware that everyone was staring at him, the soldier stood up after Boisvert had finished and "vociferously called for an encore, offering $5 if the lady would sing it over again," which she did.[8]

In a different part of town, a slave, Thomas Green Wiggins, known throughout the South as "Blind Tom," was entertaining audiences at the African Church. Born blind in Georgia in 1849, he showed such uncanny musical talent at the age of four that his owners provided him with formal musical lessons. At eight, he was giving public concerts, featuring works by Beethoven, Mozart, and other European composers. At first merely curious, audiences were soon astonished at his virtuosity. In January 1862, when he came to Richmond, he was advertised as "the Negro Boy Pianist—the Wonder of the World, A Musician, Composer, Singer, and Orator."[9] It was no exaggeration. Not only could he play works by European masters flawlessly, he could simultaneously play a different tune with each hand while singing yet another. And if that were not enough, he could also play the piano with his back to the instrument!

The New Richmond Theatre opened February 9, 1863, and stayed open until Richmond was evacuated in April 1865. Hewitt was no longer in charge. His autocratic management style had not endeared him to the actors or the theater's owner, Mrs. Elizabeth Magill, and in June 1862 Magill fired him and replaced him with D'Orsey, also appointing C. A. Rosenberg as musical director. Advertisements announced:

> The Company will consist of all those favorite and artistic Ladies and Gentlemen now performing at the Varieties, together with such additions as the material now in the South will furnish. Native talent will always receive every encouragement from the Management, in the hope to build up a corps of Dramatic Artists from such material as they feel our own South can furnish. The Management solicits from their patrons and the citizens of Richmond the generous encouragement and forbearance they have hitherto extended them, and with renewed energies, they promise to spare neither trouble nor expense.[10]

There would also be some new rules for the audience. No longer would liquor be sold in the theater; drunken patrons had frequently ruined performances in the past. Audience members were also prohibited from smoking, swearing, and cheering favorite actors or booing those less well regarded. Patrons who broke these rules, the theater warned, would be thrown out and jailed.[11]

On opening night the theater was packed. A $300 prize for the best "Inaugural Poem" was offered for the occasion, a contest won by poet Henry Timrod, who overnight became the highest-paid poet in the Confederacy. After actor Walter Keeble read the winning entry, the whole company came onstage and sang the "Virginia Marseillaise."[12]

One of the New Theatre's most popular musicals was *The Virginia Cavalier,* with lyrics by George W. Alexander, commandant of Castle Thunder, a Confederate prison in Richmond for deserters and civilians suspected of aiding the North. Critics sniped at it as "an abominable play, with absolutely nothing to recommend it." The theater critic for the *Southern Illustrated News* wrote that it was "the same old story of 'virtue rewarded—villainy foiled'—

interspersed with singing and dancing."[13] Few Southerners paid attention to the critics. Virtue rewarded and villainy foiled was what audiences wanted, and *The Virginia Cavalier* became Richmond's favorite musical, returning again and again to the Richmond Theatre.[14] In large part, the show's popularity was due to its star performer, Sallie Partington. Imagining themselves as Bob Roebuck, the "Southern soldier boy," the "darling of her heart," teenage soldiers cheered, "Miss Sallie! Miss Sallie!" each time she sang:

Bob Roebuck is my sweetheart's name
He's off to the wars and gone,
He's fighting for his Nannie dear,
His sword is buckled on.
He's fighting for his own true love,
His foes he does defy;
He is the darling of my heart,
My Southern soldier boy.

Oh! if in battle he was slain,
I am sure that I would die,
But I am sure he'll come again.
And cheer my weeping eye;
But should he fall in this our glorious cause,
He still would be my joy,
For many a sweetheart mourns the loss
Of a Southern soldier boy.

I hope for the best, and so do all
Whose hopes are in the field;
I know that we shall win the day
For Southrons never yield
And when we think of those who are away,
We look above for joy
And I'm mighty glad that my Bobby is
A Southern soldier boy.

The song and its singer were so popular that Richmond music publisher George Dunn published "The Southern Soldier Boy" in 1863 with the caption: "As sung by Miss Sallie Partington in, 'The Virginia Cavalier' at the Richmond New Theatre."

George Dunn was one of the few Richmond music publishers who managed to stay afloat during the war. Almost nothing is known about Dunn except that he worked for the Confederate Treasury as a lithographer, as well as running his music business, and many of his songs were published in collaboration with music publisher Julian Augustus Selby in Columbia, South Carolina.[15] Richmond publisher West and Johnston didn't stay in business, citing production costs and paper shortages.[16] What paper could be obtained was of poor quality, and it progressively worsened over the course of the war. In 1861, Confederate music publishers were printing their sheet music on heavy paper, often with brightly colored lithographed covers. By 1862, the paper was thinner and the pages smaller. Ink was also in short supply. When there was no more lampblack, music publishers turned to persimmons, pomegranate rind, bark, and leaves for ink.

Singer-songwriter Harry Macarthy was the South's most popular entertainer and often appeared in Richmond during the war. Born in England, he was short, handsome, clean-shaven, and had thick black hair. Best known as the author of patriotic songs like "The Bonnie Blue Flag," "The Volunteer; or, It Is My Country's Call," and "Missouri: A Voice from the South," Macarthy was the consummate showman, always looking for ways to improve his act, which he called his *Personation Concerts* because he specialized in impersonations. Macarthy crisscrossed the South entertaining soldiers and civilians alike. In February 1862, he and his wife, Lottie Estelle, opened at the Broad Street Theater, with a special tableau illustrating his "Bonnie Blue Flag."[17] The following month, on March 17, he was scheduled to open at the Metropolitan Hall, but he fell ill and the show had to be postponed for three days. The manager took out a front-page ad for the show in the *Richmond Daily Dispatch*; Macarthy's was the only act at any theater to receive that kind of notice up to then. The advertisement announced that his show had been "pronounced by the entire press to be the most unique, pleasing, chaste, and astonishing performance ever presented to the public."[18] A few days later, on March 24, he was the feature act at the African Church.[19] In December 1862 Macarthy was again at Richmond's Broad Street Theatre. The advertisement for the show described Macarthy as "the Author, Actor, Vocalist, Dancer, Composer, Banjoist, Mimic, and man of many parts." Each night, according to the notice, Macarthy would impersonate "nine or ten different characters selected from the English, Irish, Scotch, French, Dutch, Ethiopian and American, with their National Songs, Dialects, Costumes and Dances." The show was still playing during the first week of January and had been seen "by the Clergy and the most fastidious ladies and gentlemen in the South." Reserved seats were 75¢, but servants could get in for 50¢.[20]

After the Richmond Theatre reopened, Macarthy's show was transferred to that stage. A twenty-four-hour furlough in hand, Val Giles, serving with Hood's Texas brigade, did not want to miss it. The house was packed. There was no special seating accorded to rank, so generals, colonels, captains, lieutenants, and privates sat together wherever there was a seat. The showstopper occurred when Macarthy, dressed in full Confederate uniform representing a soldier leaving home for the war, marched onto the stage singing his "Bonnie Blue Flag." When he came to the chorus, Lottie Estelle ran onto the stage carrying the blue flag with its single star and threw her arms around her sweetheart's neck. "I have seen a great deal of enthusiasm demonstrated in theaters since then, and have seen pandemoniums in Democratic state conventions," reported Giles, "but I have never seen anything to equal the scene I witnessed that night. Men went wild. The soldiers to a man rose to their feet, many of them standing on their seats. Hats, caps, red sashes and sabers waved and flashed high over their heads. The uproar was so loud and continuous that Mccarty [sic] appeared on the stage and sang the song all over again, a song which afterwards became as famous in the south as 'Dixie.'"[21]

Vaudevillian acts like R. Bishop Buckley's *Southern Nightingales* and Harry Macarthy's *Personation Concerts* were at home at the Metropolitan Hall on the north side of Franklin between Thirteenth and Fourteenth. Originally a church, it was converted into a 1,500-seat theater in 1853. Minstrel shows ("Ethiopian Operas") were popular at the Corinthian Hall (also known as the Mechanics Hall Institute and renamed the Opera House in 1864 because of all the minstrel shows it featured). It was destroyed in the evacuation fire in April 1865.

Throughout the war, people in Richmond never stopped going to the city's many theaters, and even when the city was on the verge of capture in 1865, there were still theatergoing diehards. On the eve of Richmond's surrender in April 1865, "Budd and Buckley's Minstrels and Brass Band" were still being "received nightly with shouts of applause."[22] John Lansing Burrows, pastor of the First Baptist Church, was among the few who objected to all the money being frittered away on such frivolity. "With surprising energy, and regardless of cost, in these pinching times of war, a splendid building [the Opera House] with most costly decorations, has been reared from the ashes of the old," he complained.

> A strong corps of actors, male and female, have been secured, and, in addition to them, "twenty gentlemen for the chorus and the ballet." No cripples from the battlefield are these—they can sing and dance; they can mimic fighting on the stage. For the serious work of repelling a real enemy they have neither taste nor heart. But they can sing while the country groans, and dance while the cars are bringing, in sad funeral procession, the dead to their very doors and the dismal ambulance bears the sick and the wounded under the very glare of their lights and within the sound of their music.[23]

The *Richmond Daily Enquirer* had a more balanced perspective. People, it contended, needed a diversion in these troubled times. "We must know there must be recreation even in the midst of mourning and sorrow, and it is the duty of all to take recreation. . . . It is not that people enjoy themselves that we condemn, but that in doing so they conserve the provisions required for the support of the army and the poor."[24]

When they weren't going to the theaters, Richmond's elite could always find some party to attend. Soon after President Davis and his family arrived in Richmond, his wife, Varina, began hosting fortnightly levees, rivaling the parties Mary Lincoln was hosting at the White House. War Department officer Thomas De Leon called Varina's levees "social jambalayas" because they were attended by cabinet ministers, congressmen, heads of departments, generals, admirals, diplomats, dainty debutantes and belles, together with sturdy artisans, their hands scrubbed to whiteness so that they would be clean enough to shake the president's, and speculators looking for a chance to make valuable political contacts. Parties at the homes of Richmond's leading families, the Standards, the Semmeses, the Macfarlands, the Ives, and the Pegrams "were the perfect mixture of easy elegance and brains in evening dress," said De Leon, but they could not compare with Varina's levees. The first winter of the war, said De Leon, "was one written in red letters, for old Richmond rang with a chime of merry laughter that for the time drowned the echo of the summer's fights and the groans of the wayside hospitals."[25]

The city's intellectual elite—its writers, artists, musicians, clergymen, and statesmen—single and married, also got together in what came to be called the Richmond Mosaic Club. The club was completely informal. It had no officers, no fixed membership, and no special meeting place. Participants simply met by chance at various homes throughout the city. Those back from the war related their experiences over drinks, and others shared their experiences on the home front. After the potluck dinners, the members entertained one another with songs and poems.[26]

"Madame" Ruhl, a well-known soprano in the South during the war who also gave singing lessons in Richmond, often entertained the members, as did amateurs like Mrs. Myra Semmes and Mrs. Clara Fitzgerald, both of whom played the harp. The guests often entertained one another by reading well-known poems or poems they themselves had written. John R. Thompson, editor of the *Southern Literary Messenger* and best known for his song "Richmond Is a Hard Road to Travel," was a frequent guest at these gatherings. Very sensitive to criticism, Thompson listened nervously to critiques of his latest efforts. John Esten Cooke, the "Walter Scott of the South," was also a frequent attendee when his duties on Gen. Jeb Stuart's staff permitted a "flying visit to Richmond." So, too, was Innes Randolph, who also served under Stuart and is best known for writing the unrepentant "Oh, I'm a Good Ole Rebel." Sometimes Stuart himself attended, singing "Jine the Cavalry" as he rode back to camp. Gen. John Pegram also liked to drop in. Though he did not play any musical instruments very well, he was regarded as an "artistic whistler."[27]

Songs sung at the Mosaic Club and in other private homes have been dubbed "parlor music" from the room in which they were typically performed. Sentimental, often maudlin, the songs were easy to sing and play and were meant to be accompanied unobtrusively by soft-stringed instruments like the parlor piano or guitar. All the stanzas in a song had the same tune, and the same notes and chords were used over and over so they were easy to learn and play. At the time, no family in America was considered cultured if it did not have a piano in its parlor, the modern-day "living room" of the house. No girl in America could be considered "accomplished" unless she could play the piano.[28] The piano was such a prominent part of America's musical world before and during the war that few music publishers would consider any song that did not have a piano arrangement.

Men were as likely as women to be familiar with the keyboard; Gen. "Jeb" Stuart often accompanied himself as he entertained friends in their family parlors. Stuart's favorite song was "Sweet Evelina, Dear Evelina," the "dove" who lived "down in the valley" who was "fair like a rose," "meek like a lamb," with "raven black hair," and who "smells so sweet" "she never requires perfumery."[29]

Southerners were particularly partial to "Lorena," a song about a frustrated love affair and reconciliation beyond the grave ("'Tis dust to dust beneath the sod; but there, up there, 'tis heart to heart"), written by the Reverend Henry D. L. Webster in 1853 and put to music by Joseph Phillbrick Webster, who also wrote the hymn "In the Sweet By and By." In her diary, Mary Chesnut quoted a friend of hers who said that "there is a girl in large hoops and a calico frock at every piano between this place [Richmond] and the Mississippi, banging on the out-of-tune thing—and looking up into a man's face who wears Confederate uniform. Very soiled is that uniform and battle-stained, but the man's heart is fresh enough, as he hangs over her, to believe in Lorena."[30]

Dancing was always a popular pastime and grand balls were common. Affluent Southerners learned the fashionable dances of the day, like the waltz, polka, and schottische, from self-styled "professors," many of whom came from Europe.[31] One such professor, J. S. St. Maur Bingham, had a "Fashionable Dancing Academy" in Richmond's Exchange Hotel, where he gave afternoon dance lessons to ladies at 4:00 and evening lessons to gentlemen at 8:00.[32] Those feeling proficient in their skills were encouraged to attend the balls he began sponsoring in April 1863 at the Monticello Hall. Admission was $10. By May they had become so popular he started naming them "Beauregard Socials" in honor of Confederate general P. G. T. Beauregard.[33] In January 1864, the professor booked the Concert Hall for his Children's Grand Fancy Ball, where he "introduced several new and beautiful dances."[34]

There were also many less formal dancing get-togethers. When food and other supplies became scarce in 1864, the weekly social gatherings formerly called "danceable teas" became "starvation parties" featuring vintage "eau de James" (water from the James River). [35] The only expense was the musicians. There was nothing to eat, but soldiers on leave could relax or whirl for hours. If they did not care for the starvation party, there was always an impromptu "shindig" where some of the dancers were "high kickers and not overly graceful."[36]

Myra Semmes, wife of Thomas J. Semmes, senator from Louisiana and cousin to Adm. Raphael Semmes, often hosted a starvation party. The guest list for one of her parties in January 1864 included President Davis and his wife, Varina, Secretary of State Judah Benjamin, Secretary of the Navy Stephen Mallory and his wife, and the president's personal secretary Burton Harrison and his fiancée, Constance Cary. But the guest that everyone swarmed around when he arrived was General Stuart.

James Ewell Brown Stuart was one of the most adored of the Confederacy's generals, a "man's man" and the idol of the female Confederacy. Brave, resourceful, and colorful, he was the kind of cavalry officer songs like "Riding a Raid" were written about. The song was issued with two distinct covers by its Richmond publisher, J. W. Randolph. One cover had a lithograph of Stuart on horseback, sporting a wide sash, high boots, and his trademark plumed hat; the other pictured "Stonewall" Jackson, under whom Stuart served. Written to the tune of the Scottish folksong "Bonnie Dundee," which goes back to the 1620s, the song gave Jackson top billing, but the real hero was Stuart: "Each cavalier that loves Honor and right" is urged to "follow the feather of Stuart to-night."

In the winter of 1864 Stuart was making more and more visits to Richmond and was on everyone's invitation list, but it was still a social coup for Myra Semmes that he attended her party. During a pause in the dancing, the band struck up "Hail, the Conquering Hero Comes!" and Stuart strode onstage, dressed in full uniform, his sword unsheathed, and laid the blade at the foot of the altar. Next came two women dressed as nuns, who blessed the sword, followed by two pilgrims, who prostrated themselves before the weapon. Stuart's appearance made the night one that was not soon forgotten in Richmond, during or after the war.[37]

Regardless of the misery felt throughout the South in the later years of the war, Richmonders always kept themselves entertained. In the winter of 1864, while the South was beginning to disintegrate, the city was unusually blithe. The *Richmond Whig* railed at the incongruity between all the festivities going on in Richmond's homes and the desperation outside:

> There has never been a gayer winter in Richmond. Balls and parties every night! One night last week there were seven parties. . . . Go on, good people. It is better to be merry than sad. The wolf is far away from your doors, and it signifieth nothing to you that thousands of our heroic soldiers are shoeless and comfortless; or that a

multitude of mothers, wives, and children of the gallant defenders of our country's rights are sorely pinched by hunger and want.[38]

But William Owen, one of those "shoeless and comfortless" soldiers, looked forward to these parties. Owen recalled that there were "some demure, long-faced people" saying "it was a shame to be dancing while our soldiers were suffering in the field," but he welcomed the chance to dance, "for who could tell how soon any of us might fill a ditch, or a soldier's grave."[39]

Gen. Robert E. Lee felt the same way. When Constance Cary and her friends decided to put on their "starvation parties" for soldiers on leave, they first asked Lee's permission.

> "If you say no, general, we won't dance a single step!" one of the spokeswomen said.
>
> "Why, of course, my dear child," Lee quickly responded. "My boys need to be heartened up when they get their furloughs. Go on, look your prettiest, and be just as nice to them as ever you can be!"[40]

Even in the bleakest moments of the war, with Federal troops outside the city, parties were a nightly occurrence. "What a dazzling, wholesome highbred little society it was," a veteran later recalled. "Night after night, I galloped into town to attend dances, charades, and what not? and did not get back to my camp until two—three—what matter the hour?"[41] Henry Kyd Douglas, a member of the old Stonewall Brigade, recalled that even in the dying moments of the war, with the booming of the enemy's cannons audible, officers would often stop at a home where a party was going on for a waltz, dancing in their spurs while orderlies outside held their horses.[42]

Looking back on those times, Mrs. Roger Pryor reflected that these spasms of frivolity were merely the last feverish gasps of a dying country. "All who remember the dark days of the winter of 1864–1865 will bear witness to the unwritten law enforcing cheerfulness. It was tacitly understood that we must make no moan, yield to no outward expression of despondency or despair."[43] Mary Chesnut rationalized the gaiety of those somber days, saying she couldn't see how sadness and despondency would help anyone. "If it would do any good," she wrote in her diary, "we could be sad enough."[44]

Notes

1. John Smith Kendall, *The Golden Age of the New Orleans Theater* (Baton Rouge: Louisiana State University Press, 1952), 2; Henry A. Kmen, *Music in New Orleans: The Formative Years, 1791–1841* (Baton Rouge: Louisiana State University Press, 1966), 141–42.

2. For theater practices prior to and during the war, see James H. Dormon Jr., *Theater in the Ante Bellum South, 1815–1861* (Chapel Hill: University of North Carolina Press, 1967); Terry Theodore, "The Confederate Theatre in the Deep South," *Lincoln Herald* 77, no. 2 (1975): 102–14; 77, no. 3 (1975): 158–67.

3. Albert Stoutamire, *Music of the Old South: Colony to Confederacy* (Rutherford, N.J.: Farleigh Dickinson University Press, 1972), 208.

4. *Richmond Daily Enquirer,* January 3, 1862.

5. *Richmond Daily Dispatch,* January 27, 1862.

6. Ibid. On Hewitt, see E. Lawrence Abel, "Music Man of the Confederacy," *Civil War Times Illustrated,* August 2003.

7. E. Lawrence Abel, "The Best-Loved Song of the Civil War," *America's Civil War.* May 1996, 10–12, 78–80.

8. *Richmond Whig,* January 20, 1863.

9. *Richmond Daily Dispatch,* January 21, 29, 1862. The definitive biography of "Blind Tom" is Geneva Handy Southall, *Blind Tom: The Post–Civil War Enslavement of a Black Musical Genius* (Minneapolis: Challenge Productions, 1979–1983).

10. Quoted in Richard Harwell, "'New Richmond Theater' of 1863 Aimed High but It Missed the Mark," unidentified newspaper clipping, Valentine Museum, Richmond. See also *Richmond Daily Dispatch,* January 27, 1862. In October 1864, when performers were routinely being conscripted, D'Orsey was taken prisoner while trying to escape to the North. D'Orsey claimed he was a British citizen and therefore not subject to conscription, but his contention was ignored and he was imprisoned in Richmond's Castle Thunder. When he was subsequently found to be physically unfit for military service, he returned to the New Richmond Theatre as manager (*Richmond Whig,* October 25, 1864; *Richmond Daily Enquirer,* January 26, 1865).

11. *Richmond Daily Dispatch,* February 9, 1863.

12. Ibid., November 8, 1862; E. Lawrence Abel, *Singing the New Nation: How Music Shaped the Confederacy, 1861–1865* (Mechanicsburg, Pa.: Stackpole, 2000), 240.

13. Frances H. Casstevens, *George W. Alexander and Castle Thunder: A Confederate Prison and Its Commandant.* (Jefferson, N.C.: McFarland, 2004), 46, 56.

14. Ibid. lists the following dates on which it was performed: March 16–26,

April 2, May 7, 18, October 10, 17, November 25, December 19, 29, 1863, January 1–2, February 8, 20, April 19, June 22, 1864.

15. Abel, *Singing*, 259–64.

16. *Southern Illustrated News* (Richmond), July 11, 1863.

17. *Richmond Daily Dispatch*, February 10, 1862.

18. Ibid., March 10, 1862.

19. Ibid., March 24, 1862.

20. *Richmond Examiner*, January 6, 1863.

21. Val C. Giles, *Rags and Hope: The Recollections of Val C. Giles; Four Years with Hood's Brigade Fourth Texas Infantry, 1861–1865*, ed. Mary Lasswell (New York: Coward-McCann, 1961), 90–91.

22. Bromfield Lewis Ridley, *Battles and Sketches of the Army of Tennessee* (Mexico, Mo.: Missouri Printing and Publishing, 1906), 439.

23. Quoted in Ernest B. Furgurson, *Ashes of Glory: Richmond at War* (New York: Knopf, 1996), 181.

24. *Richmond Daily Enquirer*, February 16, 1864.

25. Thomas Cooper De Leon, *Four Years in Rebel Capitals: An Inside View of Life in the Southern Confederacy, from Birth to Death* (Mobile, Ala.: Gossip, 1890), 149.

26. Virginius Dabney, *Richmond: The Story of a City* (Garden City, N.Y.: Doubleday, 1976), 179.

27. De Leon, *Four Years*, 201–12.

28. Abel, *Singing*, 139–40.

29. Giles, *Rags and Hope*, 78.

30. Mary Boykin Miller Chesnut, *Mary Chesnut's Civil War*, ed. C. Vann Woodward (New Haven, Conn.: Yale University Press, 1981), 457.

31. Abel, *Singing*, 170–74.

32. *Richmond Daily Enquirer*, September 15, 1863.

33. Ibid., May 2, 1863.

34. *Richmond Whig*, January 5, 1864.

35. Mrs. Burton Harrison, *Recollections Grave and Gay* (New York: Scribner's, 1911), 150; Alfred Hoyt Bill, *The Beleaguered City: Richmond, 1861–1865* (New York: Knopf, 1946), 187.

36. Robert Emory Park, "War Diary of Captain Robert Emory Park, Twelfth Alabama Regiment," *Southern Historical Society Papers* 26 (1898): 3.

37. Thomas Cooper De Leon, *Belles, Beaux, and Brains of the 60's* (New York: Arno, 1974), 217, 222; Harrison, *Recollections*, 129–30.

38. *Richmond Whig*, February 10, 1864.

39. William Miller Owen, *In Camp and Battle with the Washington Artillery of New Orleans* (Boston: Ticknor, 1885), 299.

40. Harrison, *Recollections,* 150.

41. Ibid., 151.

42. Henry Kyd Douglas, *I Rode with Stonewall: Being Chiefly the War Experience of the Youngest Member of Jackson's Staff from the John Brown Raid to the Hanging of Mrs. Surrat* (Chapel Hill: University of North Carolina Press, 1940), 322.

43. Sara Agnes Rice Pryor, *Reminiscences of Peace and War* (New York: Macmillan, 1905), 327.

44. Chesnut, *Mary Chesnut,* January 15, 1864.

To Danville

"A government on wheels"

F. Lawrence McFall Jr.

An umbilical of iron rail tethered Danville to the capital of the Confederacy, 140 miles to the northeast. In 1847 the Virginia General Assembly allowed the construction of the Richmond & Danville Railroad, though it was not until 1856 that the line reached Danville, the terminus. A telegraph line ran alongside, and by 1865 both had become vital lifelines for the Confederate capital.[1] Moreover, Danville itself hosted an arsenal as well as rifle works and manufacturers of necessary accoutrements. Vacant tobacco warehouses had been converted for military use: a military hospital, a prison and, most important of all, a huge complex of commissary storehouses and a quartermaster depot run by local resident Maj. William T. Sutherlin, whose large Italianate mansion on the western edge of town was one of the finest homes in Danville.[2] During the course of the war, more than 3,000 refugees from northern and eastern Virginia found their way to Danville, many of them professionals seeking a safe haven from which to conduct their business. Early in 1864, another railroad opened, connecting Danville to Greensboro, North Carolina, and providing another vital line for Richmond in the closing months of the war.[3]

Danville was thus already of major importance to the Confederacy as the end of the war neared; as early as February 1865, all departments of the Confederate government were told to begin preparations to relocate to Danville should that prove necessary. Some acted swiftly. That same month Josiah Gorgas began moving his Ordnance Department's machinery and workshops to Danville. Secretary of War John C. Breckinridge instructed clerks to pack his department's papers and archives for shipment to the town. Secretary of State Judah Benjamin, likewise, sent three trunks of records and a number of boxes of papers to Danville before later shifting them to Charlotte, North Carolina.

On a rainy March 4, 1865, General Lee and President Jefferson Davis met in Richmond, where Lee outlined his plan of retiring to Danville and establishing new defensive lines behind the Dan and Roanoke rivers should he be forced to evacuate his lines around Petersburg. The rain seemed to emphasize the bleakness of the situation, as Lee stated that this move was but a matter of time. Moving his army's position would leave the capital open to invasion and capture. His strategic plan involved fortifying Danville, then joining his army with that of Gen. Joseph E. Johnston in North Carolina. He hoped that together they could defeat Gen. William T. Sherman's army, coming from the south, before Gen. Ulysses S. Grant could come to its relief. Then, with combined forces they could turn to face Grant and focus on his army's destruction.[4] Danville was the only practical choice for the new capital should Richmond be abandoned. Its position between the armies of Lee and Johnston provided protection for the government. The repair shops of the R&D Railroad, the well-stocked quartermaster and commissary departments, and the equipment from the Richmond Arsenal, recently sent down from the capital, enabled resupply of the army.[5]

Aware that the time for Lee to abandon his lines was near, President Davis instructed Burton N. Harrison, his personal secretary, to escort the Davis family to Charlotte late on March 31. Their special train departed Richmond but broke down and did not arrive in Danville until Sunday morning, April 2. The party's baggage required transfer from the R&D train to a Piedmont train because of the gauge difference of the two roads. This delay afforded Harrison ample time to visit his friend Major Sutherlin at his Main Street home, where President Davis would soon set up residence in response to Sutherlin's offer of accommodations. After safely escorting the president's family to Charlotte, Harrison himself would return on Saturday, April 8, to spend two nights in Sutherlin's spacious dwelling.[6]

The bright sunlit morning of Sunday, April 2, found Jefferson Davis and his aide Francis Richard Lubbock seated in the presidential pew, number 63, at St. Paul's Episcopal Church. Another aide and kinsman by marriage, John Taylor Wood, sat nearby. Wood, the grandson of President Zachary Taylor and nephew of Davis's first wife, had enjoyed a distinguished naval career before becoming an aide to the president. As the worship service began, Davis wore "a cold stern expression" and displayed a reserved manner as he sat erect in the pew. As the service progressed, a young courier entered the church with a dispatch for the president from General Lee. The dreaded news that Richmond must be evacuated had come at last.[7]

That afternoon and evening, officials of various governmental departments packed their important documents for transfer to Danville. They burned less important papers to prevent their capture by the Union army, which some feared was at their doorstep. The streets of Richmond bustled with activity but, according to a visitor, "there was no panic—rather, a measured hurrying—as men, many in uniform, moved about carrying trunks to the railroad depot." Yet amid the activity, "there seemed a deathlike stillness to pervade the city; everyone wore a haggard, scared look, as if apprehensive of some great impending calamity."

In Danville, the trainmaster J. H. Averill received conflicting messages from Richmond, adding to the developing confusion. Around noon, a dispatch directed him to hold all trains in Danville. Soon afterward, he received a message to send all available trains to Richmond. A shortage of workers prevented him from responding quickly to the latter order, but Averill succeeded in getting the boilers fired on four engines and added cars to each locomotive. Just as the trains prepared to depart, another order came by telegraph instructing him to hold everything in Danville and have all tracks in the rail yard made available. The government was evacuating Richmond.[8]

Eight trains assembled in Richmond provided adequate space for the various departments to accomplish a quick departure from the depot on Cary Street. Announcements circulated among the agencies that anyone or anything not on board these trains would not get out of Richmond. The third train set to leave the station, the one carrying the president and other dignitaries, had been scheduled to depart at 8:30 p.m., but last-minute details forced delay after delay. About nightfall, Horatio Washington Bruce, a Kentucky congressman, rushed to get aboard the presidential car but then found himself and his fellow passengers sitting in silence for several hours as they endured the delayed departure. Bruce later recalled, "I never knew so little conversation indulged in by so large a number of acquaintances. Very few words were exchanged."[9]

Breckinridge and the president sat in the office with the railroad's president, Lewis Harvie, for almost an hour "in anxious anticipation of better news from Lee." None arrived. Around 11:00 Davis and Harvie boarded the train, while Breckinridge stayed behind to attend to the destruction of supplies and the evacuation of remaining troops.[10] All other members of the president's cabinet found seats in the same coach, since it accommodated thirty-one people. Finally on its way, the train crept slowly forward over the James River. Everyone aboard hoped for an uneventful journey to Danville. All were aware that Union general Philip H. Sheridan's cavalry was free to advance now that Lee's lines were evacuated, and that it might attempt to cut the R&D Railroad. (One of the cars on the train carried enough horses to allow the leaders to escape should Sheridan's horsemen intercept them.) The same anxiety experienced by those on the president's train was felt by others waiting to leave Richmond. By morning, six more trains would leave the capital, bound for the government's new home.[11]

Track conditions frequently slowed the president's train as it pressed on into the darkness. Its average speed was but ten miles per hour. Those who knew Davis best detected that beneath his outwardly calm demeanor, he was near physical and mental exhaustion. His personal physician, Dr. Alexander Yelverton Peyton Garnett, was keenly aware of the president's condition and kept his eye on him throughout the long night.[12]

After daybreak, sunshine filtering through the dingy windows of the coach brought new hope to the passengers. They were aware that they were now beyond the reach of Sheridan's cavalrymen. The sunshine, however, was short-lived, and about midmorning ominous clouds brought rain that in hindsight seemed prophetic.[13] Well into the morning, after covering ninety-four miles and crossing the Staunton River into Halifax County, the train stopped for fuel at Clover Station. The final leg of the journey was just forty-six more miles.[14]

Lt. John Sergeant Wise, the young son of a former Virginia governor, was on duty at the station. He boarded the presidential car to speak briefly with his brother-in-law, the president's physician, Dr. Garnett. Wise noted that Davis's face "showed physical and mental exhaustion." In less than a week, Wise would see an even more pronounced expression of anxiety on the president's face. Throughout that Monday, Wise witnessed the other trains stopping to fuel their engines at the station. One transported the employees and archives of the State Department, another the Post Office Department, and yet another the War Department. Fascinated and entranced, Wise noted, "I saw a government on wheels."[15]

Averill notified Danville's town fathers of the train's pending arrival, but it would be delayed because of the derailment of an earlier train just east of South Boston, thirty miles to the northeast.[16] Mayor James M. Walker organized a committee for the "hospitable reception and entertainment of their expected guests." Riding in the lead carriage, Walker led the delegation, which followed in dozens of wagons and other conveyances parading down cobblestoned Craghead Street to the railroad depot. A large gathering of bystanders attested to the perceived magnitude of the event.[17] All awaited the approach of the train in the mid-afternoon rain. Finally, around 5:00 p.m., the sound of the engine trumpeted the train's arrival through the open end of the covered bridge that spanned the Dan River.[18]

Stephen Russell Mallory, the secretary of the navy, observed that the president received a cordial greeting "with that spirit of hospitality as universal in Virginia as the dews of Heaven." Davis himself recalled that he got "an old Virginia welcome," and that nothing could have exceeded "the kindness and hospitality of the patriotic citizens of Danville."[19]

The town's wealthiest citizens opened their homes to Danville's distinguished visitors. In fact, few houses that night went without guests. Major Sutherlin opened his mansion to Davis, his physician, and his aides, also extending an invitation to the ailing secretary of the treasury George A. Trenholm and his wife. The secretary had suffered throughout the long train ride from Richmond with a severe case of neuralgia. His wife, Anna, the only lady in the president's car, accompanied him on the trek to care for him, often holding his head on her lap.[20]

Col. Robert Enoch Withers, commandant of the Danville Post, had shared his Wilson Street home with guests throughout the war, including a two-week stay by Gen. John Hunt Morgan after his 1863 escape from an Ohio prison. Morgan's wife, Mattie, stayed with Withers, her cousin, during her pregnancy before the general's prison break. Sadly, the female infant died before the general reached Danville. Alabama congressman Clement Claiborne Clay, another cousin of Withers, now enjoyed his hospitality.[21]

Other government dignitaries found accommodations in the town's best homes. Judah Benjamin, the secretary of state, and the Reverend Moses Hoge, a Richmond Presbyterian minister, shared a room in the home of John M. Johnston, president of the Danville Bank. The Kentucky congressman Bruce secured lodging, along with his old friend Judge James D. Halyburton, in Witcher Keen's Main Street home.[22] The Exchange Hotel at the foot of Main Street somehow managed to find quarters for twenty men from the Richmond Arsenal responsible for getting the previously moved machinery in working order.[23]

The Danville Town Council moved swiftly to find office space for the departments of the Confederate government. It rented the vacant Benedict House, a large two-story brick building formerly used as a school by a Northern teacher, Ann Benedict. The War Department began moving its documents and supplies into this substantial structure on Wilson Street. In the absence of Secretary Breckinridge, Gen. Samuel Cooper assisted Robert Garlick Hill Kean, head of the Bureau of War, in setting up the department. There was little they could do until they received information from General Lee, so they all busied themselves opening and sorting mail brought with them on the train.[24]

Josiah Gorgas made an effort the following morning to get his Ordnance Bureau functioning at Hutter's Danville Arsenal with the twenty workers who found lodging at the Exchange Hotel, but little could be accomplished. When the men arrived at the arsenal, they discovered much of the material and machinery sent down from Richmond and Lynchburg on April 1 scattered about the yard without any protection from the elements. Postmaster General John H. Reagan, though somber during the train ride, sprang into action upon arrival in Danville. He set up his department in the Masonic Hall on Main Street and was conducting routine business in a short time.[25]

Two cars of the presidential train transported the personnel, records, and specie of the Treasury Department to Danville. Around noon on April 2, Secretary of the Navy Mallory ordered Capt. William H. Parker, superintendent of the Confederate Naval Academy, to move the corps of midshipmen, fifty or sixty cadets, from their downtown quarters to Richmond's R&D depot, their task to guard the train carrying the holdings of the Treasury Department. After the train arrived in Danville and the dignitaries departed to their places of lodging, Captain Parker had the train moved to a sidetrack. One of the midshipmen, John W. Harris, later said, "Our train stood on the track not far from the depot and our encampment was in a grove [of trees] not far from the train." Later, too, Captain Parker recorded these words: "We did not unpack the treasure from the cars in Danville. Some, I believe, was taken for the use of the government . . . but the main portion of the money remained with me."[26] Officials deposited some money removed from the train in local banks to "take care of operating expenses."

Department clerks did exchange some specie at the rate of 70:1 for currency, with military personnel being paid with currency.[27]

Monday, April 3, was a day of intermittent showers that continued throughout the evening. Tuesday dawned overcast and dreary, and a light drizzle fell all morning. The weather, however, did not deter President Davis from rising early and leaving the comfort of Major Sutherlin's home. He was eager to hear from General Lee and to see for himself what kind of protection had been constructed for the army's defense. Maj. Gen. Jeremy F. Gilmer, head of the Bureau of Engineers, had stayed behind in Richmond on Sunday and by this time was with Breckinridge and his party seeking to contact General Lee. In Gilmer's absence, Davis secured the services of his assistant, Col. Alfred L. Rives. Together they inspected the earthworks that completely surrounded the town. Davis's engineer noted that the fortifications were "as faulty in location as in construction." Immediately, he ordered Rives "to correct the one and improve the other."[28]

After his inspection of Danville's defenses, Davis called a cabinet meeting at the Benedict House. Everyone was there but Breckinridge. Later that afternoon, the president, after consultation with his cabinet, penned a proclamation to the citizens of the Confederacy. Composed at Sutherlin's mansion, it was hand carried by Judah Benjamin to the nearby office of the *Danville Register*. The newspaper published the document three days later. It conveyed the message that the government would be maintained at all costs and that the capital would remain within the borders of Virginia. It appealed to the resolve of the people to support the crumbling government.[29] Davis spoke, too, of the war entering a new phase, with the advantage of having Lee's Army of Northern Virginia free to choose its own fields of battle.

But Davis was quickly learning that with Lee's freedom of movement, communications became difficult. He had not heard from Lee since receiving that dispatch in church two days previously.[30] The chaotic situation in Richmond the day of the evacuation prevented the receipt of an appeal from Lee to Davis for supplies to be sent to Amelia Court House for his army. As a result, neither Commissary General Isaac M. St. John nor any member of his staff received the requisition.[31] Now on Tuesday, April 4, Lee requested by telegraph that 200,000 rations from Danville and Lynchburg be sent to Burkeville Junction, where the R&D and Southside railroads crossed. At that moment, freight cars in Danville held 1.5 million rations of meat and 500,000 rations of bread, ready for delivery. Tragically, Federal soldiers intercepted the order and sent a false follow-up order to Averill to hold the train instead. The first train was ready to leave the rail yard when Averill got the decoy message, thus preventing the foodstuffs from reaching Lee's hungry army.[32]

On the same day, Adm. Raphael Semmes and four hundred sailors from his James River Squadron manned the inner earthworks in Danville, since soldiers already occupied most of the outer fortifications. The navy men had entered the town the night before on the last train out of Richmond. They had stayed behind to wreck the navy yard and scuttle the naval academy's training ship, the CSS *Patrick Henry.* For Semmes to command land troops, Davis appointed him a brigadier general of artillery. Seemingly bored by the lack of action, many of Semmes's sailors appeared to Mallory to be "grave and silent"; he noted that "they presented a pretty fair illustration of 'fish out of water.'"[33]

Meanwhile, in Raleigh, North Carolina, on April 2, Gen. Pierre G. T. Beauregard was aware of Richmond's evacuation and Lee's plans to retire to Danville. More ominously, Beauregard received intelligence that Union brigadier general George Stoneman's cavalry was moving eastward from Tennessee and fast approaching the Yadkin River in North Carolina. Fearing an attack on Danville or the Piedmont Railroad, Beauregard wired Danville to ascertain the size of the available force under Col. Robert Withers's command.[34] The next day, Beauregard moved from Raleigh to Greensboro. From there, he informed Withers that he would be receiving 400 infantrymen. Later that afternoon, Beauregard ordered three artillery batteries from Hillsborough to Danville. Three days later, the Seventh North Carolina, with an unknown number of men, arrived to assist in Danville's defense. By April 9, more than 3,000 Confederate troops were in town under the control of Brig. Gen. Henry H. Walker.[35]

Compounding the concerns of both the military and the town fathers, large numbers of refugees were pouring into Danville. Overcrowding in the town, a problem since the war's inception, now reached a point of overflow, as ordinary citizens from across the state attempted to reach safety. Finding lodging was now impossible. Many were simply "herding together" with friends and acquaintances beneath any shelter available. A sidetracked boxcar was deemed suitable for a large group of ladies, including a bridal party forced prematurely from a planned ceremony in Richmond. Fires appeared throughout the rail yard as the homeless prepared their meager meals.[36]

Except by telegraph from the south, no news arrived in Danville other than by courier. The lack of news brought despair to the town. Rumors spread about the plight of Lee's army. President Davis, although inwardly pessimistic, maintained a brave front. The ever-jovial Judah Benjamin thought positively, stating, "No news is good news." Others, with the utmost confidence in General Lee, declared that he was "too busy fighting to send out couriers." None of the circulating rumors involved the possibility of Lee's defeat. Mallory observed the president's countenance and was not deceived by that brave front, for he knew that Davis "looked for disaster."[37] With everyone waiting for news from Lee, little government business was being conducted, and government workers arriving daily from Richmond on horseback and on foot found their services no longer needed.

On Wednesday, April 5, the president ordered General Walker to send a trusted officer up the railroad to try to find Lee. Walker chose John S. Wise, the young lieutenant who had boarded the president's car at Clover Station four days earlier. Encountering Union cavalry at Green Bay, a village eight miles south of Burkeville, Wise detrained and continued on horseback.[38] It was past midnight on Thursday, April 6, when he found Lee encamped north of Rice's Station after the disaster at Sayler's Creek. Lee gave Wise a brief message for Davis, and the lieutenant left before dawn after speaking briefly with his father, Brig. Gen. Henry A. Wise.[39]

Around 8:00 in the evening of Saturday, April 8, Burton Harrison welcomed Wise at the door of the Sutherlin mansion. A cabinet meeting was under way in the dining room. Wise was the first courier with news directly from General Lee. After reading the report, Davis asked the lieutenant if he thought Lee could reach a point of safety with his army. Wise replied, "I regret to say, no. From what I saw and heard, I am satisfied that General Lee must surrender." At his news, Wise thought he saw a simultaneous shudder pass through the cabinet.[40]

The next day, Palm Sunday, a dispatch sent by Lee in the early hours of April 6 before his defeat at Sayler's Creek finally reached Davis. The president immediately responded by telling Lee that ample supplies awaited him in Danville, stressing the need for him to win a victory north of the Roanoke [Staunton] River. Davis's almost complete inability to control the situation now, and the frustration and anxiety of the long week, manifested themselves in his reply, as he went on to complain that "the Secretary of War, Quartermaster General, Commissary General and Chief Engineer have not arrived; their absence is embarrassing."[41]

Earlier in the day, special services at the Episcopal church on Main Street attracted President Davis and several cabinet members. Judah Benjamin attended with his host, the banker, John M. Johnston. Benjamin's roommate, Dr. Moses Hoge, preached the morning service at the Presbyterian church a block away.[42] Before the conclusion of the services, the train carrying the midshipmen and the gold of the Treasury Department left Danville over the Piedmont Railroad. At 4:00 that afternoon, it arrived safely in Greensboro.[43]

The stress of the week had begun to affect Judah Benjamin, too. After church he spoke with Maj. Edward Hutter, the Danville Arsenal commander. From the time of his arrival in Danville three years earlier, Hutter had run an efficient operation. Benjamin asked him if he had been recently paid. Hutter replied that he had not. From his pocket Benjamin then handed Hutter $600 in gold, the amount due him, with the comment: "The Confederate soldiers had better have the gold than the Yankees."[44]

On Monday, April 10, Capt. William Pinkney Graves, former commander of the "Danville Blues," arrived in town at 3:30 p.m. and reported immediately to General Walker. Graves was the first courier to bring confirmation of Lee's surrender at Appomattox Court House the previous day. Walker hurriedly ushered Graves to the president with the news. Davis was meeting with cabinet members at the Benedict House. The president read the message and silently handed it to the others. Passing the dispatch from hand to hand, each in turn carefully read the dismaying message. Secretary Mallory later recalled that "the information fell upon our ears like a firebell in the night." To add to their gloom, around noon a thunderstorm began raging, and a steady downpour continued the remainder of the day. Mother Nature seemed to be mocking the Confederacy's failure.[45]

Although the government's departure from Richmond a week earlier had appeared chaotic, at least it had been planned for some time. It could have been considered a strategic withdrawal for the readjustment of Lee's defensive position. However, there were no plans in place to respond to being forced from Danville—only flight.[46] Davis continued working in the executive office late into the evening as Burton Harrison arranged with Averill to have a train readied by 8:00 p.m. for the government's departure. Delays plagued the evacuation just as they had the previous week in Richmond.[47] Finally, at 11:00 p.m., an underpowered engine pulled away from the Piedmont depot, its anxious passengers aware that Stoneman's cavalry could be waiting in ambush in the rainy darkness ahead of them.[48] Engine trouble stretched the normally five-hour trip to Greensboro into more than double that, and the train passed over a trestle a few miles north of Greensboro only shortly before Union cavalrymen burned it, prompting Davis to remark to Mallory that "a miss is as good as a mile." It was almost noon when the beleaguered travelers finally reached Greensboro, where they found themselves unwelcome guests.[49] With the Confederacy collapsing all around them, civilians here and elsewhere now had to worry about themselves, and they feared Yankee reprisals for harboring their fleeing leaders.

In 1902, B. Boisseau Bobbitt of the *Raleigh Morning Post* reflected on Danville's fateful week: "The last capital of the Confederacy had been vacated by the government, and from thence 'the Bonny Blue flag that bears a single star' ceased to represent a nation. Moreover, from this time the Confederate Government was no longer a government."[50] Indeed it was not. Within days it would begin to disintegrate into fugitives.

Notes

1. Malcolm Cameron Clark, The *First Quarter-Century of the Richmond & Danville Railroad, 1847–1871* (Washington, D.C.: n.p., 1959), 31, 49; L. Beatrice W. Hairston, *A Brief History of Danville, Virginia, 1728–1954* (Richmond: Dietz, 1955), 20; Robert C. Black, *The Railroads of the Confederacy* (Chapel Hill: University of North Carolina Press, 1952), 35.

2. F. Lawrence McFall Jr., *Danville in the Civil War* (Lynchburg, Va.: H. E. Howard, 2001), 4; Edward Sixtus Hutter Compiled Service Record, Record Group 109, National Archives, Washington, D.C. (an extensive record of more than two hundred pages detailing the day-to-day operations of the Danville Arsenal; hereafter cited as CSR, Hutter); J. Risque Hutter, "The Eleventh at Five Forks Fight," *Southern Historical Society Papers* 35 (January–December 1907): 357 (hereafter cited as *SHSP*); John M. Murphy, *Confederate Carbines and Musketoons* (Dallas: Taylor, 1986), 28, 138; "The Last Roll," *Confederate Veteran*, February 1900, 84; *Richmond Daily Dispatch*, May 30, 1862; Richard D. Goff, *Confederate Supply* (Durham, N.C.: Duke University Press, 1969), 10–11, 77.

3. Black, *Railroads*, 207; Harold F. Round, "The Piedmont Railroad," *Civil War Times Illustrated*, October 1968, 34–36; Cecil Kenneth Brown, "A History of the Piedmont Railroad Company," *North Carolina Historical Review* 3 (April 1926): 208.

4. Josiah Gorgas, *The Journals of Josiah Gorgas, 1857–1878*, ed. Sarah Woolfolk Wiggins (Tuscaloosa: University of Alabama Press, 1995), 153, 155;

John B. Jones, *A Rebel War Clerk's Diary,* ed. Earl Schenck Miers (1866; repr., Alexandria, Va.: Time-Life Books, 1982), 2:439, 441; Michael B. Ballard, *A Long Shadow: Jefferson Davis and the Final Days of the Confederacy* (Jackson: University Press of Mississippi, 1986), 42; William B. Smith, "Recovery of the Great Seal of the Confederacy," *SHSP* 41 (January–December 1913): 30–31; Jefferson Davis, *The Rise and Fall of the Confederate Government* (New York: Appleton, 1881), 2:550–51, 573; Douglas Southall Freeman, *R. E. Lee: A Biography* (New York: Scribner's, 1936), 4:91.

5. Ballard, *A Long Shadow,* 53–54.

6. Robert L. Scribner, "Seven Days in a Quandary," *Virginia Cavalcade* 13 (Winter 1963–1964): 6; *Danville Register,* March 31, 1965, Special Centennial edition.

7. Royce Gordon Shingleton, *John Taylor Wood: Sea Ghost of the Confederacy* (Athens: University of Georgia Press, 1979), 148; "Last Days of the Southern Confederacy," *SHSP* 19 (January 1891): 329.

8. J. H. Averill, "Richmond, Virginia: The Evacuation of the City and the Days Preceding It," *SHSP* 25 (January–December 1897): 267–68.

9. Shingleton, *John Taylor Wood,* 148; James C. Clark, *Last Train South: The Flight of the Confederate Government from Richmond* (Jefferson, N.C.: McFarland, 1984), 14; H. W. Bruce, "Some Reminiscences of the Second of April, 1865," *SHSP* 9 (May 1881): 209.

10. Robert Douthat Meade, *Judah P. Benjamin: Confederate Statesman* (New York: Oxford University Press, 1943), 312; Stephen R. Mallory, "The Flight from Richmond," *Civil War Times Illustrated,* April 1972, 28; Ballard, *A Long Shadow,* 46.

11. J. Frank Carroll, *Confederate Treasure in Danville* (Danville, Va.: Ure, 1996), 82; Mallory, "Flight," 29; Ballard, *A Long Shadow,* 46.

12. Mallory, "Flight," 29; Bruce, "Reminiscences," 209; Ballard, *A Long Shadow,* 48; John S. Wise, *The End of an Era,* ed. Curtis Carroll Davis (New York: Thomas Yoseloff, 1965), 415; Clark, *Last Train South,* 26–32.

13. Ballard, *A Long Shadow,* 53.

14. Mallory, "Flight," 29.

15. Wise, *End of an Era,* 415.

16. Ballard, *A Long Shadow,* 53.

17. Mallory, "Flight," 25; Burke Davis, *The Long Surrender* (New York: Random House, 1985), 21; Shingleton, *John Taylor Wood,* 148; Robert Garlick Hill Kean, *Inside the Confederate Government: The Diary of Robert Garlick Hill Kean, Head of the Bureau of War,* ed. Edward Younger (New York: Oxford University Press, 1957), 205; Gorgas, *Journals,* 158–59.

18. Mallory, "Flight," 30; Edward Pollock, *Illustrated Sketch Book of Danville,*

Virginia: Its Manufactures and Commerce (1885; repr., Danville, Va.: Womack, 1976), 51; Kean, *Inside the Confederate Government,* 205; Bruce, "Reminiscences," 209; Gorgas, *Journals,* 159. The train's time of arrival in Danville varies widely in postwar accounts, from 11:00 a.m. to 5:00 p.m., with Davis citing the earliest and Mallory the latest. Since Mallory's work was the only contemporary account by a major participant, 5:00 is preferred by the author.

19. Mallory, "Flight," 30; Davis, *Rise and Fall,* 573.

20. Alfred Jackson Hanna, *Flight into Oblivion* (Bloomington: Indiana University Press, 1959), 14–15; Shingleton, *John Taylor Wood,* 149; *SHSP* 31 (1903): 80; Ballard, *A Long Shadow,* 53.

21. *Danville Register,* January 15, 1864; *Proceedings of Council,* December 12, 1863; Dave Roth, "John Hunt Morgan's Escape from the Ohio Penitentiary," *Blue and Gray,* October 1994, 24.

22. Davis, *Long Surrender,* 57; Meade, *Benjamin,* 313; Bruce, "Reminiscences," 209.

23. Joseph R. Haw, "The Last of C.S. Ordnance Department," *Confederate Veteran,* December 1926, 450.

24. Pollock, *Sketch Book,* 58–59; Ballard, *A Long Shadow,* 55; Micajah H. Clark, "Retreat of Cabinet from Richmond," *Confederate Veteran,* July 1898, 293.

25. Mallory, "Flight," 30; Haw, "Last of C.S. Ordnance Department," 450; Josiah Gorgas, "Contributions to the History of the Confederate Ordnance Department," *SHSP* 12 (January–February 1884): 83; Ballard, *A Long Shadow,* 55.

26. John F. Wheless, "The Confederate Treasure," *SHSP* 10 (March 1882): 138–39; William H. Parker, "The Gold and Silver in the Confederate States Treasury," *SHSP* 21 (January–December 1893): 305–6; John W. Harris, "The Gold of the Confederate States Treasury," *SHSP* 32 (January–December 1904): 160; U.S. Navy, Naval History Division, *Civil War Naval Chronology, 1861–1865* (Washington, D.C.: Government Printing Office, 1971), 5:76.

27. Micajah H. Clark, "The Last Days of the Confederate Treasury and What Became of Its Specie," *SHSP* 9 (October–December 1881): 545.

28. Ballard, *A Long Shadow,* 56; Mallory, "Flight," 30; Hanna, *Flight into Oblivion,* 19; Davis, *Rise and Fall,* 573.

29. Ballard, *A Long Shadow,* 56; Pollock, *Sketch Book,* 55; *Danville Bee,* January 19, 1937; *New York Herald,* April 15, 1865.

30. Ballard, *A Long Shadow,* 46.

31. Davis, *Rise and Fall,* 573.

32. Janet B. Hewett et al., eds., *Supplement to the Official Records of the Union and Confederate Armies* (Wilmington, N.C.: Broadfoot, 1994–2001), 8:22; Mrs. A. M. Houston, "The Evacuation of Richmond," *Confederate Veteran,* April 1916,

165; Isaac M. St. John, "Resources of the Confederacy in 1865," *SHSP* 3 (March 1877): 99; Averill, "Evacuation," 269.

33. Patricia L. Faust, ed., *Historical Times Illustrated Encyclopedia of the Civil War* (New York: Harper and Row, 1986), 666; Parker, "The Gold and Silver in the Confederate States Treasury," 306; U.S. Navy, *Civil War Naval Chronology,* 5:76; Mrs. Bryan Wells Collier, "Raphael Semmes, C.S. Navy," *Confederate Veteran,* September 1931, 344; Bruce S. Allardice, *More Generals in Gray* (Baton Rouge: Louisiana State University Press, 1995), 207; Mallory, "Flight," 30.

34. U.S. War Department, *War of the Rebellion: A Compilation of the Official Records of the Union and Confederate Armies* (Washington, D.C.: Government Printing Office, 1880–1901), series 1, vol. 47, pt. 3, 742 (hereafter cited as *OR;* all references are to series 1).

35. Ibid., vol. 47, pt. 3, 742, 746; vol. 46, pt. 3, 1390–91; Weymouth T. Jordan Jr. and Louis H. Manarin, eds., *North Carolina Troops, 1861–1865: A Roster* (Raleigh: North Carolina Department of Archives and History, 1990), 4:405.

36. George Benjamin West, *When the Yankees Came: Civil War and Reconstruction on the Virginia Peninsula,* ed. Parke Rouse Jr. (Richmond: Dietz, 1977), 90; Mallory, "Flight," 30.

37. Hewett, *Supplement to the Official Records,* 7:774; Mallory, "Flight," 30.

38. Davis, *Rise and Fall,* 575.

39. Wise, *End of an Era,* 428–29.

40. Ibid., 443.

41. *OR,* vol. 46, pt. 3, 1390–91.

42. Hanna, *Flight into Oblivion,* 20; Meade, *Benjamin,* 313; "Appeal for Last Confederate Capitol," *Confederate Veteran,* May 1913, 221.

43. John W. Harris, "Confederate Naval Cadets," *Confederate Veteran,* April 1904, 170; Harris, "The Gold of the Confederate States Treasury," 160.

44. CSR, Hutter; Meade, *Benjamin,* 311.

45. Pollock, *Sketch Book,* 58; Mallory, "Flight," 31; Joseph T. Durkin, *Confederate Navy Chief: Stephen R. Mallory* (Columbia: University of South Carolina Press, 1987), 339; Burton Harrison, "Retreat of the Cabinet," *SHSP* 26 (January–December 1898), 98; Ballard, *A Long Shadow,* 65.

46. McFall, *Danville in the Civil War,* 93.

47. Averill, "Evacuation," 269; Mallory, "Flight," 31; *OR,* vol. 46, pt. 3, 1391; Hanna, *Flight into Oblivion,* 22.

48. Scribner, "Seven Days in a Quandary," 15; Hanna, *Flight into Oblivion,* 25; *OR,* vol. 46, pt. 3, 1393–94.

49. Averill, "Evacuation," 270; Mallory, "Flight," 31; Davis, *Long Surrender,* 62.

50. "Our Last Capital," *SHSP* 31 (January–December 1903): 335.

"When Johnny comes marching home"

The Demobilization of Lee's Army

Kevin Levin

Lawrence Taliaferro's Civil War should have ended on very familiar ground when he crossed the Rappahannock River near Fredericksburg shortly after the surrender of the Army of Northern Virginia at Appomattox Court House on April 9, 1865.[1] Instead Taliaferro, who served in the Forty-seventh Virginia Infantry, was struck by the drastic changes to the landscape. Abandoned and rusting war machinery littered the ground as well as the bones of mules and horses. The surrounding forests had been leveled to serve the needs of warring armies throughout the conflict. As Taliaferro traversed those final twelve miles to what he hoped would be the comforts of his family's estate, he became disoriented by the numerous paths that obscured a well-known road. Eventually he lost his way and was forced to ask for directions. An elderly black man, who Taliaferro later learned was an ex-slave of the family, escorted the confused and tired young man to his home.

Taliaferro reunited with his father and sister and shortly thereafter an older brother who had also served in Lee's army. With the help of only one mule, one horse, and a few ex-slaves who remained with the family, the Taliaferros began the process of rebuilding their estate by collecting old bones and iron from the surrounding area for resale. The Federal army, in recognition of the family's hospitality during the war, supplied mules and food, which no doubt furthered the process of rebuilding and perhaps even fostered a sense of optimism that a brighter future was possible. No amount of succor from the Federal army, however, would have blinded Lawrence Taliaferro and his family to the challenges they faced in the immediate future.[2]

The confusion and uncertainty that Lawrence Taliaferro experienced on his journey home was repeated along countless roads and paths throughout Virginia. Unfortunately, much of the literature on the Army of Northern

Virginia and the Civil War ends with the furling of flags and the stacking of arms on the surrender field at Appomattox. Although the army ceased to function as the military arm of the Confederate government, it did not cease to exist after the surrender ceremony on April 12; rather, it slowly dissipated along the roads as small groups of men headed off to destinations around the South. Ending the Civil War narrative abruptly at Appomattox or focusing on stories of reconciliation and reunion obscures or minimizes the connections between the war and the postwar challenges surrounding emancipation and subjection to Republican rule, which defined the era of Reconstruction.[3]

A survey of the experiences of Lee's men in the first few weeks after their surrender at Appomattox challenges the tendency to see a sharp break between the war years and Reconstruction. Indeed, many of the fears and lingering questions that Confederates carried home with them would play out in the following decades. For the newly minted veterans of Virginia, the journey home may have been particularly emotionally and psychologically taxing, given that they had fought four years on familiar ground, framing the war effort as a defense not only of nation but of home.[4] It is not a stretch to imagine soldiers contemplating whether they would face retribution from the Federal government in the form of disfranchisement or property confiscation. Many worried about what a post-emancipation social order would look like, with the Federal government now in control and the U.S. Army in a position to realize the worst fears of white Southerners, associated with images of racial amalgamation and "Negro rule"—the very social order the Confederate army was meant to prevent from taking hold. The end of the war raised profound questions of identity that civilians and soldiers must answer. White Southerners occupied a precarious position in the days and weeks after the end of the war, as they clung to their former Confederate selves and wrestled with the question of whether they could once again embrace their prewar identification as Americans.[5]

More immediate concerns centered on the challenges of providing for themselves and their families—even as they were reminded of the physical destruction the war had wrought in the Shenandoah Valley, the cities of Richmond, Petersburg, and Fredericksburg, and elsewhere. Extending the story into the first few weeks after the surrender at Appomattox to include "these final acts of soldiering," according to historian Jason Phillips, will "change the tone and meaning of the war's outcome."[6]

The suddenness of the collapse and surrender of Lee's army left no time to plan and execute an orderly demobilization. Life in the trenches of Petersburg may have been taxing on the mind and body, but it also conditioned Lee's men to maintain the belief that continued resistance to Grant and the Federal army was not only possible but likely to bring about independence.[7] In short, within less than two weeks Confederates went from resistance with some sense of hope to defeat and surrender.[8] The march west out of the trenches of Petersburg on April 2, 1865, was not carried out in preparation for an eventual surrender; it was intended as the first stage of an eventual linkup with Joseph Johnston's army in North Carolina. Writing ten years after the war, George C. Eggleston recalled the sense of optimism that he believed pervaded the ranks even late in the war, noting, "We refused to admit, even to ourselves, the possibility of failure."[9]

For thousands of Confederates the war ended along the roads leading west out of Petersburg as entire units disintegrated out of sheer exhaustion or the realization that the war was lost. Those Virginians who lived within close proximity perhaps found it easier to justify breaking ranks, given the army's bleak future. Not only did these men lack information regarding the status of the army in the coming days, they failed to procure the requisite parole papers that would eventually be distributed at Appomattox. Samuel Howard learned of Lee's surrender from Federal cavalry miles from the main body. At first he considered the news a hoax, until "party after party pass us unarmed repeating the same story." Confederates who abandoned the army during the retreat, as did Howard, proceeded without parole papers, which left them "uncertain what would be our fate in the event of our capture." As a result, Howard and his comrades tried to "avoid the Yanks as we would a pestilence." Only later did these men proceed with the confidence that they would be unmolested by Federal soldiers.[10]

Those who remained with the army as far as Appomattox Court House and who formally surrendered their arms were afforded the opportunity to bring some measure of closure to their four-year struggle. Between April 9 and April 13 Confederates interacted with Union soldiers, listened to their commanders for one final time, and said good-bye to friends who had shared the hardships of war. Lee addressed his men one final time in General Order No. 9, sharing his "admiration of your constancy and devotion to your country . . . and duty faithfully performed."[11]

Popular perceptions of the surrender at Appomattox are shaped by images of Lee and Grant seated in the McLean House, Union soldiers sharing rations with hungry Confederates, and by the earliest symbols of reconciliation and reunion, associated with the famous salute shared by major generals John B. Gordon and Joshua Chamberlain during the surrender ceremony itself. Grant's own lenient terms of surrender, which allowed soldiers to keep their horses and gave permission "to pass through the lines of the Union armies" and utilize "Government transportation and Military rail-roads," contribute to our continued emphasis on the theme of reconciliation.[12]

While acts of benevolence and peaceful interactions between one-time enemies no doubt occurred at Appomattox, these attractive stories tend to lead to a superficial understanding of the war's end, and certainly fail to acknowledge the strong feelings of bitterness that pervaded Confederate ranks. Even before the army's surrender, retreating Confederates expressed horror at the news that Richmond and Petersburg had fallen. "Words cannot fathom the depth and breadth of my soul's anguish at this unexpected news," wrote William L. Wilson of the Twelfth Virginia Cavalry. The experience of formally surrendering arms was no less painful; a second lieutenant in the Nineteenth Virginia Battalion, Crutchfield's Artillery Brigade, described the scene as "the saddest day of my life." This same officer held out hope even after parole papers were distributed that "there is life in the old land yet—and I cannot believe that the southern people are subjugated." James Whitehorne admitted that "all of us are fleeing Appomattox as if we could run away from the horrible memories of the place." Even years after the war, former Rockbridge Artillery officer William Thomas Poague admitted that "there has never been a day since, when I could dwell on that last scene without experiencing emotions of deepest grief and sorrow."[13] For Confederate soldiers, Appomattox was a scene of defeat and humiliation, not of reconciliation and reunion.

For the most diehard Confederates, an unwillingness to surrender and admit defeat reflected their inability to return to their prewar identity as Americans. These men contemplated the roads that would take them to Gen. Joseph E. Johnston's army in North Carolina or the Blue Ridge Mountains to fight another day; some considered destinations as far away as Texas and Brazil rather than face the humiliation of defeat and Republican rule. Henry McNeill, who served in the Seventh Virginia Cavalry, McNeill's Partisan Rangers, continued to hold out hope for "foreign intervention" when he informed his mother on April 24 that he would wait in the mountains and woods "until we can learn the fate of the Confecy more fully." Even after learning of the fall of Richmond and the anticipation of Lee's surrender, John Dooley felt "honour bound to follow the fortunes" of the escaped Confederate government, "until its cause is hopeless or its hopes of success revive."[14] Dooley traveled as far as Charlotte, North Carolina, before deciding to return to his home in Richmond.

The members of what Peter Carmichael has dubbed the "Last Generation"—those soldiers who served as junior-grade officers in Lee's army and proved to be some of the most aggressive on the battlefield—remained steadfast and confident of victory even late in the war. Their commitment to the South's ruling class and to the maintenance of slavery, together with their strong sense of Confederate nationalism, reinforced their unwavering faith that God would not abandon their righteous cause. Defeat demanded acceptance of a new order, which was more than some could bear. Young Virginians of the slaveholding class who had matured throughout the most politically divisive years of the 1850s were especially defiant. Ham Chamberlayne refused to take part in the "funeral at Appomattox C. H." and instead made plans to fight with Johnston in North Carolina or move on to Texas: "I am not conquered by any means & shall not be while alive—My life is of no further value—Farewell to my beloved Virginia."[15] Such decisions attest to the difficulty some of Lee's men had imagining themselves adjusting to and living peacefully with freed slaves and their enemies.

The vast majority of the men in the Army of Northern Virginia chose to return home to rebuild their lives and communities. The time it took to walk home depended on the number of miles to be traversed as well as unanticipated obstacles experienced along the way. The most serious challenge was the logistical nightmare of having to secure supplies from civilians who, in many cases, were overwhelmed by the demand. William B. Grove's journey home took less than two weeks. While his diary entry of April 7 indicates that he was "determined with the help of God to resist to . . . the last," by April 28 he was working his plow and considering planting watermelon seeds for his next crop.[16] Samuel Howard's diary entries no doubt reflect the experiences of many. On his journey home he depended to a great extent on the hospitality of those encountered along the way in procuring food and other supplies. On April 12, Howard and his small party arrived at the home of Phil Withers, where they met "with a cold reception." Withers agreed to "take us out of the rain" but was unable to feed them, not because he was unwilling to do so, but because soldiers had "eaten him out." The following morning the group walked eight miles to Pleasant Rosser's farm, where they were once again forced to compete with a large group of soldiers seeking food. From there it was on to William Person, whom Howard found to be a "shrewd and hospitable gentlemen"; there they stayed for two days. Howard reached the Barksdale Ferry Depot on April 20, and there he crossed the Dan River.[17]

A few lucky souls took advantage of functioning railroads and steamships. Four years of war had severely taxed Virginia's transportation infrastructure, but many of the lines remained intact, even if their tracks had been worn down for military purposes.[18] Lee's chief of artillery, Brig. Gen. Edward P. Alexander, took advantage of a railroad linking City Point, Petersburg, and Burkeville on what was to be the first stage of a long journey to Brazil, where he intended to join the military in the war against Paraguay. Pvt. Edgar Warfield, who served in the Seventeenth Virginia Infantry, reached Richmond by April 15 and attempted to secure transportation home to Alexandria in northern Virginia. Although the provost marshal was unable to help, Warfield managed to purchase a ticket on the steamship *Kelso* for the final leg of his journey.[19]

Crowded country roads, limited supplies, and thousands of men desperate to return to their families as quickly as possible all contributed to a breakdown in discipline and increased tension and violence. This was acknowledged almost immediately after the surrender at Appomattox by a chaplain, who observed "more stealing in camp . . . than I ever knew." Violence on the roads home was sometimes targeted, but often indiscriminate. David Walker of the Otey Battery returned home to Amelia Court House only to find that "all our neighbors had been pillaged and abused . . . by stragglers." While resting at William Person's home, William Grove learned that a soldier had destroyed his host's map, cutting out various states to use for directions home. Though the theft might be considered trivial, Grove described the perpetrator as a "miscreant" who "had degraded the very name of Soldier." Grove also experienced a more serious breakdown in discipline when he witnessed a group of "ragamuffins" break into a government storehouse at News Ferry Depot to steal harnesses and other accoutrements. It is unclear whether the men involved were former soldiers, but such actions were often justified as a means to prevent the items from falling into the hands of Yankees or as compensation for back pay never received.[20]

The sudden breakdown in authority forced many counties to quickly

organize patrols to deal with deserters, paroled soldiers, and bands of outlaws who stole horses, cattle, and sheep, and preyed on innocent civilians.
In Lexington, ex-Confederates assisted with law enforcement and managed
to track down thieves who had stolen the Communion service at the Falling
Springs Presbyterian Church. The residents of Culpeper worked to repair the
county jail in response to an increase in cattle theft and other disturbances
attributed to returning soldiers.[21]

More severe lapses in authority could be found in places such as Lynchburg and Danville in the immediate aftermath of Appomattox. Lynchburg's
close proximity to Appomattox made it an obvious destination for renegade
Confederates and newly paroled soldiers seeking transportation and supplies for their journeys home. The large influx of soldiers taxed the town's
infrastructure and economy, which had been in decline throughout the war.
Fearful of riots and plundering, local business owners shut their doors and
city services were suspended. This led to the looting of Confederate supply
stores by both soldiers and destitute white civilians who sought clothing,
shoes, and other valuables. A quick decision was made to restore order with
the Union army—no doubt an indication that "Yankee rule" was preferable
to chaos. Brig. Gen. John W. Turner assumed control of the town and issued
an order stating that any Union or Confederate soldier "caught pillaging
private houses, or committing any outrageous acts upon the persons of
citizens" would be hanged. Instead of securing the city's military stores and
businesses, however, Turner decided to hand over all remaining supplies
to the town's poor black and white population as well as to convalescing
ex–Confederate soldiers. On April 16 Turner's force departed Lynchburg,
leaving a city of fearful residents who rarely ventured beyond their front
doors in the ensuing weeks.[22]

The situation in Danville—a town of roughly 5,000 in 1861—was much
worse. Situated on the border with North Carolina, the town served as the last
Confederate capital after the abandonment of Richmond on April 2. Danville
was chosen because of its location between Lee's army and General Joseph
Johnston's army in North Carolina. In addition, the town included a well-
stocked quartermaster department, repair shop, and ordnance machinery;
most important, it allowed President Davis to maintain the capital within
Virginia as well as the public perception that the government continued to
function. Between April 2 and April 10 Davis conducted affairs to the best of
his ability while the town itself served as a magnet for stragglers from Lee's

retreating army hoping to link with Johnston in North Carolina or attempting to get home. The situation quickly deteriorated after the surrender of the army. On his approach to the town, John Dooley observed that "Danville is in a perfect uproar." Throngs of soldiers and civilians poured into the overcrowded town, while the streets leading out of town were "choked with government wagons trying to force their way out." Rioting and plundering soon followed, halted only when Confederate ordnance was accidentally ignited. On his way out of the city amid rumors that the enemy had cut the Greensboro road, Secretary of the Navy Stephen Mallory recalled "scenes of confusion such as it was never before the fortune of old Danville to witness." Meanwhile, Davis and what was left of the government continued south.[23]

Reminders of defeat could be found throughout Virginia, from the burned-down business district of Richmond to the leveled countryside of the Shenandoah Valley and northern Virginia. A *London Times* correspondent reported that "the once fertile fields" between Winchester and Martinsburg "are lying barren, for their owners have lost all their means, their negroes having fled and their horses and money having been carried off." As if the physical destruction were not enough, he went on to note that "graves are scattered by the roadside." The same scenes were witnessed east of the Blue Ridge Mountains in the area between Manassas and Alexandria. The constant movement of armies along with the two major battles near Manassas left miles of entrenchments, scores of naked chimneys, and few trees standing; one observer described the area south of Alexandria along the railroad lines as a "prairie."[24] Such scenes of destruction would have exacerbated the anxiety that returning soldiers felt as they anticipated what awaited them at their own homes.

While the physical manifestations of war painted a bleak picture of the immediate future, news of the assassination of Abraham Lincoln on April 14 presented ex-Confederates with the likelihood of more severe retribution from the Federal government as well as immediate repercussions from a saddened and even vengeful Union army. Edgar Warfield learned of Lincoln's assassination while waiting for a steamship in Richmond for the final leg of his journey to Alexandria. As he stood with other ex-Confederates among a large crowd of white and black ("but mostly black") Union soldiers, "a feeling of uneasiness crept over us as we momentarily expected something unpleasant to happen." Edward P. Alexander in Washington, D.C., found that "the passion & excitement of the crowds were so great that anyone on the street recognised merely as a Confederate, would have been instantly mobbed & lynched." One eyewitness reported that when news of the assassination arrived in Richmond, Union troops "pounced with the ferocity of wild beasts upon every rebel soldier they could lay hands upon, beating and driving them from the streets, the poor fellows all the while in ignorance of the cause of their bad treatment."[25]

News filtered throughout Virginia slowly and was laced with rumor. Not until April 20 did Samuel Howard learn that Lincoln had "been shot & killed his son wounded, and Seward desperately wo[u]nded." While William Grove's diary entry includes a note indicating that Lincoln had been shot and "Seward mortally wounded," as late as April 25 he was also contemplating more recent rumors that both Ulysses S. Grant and Horace Greeley had been assassinated.[26] It is almost impossible to find an accurate account of events in Washington among returning soldiers. This is not surprising, given the state of communications in the immediate post-Appomattox period. It is important, however, to understand that Lincoln's assassination was an ongoing event for these men, the scale of which could not be properly understood. In the most extreme cases, men walked home under the impression that the president, vice president, secretary of state, and highest-ranking general had all fallen victim to John Wilkes Booth's conspiracy; for these individuals there was no Federal government.

Although many white Southerners agreed that Lincoln's actions since 1861 were best understood as those of a "tyrant," they remained ambivalent about his murder. Reactions ranged from public declarations that the South had been properly avenged to genuine sadness—though, as Anne Sarah Rubin asserts, most fell somewhere in between. John Dooley noted in his diary that "people don't know whether to rejoice or to be sad." "And the reason," Dooley went on to state, "appears to be that they are not sure whether it be better for the South that Abraham should be king, or some Successor." For those with access to more reliable news, the realization that Andrew Johnson would assume the presidency led to additional doubts and questions. Even though Johnson proved to be lenient toward the white South, ten years later George Eggleston recalled that his neighbors in Amelia County believed the new president to be a "renegade Southerner" who "would endeavor to prove his loyalty to the Union by extra severity to the South."[27] It is likely that returning soldiers, along with their civilian counterparts in the Confederate government, expected to be the targets of the Johnson administration's retribution.

Virginia's veterans were confronted with more ominous signs of the Confederacy's demise and with it the undermining of central pillars of the antebellum South. There was no more critical an indicator of this than the abrupt end of slavery, and by 1865 both those who had owned slaves and those who had not understood its significance on a daily basis as they traversed the roads home. Long before Lee's surrender at Appomattox, Confederate soldiers were forced to confront the threat to their slave society. In 1861 Virginians decided that slavery would be safer outside the Union, as they perceived the Republican president to be a threat to their way of life. By the end of the year, thousands of Virginia slaves had demonstrated the lengths they would go to assert their desire for freedom by running from their masters in areas controlled by the Union army. Their doing so undermined the Confederate war effort in innumerable ways, from depriving the government in Richmond of their services to providing the Union army with intelligence. By 1863 those same slaves had helped to transform a war that had originally been framed around the preservation of the Union into a war to end slavery itself. Beginning with Ulysses S. Grant's Overland Campaign, and increasingly in the trenches around Petersburg in the summer of 1864, the Army of Northern Virginia was forced to confront United States Colored Troops on the battlefield. This culminated on July 30, when a division of black soldiers took part in a failed Federal offensive outside of Petersburg, dubbed the battle of the Crater. Although the battle was a decisive Confederate victory, the experience of fighting black soldiers in close quarters served to reinforce the close connection between the maintenance of Southern armies and the protection of home, families, and the institution of slavery. The turn toward emancipation, however, meant that only with victory and independence would Confederates' homes as well as the political and social structures of their communities be maintained.[28]

While the two armies were camped around Appomattox awaiting the surrender ceremony, Federal authorities made it a point to keep black troops away from Confederate soldiers for fear that contact would exacerbate an already emotional and tenuous situation.[29] Once on the road, however, former Confederates were forced to confront both occupying black troops and newly freed slaves who chose to exercise their freedom in ways that often confirmed white Southerners' antebellum racial notions. Aaron Sheehan-Dean has noted that "from the crisis of secession through the debates over slave soldiers, white Virginians had made protection of the institution of slavery a central war aim."[30] In Petersburg, white residents and returning soldiers were forced to confront both African American garrison troops and a sizeable free black population. Henry Bird, who had served in the Twelfth Virginia Infantry, observed that "it is both sad and laughable to see the smoked Yankees parading in the streets in all their Sunday finery and then to think of the change that will come over the spirit of their dream in less than six months." Bird's hope for a quick return to prewar racial hierarchies would have to wait, but such encounters fueled animosity against both occupying soldiers and former slaves, and ultimately would contribute to white Southerners' self-identification as victims of "Yankee" Reconstruction.[31]

The former capital of Richmond fared even worse. The fires the Confederates had set in an attempt to prevent Federal forces from claiming large military stockpiles accidentally burned a large section of the business district along the James River. Naked facades presented an ominous sight for Robert E. Lee, who entered the city on April 15, as well as for countless others who had once called Richmond home or who were looking for passage elsewhere. Returning Confederates, such as Kena King Chapman, who were without accurate information surrounding the city's destruction, "blamed immigrant hordes from the North and slaves."[32] For ex-Confederates, Richmond did fare better than Petersburg in one respect when Gen. Edward Ord ordered black units stationed in the city to leave.[33]

Upon their return home, veterans from slave-owning families experienced the loss on a personal level, as they had to make the shift from toil on fields of battle to labor on fields of corn and other crops—work they had never had to do previously, and which reinforced white bitterness. Samuel Buck recalled "doing as much work as any slave my father ever owned." Young Carlton McCarthy's experience on a farm outside Richmond would have been sufficient to drive home the intimate connection between defeat and emancipation for any former veteran. Rather than head directly into Richmond, McCarthy and a companion chose to work on a plantation in exchange for lodging and cash. Such "manual labor," which had been formerly carried out by slaves, clearly left an indelible imprint on McCarthy's memory. Writing in 1882, he recalled: "The negro men and women in the neighborhood, now in the full enjoyment of newly-conferred liberty, and consequently having no thought of doing any work, congregated about the garden, leaned on the fence, gazed sleepily at the toiling soldiers, chuckled now and then, and occasionally explained their presence by remarking to each other, 'Come here to see dem dar white folks wuckin.'"[34] Similar scenes took place throughout Virginia, serving to remind white Southerners that their labor system had been subverted and that their perceptions of blacks as obedient and faithful servants were perhaps misplaced.

Once home, the challenges of postwar adjustment and recognition of Confederate defeat continued as occupying Federal forces regulated the behavior of returning veterans and kept a sharp lookout for any hint of further aggression against the Federal government. Military authorities cautioned veterans to remove the brass buttons from their uniforms or face arrest, and encouraged oaths of allegiance to the United States.[35] Isaac Russell, who worked as a hospital steward in Winchester, chose to cover his brass buttons with black cloth after he was forced to appear at the provost's office, as did Samuel Buck, who described the order as "galling to me." Edgar Warfield arrived home in Alexandria to find two American flags hanging over his doorstep, which were placed "by the authorities, who anticipated my father's return and mine, so that we would have to walk under them on entering." Those same authorities forced Warfield to report to the city's provost marshal, which he did for two weeks.[36] Although these policies were nonviolent, they served to remind Virginia's veterans of the completeness of their defeat as well as their inability to control their individual and collective destinies. The order for soldiers to remove military buttons from their uniforms served to minimize tangible connections to their former identities as soldiers of a Confederate nation.

The historical record is filled with joyous accounts of reunions for countless numbers of returning soldiers. Further removed from our popular memory of the initial postwar period, however, are the accounts of soldiers who experienced a profound crisis of confidence and depression or were unable to cope with the demands of a post-emancipation world and who fervently believed that defeat was somehow to be explained by a vengeful God. Others missed the predictable rhythms of camp life and the excitement of battle. Many anticipated a dark future. Nineteen-year-old William Selwyn Ball rode home to his family's estate in Fairfax County only to find it completely destroyed. His brother and cousins, who had also served in Lee's army, were "sprawled out on the lawn . . . dazed and unable to realize that actually all was lost." Though his older brother was eventually able to begin a law practice, Ball was unable to regain his confidence and sense of purpose; with the loss of the war, "the world seemed to . . . come to an end," leaving him with "no ambition." Newspapers in Alexandria reported an increase in "houses of entertainment," and one editorial observed that these "degrading dens of destruction" turned men who four years earlier had been "prominent church members, honored esteemed and loved" into "dancing theatre-going, rum-guzzling mutilated images of manhood." Farther south in Richmond, newspapers complained that "thousands of our most gifted and promising young men are fast becoming confirmed sots."[37]

The reference to "mutilated images of manhood" stretches the conception of the damage wrought by war beyond the physical. The failure on the part of Lee's men to protect their homes and communities as well as the realities of occupation and emancipation tugged at their own sense of identity and place within a political and social hierarchy based on white supremacy. However, accounts of psychological breakdown or signs of weakness and despair are difficult to judge, given the culture's emphasis on public displays of strength and the public reputations that white Southern families wished to maintain.[38]

It would take between fifteen and twenty years for ex-Confederates to arrive at a point where they could begin to put pen to paper and make sense of their war experiences within a postwar world that now included a revival of confidence and a sense of regional identity. With the exception of the four short years of Readjuster Party control, by the mid-1870s white Virginians had successfully rebuilt a social and political hierarchy based on white supremacy. Racial controls hardened in the years after the Supreme Court's 1896 decision upholding segregation in *Plessy v. Ferguson* and through the Jim Crow era. Confederate memoirs written throughout this period are filled with stories of battlefield heroics, colorful generals, obedient and loving slaves, and other nostalgic episodes. Gone in large part are the stories of war's devastation, the sense of utter despair, and the strong feelings of humiliation associated with defeat that colored the accounts of Confederates in the weeks after Appomattox. The experiences of these men along the roads and paths leading away from Appomattox served as the foundation from which they proceeded to rebuild their lives and collective identities as white Southerners. More important, the experience of defeat in its various forms provided many with the impetus to eventually challenge occupation forces as well as the steps that Virginia's ex-slaves had taken to secure their freedom.

Notes

1. Taliaferro enlisted in the Fredericksburg Artillery on November 4, 1861, and on May 1, 1862, was commissioned first lieutenant in the Forty-seventh Virginia.

2. Ida Tarbell, "Disbanding of the Confederate Army," *McClure's*, April 1901, 534–36, reprinted in B. A. Botkin, ed., *A Civil War Treasury of Tales, Legends, and Folklore* (Lincoln: University of Nebraska Press, 2000), 558–60.

3. One of the best examples of a recent study that utilizes the theme of reunion and reconciliation is Jay Winik, *April 1865: The Month That Saved America* (New York: HarperCollins, 2001). On Reconstruction in Virginia, see Peter Wallenstein, *Cradle of America: Four Centuries of Virginia History* (Lawrence: University Press of Kansas, 2007), 213–29.

4. See Aaron Sheehan-Dean, *Why Confederates Fought: Family and Nation in Civil War Virginia* (Chapel Hill: University of North Carolina Press, 2007).

5. Anne Sarah Rubin, *A Shattered Nation: The Rise and Fall of the Confederacy, 1861–1868* (Chapel Hill: University of North Carolina Press, 2005), 117–38.

6. Jason Phillips, *Diehard Rebels: The Confederate Culture of Invincibility* (Athens: University of Georgia Press, 2007), 178.

7. George C. Rable, "Despair, Hope, and Delusion: The Collapse of Confederate Morale Reexamined," in Mark Grimsley and Brooks D. Simpson eds., *The Collapse of the Confederacy* (Lincoln: University of Nebraska Press, 2001).

8. A great deal has been written on Confederate morale in the Army of Northern Virginia during the final year of the war. See Gary W. Gallagher, *The Confederate War* (Cambridge, Mass.: Harvard University Press, 1997); J. Tracy Power, *Lee's Miserables: Life in the Army of Northern Virginia from the Wilderness to Appomattox* (Chapel Hill: University of North Carolina Press, 1998); Phillips, *Diehard Rebels.*

9. George Cary Eggleston, *A Rebel's Recollections* (1875; repr., Baton Rouge: Louisiana State University Press, 1996), 172.

10. Richard Barksdale Harwell, ed., *A Confederate Diary of the Retreat from Petersburg, April 3–20, 1865* (Atlanta: Emory University Publications Sources and Reprints, 1953), 18.

11. Robert E. Lee, *The Wartime Papers of Robert E. Lee,* ed. Clifford Dowdey (1961; repr., New York: Da Capo, 1987), 934–35.

12. U.S. War Department, *War of the Rebellion: A Compilation of the Official Records of the Union and Confederate Armies* (Washington, D.C.: Government Printing Office, 1880–1901), series 1, vol. 46, pt. 3, 1394.

13. James Whitehorne and William Wilson references can be found in

Rubin, *A Shattered Nation*, 12–21. The final Whitehorne reference is located in Chris M. Calkins, *The Final Bivouac: The Surrender Parade at Appomattox and the Disbanding of the Armies, April 10–May 20, 1865* (Lynchburg, Va.: H. E. Howard, 1988), 47. William Thomas Poague, *Gunner with Stonewall: Reminiscences of William Thomas Poague*, ed. Monroe F. Cockrell (1957; repr., Lincoln: University of Nebraska Press, 1998), 129.

14. Edward B. Williams, ed., *Rebel Brothers: The Civil War Letters of the Truehearts* (College Station: Texas A&M University Press, 1995), 217–18; John Dooley, *John Dooley, Confederate Soldier: His War Journal*, ed. Joseph T. Durkin (South Bend, Ind.: University of Notre Dame Press, 1963), 181.

15. Peter S. Carmichael, *The Last Generation: Young Virginians in Peace, War, and Reunion* (Chapel Hill: University of North Carolina Press, 2005), 213–18; Ham Chamberlayne, *Ham Chamberlayne—Virginian: Letters and Papers of an Artillery Officer in the War for Southern Independence, 1861–1865*, ed. C. G. Chamberlayne (1932; repr., Wilmington, N.C.: Broadfoot, 1992), 320–21.

16. Papers Chiefly pertaining to Virginia, 1803–1904, William B. Grove Diary, accession 8995, University of Virginia Library, Charlottesville.

17. Harwell, *A Confederate Diary*, 21.

18. Paul F. Paskoff, "Measures of War: A Quantitative Examination of the Civil War's Destructiveness in the Confederacy," *Civil War History* 54 (March 2008): 52–54.

19. Edward Porter Alexander, *Fighting for the Confederacy: The Personal Recollections of General Edward Porter Alexander*, ed. Gary W. Gallagher (Chapel Hill: University of North Carolina Press, 1989), 547–49. Alexander traveled to Washington to meet with the Brazilian foreign minister and then to New York to discuss his plans with the Brazilian consul, but was unable to gain permission. Edgar Warfield, *Manassas to Appomattox: The Civil War Memoirs of Pvt. Edgar Warfield, 17th Virginia Infantry* (1936; repr., Mclean, Va.: EPM, 1996), 175–76.

20. Calkins, *The Final Bivouac*, 54; Harwell, *A Confederate Diary*.

21. Robert J. Driver Jr., *Lexington and Rockbridge County in the Civil War* (Lynchburg, Va.: H. E. Howard, 1989), 99; Daniel E. Sutherland, *Seasons of War: The Ordeal of a Confederate Community, 1861–1865* (Baton Rouge: Louisiana State University Press, 1995), 376. In addition, see Mark K. Greenough, "Aftermath at Appomattox: Federal Military Occupation of Appomattox County, May–November 1865," *Civil War History* 31 (March 1985): 5–23.

22. Steven E. Tripp, *Yankee Town, Southern City: Race and Class Relations in Civil War Lynchburg* (New York: New York University Press, 1999), 159–61; Calkins, *The Final Bivouac*, 58–61.

23. On the Confederate government's retreat, see Michael B. Ballard, *A Long Shadow: Jefferson Davis and the Final Days of the Confederacy* (Jackson:

University Press of Mississippi, 1986), 52–73; Dooley, *War Journal*, 179–81; Stephen R. Mallory, "The Last Days of the Confederate Government," in Peter Cozzens, ed., *Battles and Leaders of the Civil War* (Urbana: University of Illinois Press, 2002), 5:675.

24. Richard Duncan, *Beleaguered Winchester: A Virginia Community at War, 1861–1865* (Baton Rouge: Louisiana State University Press, 2007), 251; Nan Netherton, Donald Sweig, Janice Artemel, Patricia Hickin, and Patrick Reed, *Fairfax County, Virginia: A History* (Fairfax, Va.: Fairfax City Board of Supervisors, 1978), 371.

25. Warfield, *Manassas to Appomattox*; Alexander, *Fighting for the Confederacy*, 547; Ernest B. Furgurson, *Ashes of Glory: Richmond at War* (New York: Knopf, 1996), 359.

26. Harwell, *A Confederate Diary*, 21; William B. Grove Diary, April 25, 1865.

27. On reactions to Lincoln's assassination in Virginia, see Rubin, *A Shattered Nation*, 126–30; Dooley, *War Journal*, 195; Eggleston, *A Rebel's Recollections*, 184.

28. George S. Burkhardt, *Confederate Rage, Yankee Wrath: No Quarter in the Civil War* (Carbondale: Southern Illinois University Press, 2007), 159–74; Chandra Manning, *What This Cruel War Was Over: Soldiers, Slavery, and the Civil War* (New York: Knopf, 2007).

29. William Marvel, *Lee's Last Retreat: The Flight to Appomattox* (Chapel Hill: University of North Carolina Press, 2002), 185.

30. Sheehan-Dean, *Why Confederates Fought*, 192.

31. A. Wilson Greene, *Civil War Petersburg: Confederate City in the Crucible of War* (Charlottesville: University of Virginia Press, 2006), 266–72.

32. Quoted in Phillips, *Diehard Confederates*, 180.

33. On the immediate aftermath of the war in Richmond, see Nelson Lankford, *Richmond Burning: The Last Days of the Confederate Capital* (New York: Viking, 2002).

34. Samuel D. Buck, *With the Old Confeds: Actual Experiences of a Captain in the Line* (Baltimore, Md.: H. E. Houck, 1925), 134; Carlton McCarthy, *Detailed Minutiae of Soldier Life in the Army of Northern Virginia, 1861–1865* (1882; repr., Lincoln: University of Nebraska Press, 1993), 178.

35. On the politics of loyalty oaths and pardons in Virginia, see Susanna Michele Lee, "Reconciliation in Reconstruction Virginia," in Edward L. Ayers, Gary W. Gallagher, and Andrew J. Torget, eds., *Crucible of the Civil War: Virginia from Secession to Commemoration* (Charlottesville: University of Virginia Press, 2006), 189–208.

36. Duncan, *Beleaguered Winchester*, 252; Buck, *With the Old Confeds*, 134; Warfield, *Manassas to Appomattox*, 177.

37. Netherton et al., *Fairfax County, Virginia*, 371–72.

38. Historians are beginning to look more closely at the emotional and psychological consequences of the Civil War in the postwar South. See Bertram Wyatt-Brown, *The Shaping of Southern Culture: Honor, Grace, and War, 1760s–1880s* (Chapel Hill: University of North Carolina Press, 2001), 255–69; Eric T. Dean Jr., *Shook over Hell: Post-traumatic Stress, Vietnam, and the Civil War* (Cambridge, Mass.: Harvard University Press, 1997).

"Traitors shall not dictate to us"

Afro-Virginians and the Unfinished Emancipation of 1865

Ervin L. Jordan Jr.

Two weeks after Lee's surrender, a Richmond newspaper reported that a committee of three slaves representing twenty-seven others politely informed their master that they were now free but would continue to work if he paid wages in Yankee greenbacks. He irately told them to go to hell and hoped they would get there soon enough. Elsewhere, Gilbert Turner, son of Nat Turner, headed north: "I have been in Hell once. Now that God is leading me out, *I don't ever mean to go back into Hell again!*"[1] The races seemed in parallel hells, and some may have believed that William Shakespeare had predicted their tribulations in the post-slavery landscape:

> Thou seest we are not all alone unhappy:
> This wide and universal theatre
> Presents more woeful pageants than the scene
> Wherein we play in. (*As You Like It,* act 2, scene 7)

When the news of freedom came, Petersburg slaves sang freedom songs around a huge bonfire that could be seen for miles, but an Elizabeth City County song seemed proof of the freedom to leave: "What do we gain by stayin' here? Hunger, shame and fear." Falls Church residents optimistically articulated homes, schools, churches, and citizenship as their foremost goals.[2] Afro-Virginians' transition from slavery to freedom during the post-emancipation period of April–December 1865 was fraught with challenges. Their new freedoms, in varying degrees, embraced but were not limited to: military service; mobility and emigration; wage employment; land ownership; reuniting of families; education and worship; access to public spaces; and voting. Possessing almost nothing except hope, the freedpeople's exercise of these freedoms was jeopardized by seething whites traumatized by defeat yet determined to maintain racial hegemony. In some respects, Richmond blacks complained in June, "we are worse than when we were slaves and living under slave law." The age of emancipation was marked by profound contradictions and complexities difficult to reassess, considering the predominance of white-created contemporary sources and the shadow of Reconstruction and Jim Crow darkening the pages. As one of a new generation of African American historians has observed, it is "in keeping with past and present racial hierarchies for blacks' stories to be accepted when they affect only other black people, but to treat their stories with super, super skepticism when they say things about white people that other whites find to be problematic."[3]

The spring of 1865 was damp and cold as despairing whites, their morale sapped by paucities and war weariness, conceded defeat. "The Times seem dark & gloomy," noted a Chesterfield County resident. Households mixed wheat with old coffee grounds to extend the flavor and hoarded dwindling supplies of ham, soap, onions, and catsup. A Culpeper County adolescent dismissed the usual rumors of armistices and European military intervention, having "heard it a hundred times before." At the Hampton Roads Peace Conference in February, three Confederate commissioners met with Abraham Lincoln and his secretary of state William Seward. When Lincoln was asked what would become of slavery if a negotiated settlement were reached, his contradictory reply was that as a wartime measure the Emancipation Proclamation would terminate when the war ended, but slaves freed under its provisions would remain free. He added an anecdote about a farmer who planted potatoes for his hogs; when the ground froze and the farmer was asked by a neighbor about the hogs' fate, he replied, "Root, hog, or die." An example of the racial status quo occurred when an Afro-Virginian boatman was sent to the commissioners' steamer with a basket of champagne as a parting gift. As the Confederates waved their thanks, Seward facetiously responded, *"Keep the champagne, but return the Negro!"*[4]

No one seriously asked the enslaved what they collectively wanted, so the slavery business continued in full vigor. J. M.C. Haden & Company of Richmond sold Jefree, a male slave, for $4,000 and guaranteed his health. Slaves were in short supply in some areas; military quartermasters sought blacksmiths, mechanics, and laborers with the promise of clothing (but not blankets), rations, health care, and an annual $1,000 payment for their owners. A "strong and healthy cook, washer, ironer and milker" had been available for hire in Albemarle County since December, likely as she had "with her one or two small children." Staunton's Michael Harman donated twenty male slaves to the Confederate war effort, probably because he could no longer afford to support them.[5]

Slaves serving as soldiers was a topic of whispered conversations, though Congressman Thomas Gholson denounced it as a hazardous racial experiment that would place whites' fate in black hands. Afro-Confederates' first public military parade raised hopes in March, but most white Richmonders were unimpressed, ignoring the event to watch a billiards game. Nor were they bothered by the contradiction of slave auctions and recruitment advertisements for black soldiers in adjoining newspaper columns. This spasmodic effort was of stragglers in a race already lost. A poignant photograph taken at the Petersburg trenches showed two dead Confederates—a uniformed white artillerist and a young black male in civilian clothes and boots, his face turned from the camera. He died too late for the Lost Cause, and probably unmourned, as most blacks despised Afro-Confederates as race traitors and "skillet heads."[6]

On Sunday morning, April 2, black sexton Richard Chiles quietly walked down the aisle of St. Paul's Episcopal Church to the pew where Jefferson Davis sat alone. He handed Davis a note. The president read it and then hurried from the church with deathly pale countenance. All this attracted the nervous attention of his fellow worshippers, who surmised that General Lee had advised Richmond's evacuation. Chiles's family was proud of his role in history; his children excelled in law, journalism, and education, with one daughter, Marietta, becoming a prominent Richmond educator. Another black Richard made history the next morning—on April 3, Richard Gill Forrester, a young slave tasked to raise state and Confederate flags, became the first person in four years to fly an American flag over the state capitol. Secessionists had discarded the Stars and Stripes in the trash in 1861, but he had secretly recovered it. Forrester became the patriarch of one of Richmond's most reputable black families and was among the first Afro-Virginians elected to municipal office.[7]

The Thirty-sixth U.S. Colored Infantry, followed by the Fifth Massachusetts Cavalry, both of the XXV Corps, Army of the James, were the first Union troops to enter Richmond on April 3, though they were initially ordered to go around it. Two other black infantry regiments, the Twenty-ninth Connecticut and the Ninth United States Colored Troops (USCT), soon followed. "It was fit that the old flag should be restored to the city by soldiers of the race striking the final blow," declared *Harper's Weekly.* Massachusetts governor John Andrew added: "The colored men received late, got in first, and this is Scripture fulfilled." Among them was Cpl. Samuel Ballton of the Fifth Massachusetts, a Westmoreland County ex-slave who had taken his wife and mother-in-law to freedom in Union-occupied Fredericksburg before enlisting in 1864.[8]

A remarkable event transpired on that extraordinary day. As black troops marched through the city, an elderly woman anxiously scanned their faces for a son who had fled to Canada from Richmond and was subsequently rumored to have enlisted in Ohio. A sympathetic soldier of the Twenty-eighth USCT took her to his regimental chaplain, Garland H. White; in an extraordinary coincidence, mother and son were soon reunited as White proved to be her long-lost son.[9]

Confederate civilians expected the worst from black troops, but they proved to be disciplined professionals. When the XXV Corps was ordered to leave Richmond, its commander, disgusted by locals' racism, insisted on marching his black troops through that city and Petersburg as a show of force. The reaction among Richmond's white women ranged from consternation to contempt. One tearful girl said the sight of black troops hurt as much as the psychological blow of Lee's surrender yet expressed surprise and relief at how well they were drilled, clothed, and equipped. A defiant Lucy Fletcher deemed them little more than imported African "savages and cannibals," and diarist Clara Shafer groused of "Negro soldiers stepping about as grandly as possible," whose presence induced the now-freed slaves to treat the new state of affairs "as a holiday frolic."[10]

Thomas Morris Chester of the *Philadelphia Press,* one of the war's few accredited black journalists, described the reaction of Afro-Richmonders: "Nothing can exceed the rejoicings of the Negroes since the occupation of this city. They all declare that they are abundantly able to take care of themselves." More than 2,000 African Americans and white soldiers attended a massive "Jubilee Meeting" presided over by Chester at the First African Baptist Church on April 7 to celebrate victory and freedom. David Stevens, chaplain of the Thirty-sixth USCT (organized in Portsmouth two years previously) delivered the sermon, becoming the first black man to preach from its pulpit.[11]

Approximately forty USCT regiments had participated in forty-five battles in Virginia during 1864–1865. "Black units did some of their best fighting in Virginia," contends one USCT historian. A white officer wrote home that "the Darkies are Bully fellows to fight." Nearly 6,000 Afro-Virginians enlisted; of the nine USCT regiments organized in the state, only three (the First U.S. Colored Cavalry and the Tenth and Thirty-sixth regiments) fought on Virginia soil, mostly during the Petersburg campaign. An unassigned infantry detachment organized in Alexandria in the fall of 1864 was the state's last organized black USCT unit and in July 1865 the first to be mustered out. The last Afro-Virginian regiment, the Thirty-eighth U.S. Colored Infantry, was mustered out in 1867 after three years' service.[12]

Defeat humiliated white Southerners as a soul-numbing harbinger of a racial apocalypse with "black governors, black judges, black legislators, black juries, black witnesses—everything black," and some embittered freedpeople sought to settle old scores. A group of men headed to Richmond from Goochland County forewarning an intent to "set things right." Brunswick County freedman Allen Wilson contemplated killing an overseer in revenge for permanently crippling his mother by frequent whippings. Some evicted white families and seized their property as compensation for enslavement and became stubborn squatters. A dismayed Fauquier County woman returned home "to a scene of ruin and desolation," with blacks in "complete possession of everything, their tubs and pots setting all around and clothes hanging about in the bushes." John Howard expropriated the Prince William County farm of his octogenarian owner and told Union authorities he had a legal right to the land because the Howards had kept it profitable during the war.[13]

For blacks, Lincoln's Richmond visit on April 4 seemed the fulfillment of biblical messianic prophecy; seeing him in person confirmed their freedom. At Capitol Square, speaking from the base of the Washington statue, he allegedly told them that liberty was their birthright, slavery a sin, and urged them "to cast off the name of slave." The Great Emancipator's assassination ten days later horrified Afro-Virginians. "To the unhappy race upon whose equal natural rights with ourselves this nation had so long trampled," noted *Harper's Weekly,* "the name of Abraham Lincoln meant to them freedom, justice, home, family, happiness." Chauncey Leonard, a military chaplain in Alexandria and one of the army's few black commissioned officers, lamented: "We mourn the loss of our Noble Chief Magistrate. We have looked for him as our earthly Pilot to guide us through this National Storm and Plant us securely on the Platform of Liberty and Equal Political rights, but God in his wise Providence has removed him. Brave men weep for him."[14]

The freeing of the South's slaves was not required by the terms of Lee's surrender, so on their own authority military officials declared Virginia slaves free during April and May 1865. Appomattox, Campbell, and Rockbridge ex-slaveholders noted May 26 as the day when slaves were "declared free by order of the military authorities." In June, Maj. Gen. Alfred Terry, commander of the Department of Virginia, received Washington's permission to issue an order abolishing slavery. The war also ended the free black caste; they, not slaves, were probably the first black caste whose freedom status was unambiguous after Appomattox. Terry's order also invalidated discriminatory laws against free blacks and declared they would henceforth enjoy the same personal liberties as white citizens. Among the last to register their residency as required by law was Anna Eliza Stewart of Lynchburg, freeborn in 1839 and registered since 1851. She did so again for the last time on April 3, 1865—the day Union troops seized Richmond. Persistent confusion over blacks' status led to ratification of the Thirteenth Amendment's forty-five words in December 1865 and blacks' citizenship in the Civil Rights Act of 1866.[15]

"The Virginia of the past we shall not know again any more than we can revive the Middle Ages," a Charlottesville newspaper dourly acknowledged, yet some slaveholders were in denial, as evinced by postwar registering of "slave" births. Antebellum state laws required the annual registering of births and deaths regardless of race or status. For a slave this included the date and place of birth, gender and name, and name of the mother and owner; more than 130,000 slave births were recorded in the Old Dominion from 1853 to 1865. One week after Lee's surrender, such births were recorded in Rockingham and Albemarle counties. Children born to three slave couples owned by one Halifax County master during May 1865 were registered, as were others in the counties of Loudoun, Orange, Rappahannock, and Warren between August and November. Campbell County led all others in the number of slave births registered after May 1865. An unnamed boy born to an Albemarle County slave named Lucinda on the first of December, and Sarah, born to Lee County "slave" parents that same month, were among Virginia's last registered slave births.[16]

Masters assumed that the Federal government would compensate them for emancipating their slaves. A Buckingham County resident listed ninety by name and age (from ten to seventy-five), with a combined value of $54,000. During the summer of 1865, a Petersburg slaveholder, "a harmless and good-natured lunatic," dutifully paid taxes on his "slaves." The Fourteenth Amendment (1868) prohibited compensation to slaveholders, yet whites were loath to give up this hope. During the 1890s Louisa County lawyer W. E. Bibb, president of the innocuously named National Adjustment Society, was an unofficial national coordinator for such efforts. A state court finally ruled in *Jones v. Jones* (1896) that Bob, a former slave, was free and owed his ex-owner's heirs nothing.[17]

When Philip Coleman asked his Halifax County master Bird Rogers for a freedom certificate, Rogers slyly demurred, saying Coleman's reputation for honesty and hard work was locally renowned. Coleman took no chances and headed north as soon and as far as he could—to Rhode Island. Testing their new freedom to travel, many former slaves initially left, without notice or a definite destination, seeking to put distance between themselves and their former masters. "Have had a great deal to contend with the *ingratitude* of servants! Gone off without saying a word on the subject," one Chesterfield County resident fumed two days before Lee's formal surrender. "We are still bothered with the servants, who make no arrangements for their future homes," an exasperated Lynchburg woman declared. "They are off one day, & back the next." An Orange & Alexandria Railroad station agent glumly noted: "No Negroes. Negroes all leaving. Many Negroes going North. All gone from around here." Black migration from the countryside to the cities was viewed by whites with revulsion and dread. "The servants hereabouts are in much commotion," declared the Reverend Richard Davis in Orange Court House. "Many have quit their old masters & are going down the road to Culpeper or to Alexandria to get work, or liberty to be idle." His former slave, Frances, characterized as "one of 1,000" for her domestic devotion, had agreed to stay only after promised fair wages.[18]

Freedpeople attempting to leave were threatened or killed. In Buckingham County Lewis Gilliam was shot dead for refusing to plow and a freedwoman was run over by a wagon driven by her former mistress. Some Gordonsville freedmen quit work in June after their request for land was rejected by their former master. When they demanded to know "what sort of freedom this was," a Union officer ordered them back to work: "If you do not behave yourselves properly the only land you will get is 6 × 3 feet [in the graveyard]." In response to complaints of Yankee and black outlaws, Union officials revived local patrol systems, arming whites who took oaths of allegiance to the Federal government. These terrorist militias infringed on freedpeople's civil rights. Three black males accosted by an Amelia County patrol one Saturday night audaciously disputed its authority and spoke of their "freedmen's rights" but were whipped for not having passes.[19]

Whites who meddled in blacks' leisure time did so at their peril. When in July a ferryboat landed a black picnic party in Smithfield, local residents' attempts to expel them led to a riot requiring two companies of Union cavalry to quell. Order was restored after one of the white ringleaders "had his scalp removed" by an officer's sword. Union soldiers, too, interfered with blacks' freedom of movement. Curfews were established in Richmond and elsewhere. A New Hampshire soldier stationed there approvingly commented in his diary, "The Niggers ordered away"; they temporarily withdrew to Petersburg, only to return within days "by the ten of thousands." Orders issued during May announced that blacks were subject to arrest if they lacked passes from their employers for visits to urban areas. But having such passes did not always exempt them from abuse or arrest. Black employers such as Richmond carriage and livery stable operator Albert Brooks found themselves in jail on the grounds that the passes they issued to their black employees were fraudulent. This discriminatory policy was revoked in June after vigorous protests by blacks and their white Northern allies.[20]

The Bureau of Refugees, Freedmen, and Abandoned Lands, known as the Freedmen's Bureau, was established by Congress in March 1865 and comprised civil servants, military officers, African American and white Northern missionaries. It collected taxes, punished crime, created and interpreted laws, and used military force to enforce its policies. It also monitored and enforced wage contracts and established schools and courts. Additional duties, as outlined in instructions to a Buckingham County official, were "to protect the Negroes in their rights as free men; to see that they, in their present state of helplessness, are not injured or oppressed by their former masters." Beginning in July, Virginia was divided into ten administrative districts: Alexandria, Fort Monroe, Fredericksburg, Gordonsville, Lynchburg, Norfolk, Petersburg, Richmond, Winchester, and Wytheville. The bureau estimated the 1865–1866 population of the state as 1.2 million, of which 500,000 were African Americans; by August it was feeding an average of 29,000 residents daily.[21]

Bureau officials, noting that "state laws are practically inoperative respecting Negroes," ordered blacks accused or arrested by civil or military officers to be handed over to the nearest bureau office, along with witness names and written charges for eventual adjudication. The bureau was not always charitable where rations were concerned and frequently considered reducing those for black soldiers' families on the grounds that their wives should work to help support their families. The assistant commissioner in Norfolk, where 2,000 black families received provisions, ended food distribution in June 1865 because black soldiers' pay and rations equaled white soldiers'.[22]

Both races wanted the bureau as their exclusive ally and complained of preferential treatment to the other as a racial spoils system. However, whoever had the bureau as an ally did not need enemies. A Luray resident grumbled, "Yankee Cavalry are all the time flying around through here, arresting some peaceable, harmless Citizens on some false report given by some Negro." One Rockingham County resident offered a sarcastic toast: "The freedmen's bureau may the Devil turn inside out! Amen!" Shortly after Richmond's capture, Union soldiers were ill-treating blacks. They prevented black assemblages on weekdays to coerce them into working or finding work. When blacks were banned from Capitol Square and street corners, white Richmonders took smug satisfaction: "These officers with all their sympathy for Negritude, treat them much worse than we do. These poor unfortunate people will repent at length for the change in their status."[23]

Whites tried to drive a racial wedge between the freedpeople and the Yankees. During a Leesburg tournament, the only black onlooker who was insulted and mistreated was knocked down by a Union soldier. A Richmond woman informed her son: "If the servants in the country knew what was good for them they would stay quietly at their good homes. Many of the colored people here are beginning to feel that they have not benefitted by the coming of the Yankees." One freedwoman, when asked by a potential employer what sort of work she could do, replied that she could not do anything. Remarking that "she could do something when he had finished" with her, a Northern soldier of Irish descent hung her up by her thumbs and whipped her. Such abuses heartened ex-Confederates. "The poor stupid negro population is entirely gone mad, & seem to think the Yankees are going to let them remain *idle,* & live off the fat of the land," noted a Chesterfield County woman. "They will soon be deceived."[24]

Slavery and agriculture were the engines that drove Virginia's antebellum economy, and whites were unconvinced that the latter could survive without the former. Afro-Virginians were mainly farmers, laborers, oystermen, and artisans (carpenters, shoemakers, blacksmiths), though whites preferred them as agricultural laborers. A plethora of military orders issued during May and June regulated black labor and mobility, including instructions to "keep the negroes on their plantations so that crops may be cultivated." A Lynchburg order stated: "The delusion which many Colored persons, formerly slaves, are laboring under concerning their rights and privileges, having been in many instances productive of evil. All colored persons are informed that it is much better for them to remain where they are." However, less than a week later, officers admonished: "Owners of plantations on which agricultural products have been sowed and planted by the present freedpeople—their former slaves—will not be permitted to turn them loose upon the community without providing for their support. The support of the laborer and his family is a just charge against the product of the land, and the owner cannot escape the payment, either as wages paid or by giving a fair proportion of the crop."[25] How blacks were to be made aware of such military orders was not addressed: the orders were posted in newspapers, but most blacks were illiterate, and they could not trust whites, who did not have their best interests in mind, to pass on the information.

Planters and farmers sought to set freedmen's wages at $5 per month, and land was not to be sold or rented to them. An order issued by Petersburg's district commander checkmated this attempt: "No more public meetings will be held to establish a fixed price for negro labor, make distinctions prejudicial to the interests and limiting the freedom of the blacks. No difference in price for the same amount, kind, and quality of labor will be permitted between whites and blacks. When a former master hires his former slaves and keeps and feeds his family . . . the cost of their maintenance will be considered part of the laborer's wages."[26]

Some whites hoped to convince Europeans to immigrate "in greater numbers [so as to] eat up the black man" and replace blacks as agricultural workers. The importation of Chinese laborers was also suggested; though Congress banned the involuntary trafficking of "coolie" labor, this ban did not extend to those who voluntarily came to America. Originating from both sides of the Atlantic, such schemes to secure compliant and cheap European and Asian labor failed.[27]

Families complained about the scarcity of cooks. "I shall probably cook for myself and my children," conceded Lynchburg resident Alice Saunders. "We all seem to be unfortunate about cooks." In Chesterfield County, Martha Robertson noted that her cook, though she had "protested most *loudly* she would never *leave* us," was "the first woman to leave!" White women were also frustrated by blacks' refusal to work on holidays. "I'll tell you what kind of Christmas I spent," groused a Campbell County housewife. "My cook left me on Christmas Day and I was left with all the cooking and housework. We have nothing like our old time Virginia Christmas now. We see very little of the coloured people during Christmas. They leave white people to wait on themselves and they enjoy their freedom." White women were annoyed by fellow whites whose misdeeds threatened the availability of domestic servants. "John Henry we hear had some difficulty with a white boy who drew a knife on him. How it terminated we don't know, but it is deserted here in some of the Cabins," one woman privately complained. "Betty leaves . . . Caryetta & Marie leave . . . and [Avis] has already left though she says it is only for a visit."[28]

Most freedmen families were propertyless, on the move, or in debt peonage. Several migrated to other states in search of fair wages and better treatment. Wage contracts were restrictive: most required laborers to remain with their employers for a year and barred them from leaving for higher pay or better working conditions. Several required passes for laborers to leave plantations during their free time. All able-bodied persons, including children, were assigned work. Various chores were required without additional compensation. The first work agreements were family-based gang-labor systems. George Hannah signed one with eleven Charlotte County freedmen families detailing weekly wages, rations, housing, and firewood; two years later only five families renewed this contract. Twenty-two former slaves of John Hartwell Cocke of Fluvanna County, octogenarian owner of plantations in Virginia and Alabama, signed a contract that acknowledged their right to leave or stay: "We whose names are subscribed do acknowledge that as soon as the Emancipation Proclamation was issued at the Close of the War, we were Called together, and the Choice was given us to accept the freedom then made known, or to remain at Service for the Management and good order of the plantation." They secured monthly wages and arbitration of disputes by federal military officers; in return Cocke promised "comfortable food & clothing and other accommodations" while retaining the right to terminate employment "for gross neglect or violation of duty." He also secured presidential amnesty and a general's order prohibiting soldiers from "molesting or troubling" his property and black workforce.[29]

Slavery had taught blacks not to trust slaveholders and oftentimes the early post-emancipation experience reinforced those lessons. Before the end of April freedmen were suing their former masters for back wages. Milton Green Burks, a Craig County freedman, worked for George Hutchinson from the day of Lee's surrender until Christmas 1865 but was paid in clothing instead of cash. After waiting more than a year, Burks filed a complaint in August 1866 and the Freedmen's Bureau ordered Hutchinson to pay him. Sixteen-year-old Lorenzo Ivy's Pittsylvania County sharecropper family believed the promises of its former master but others left because they knew him all too well. The Ivys labored from April to November, producing large crops of corn, wheat, and tobacco. "I never worked harder in my life," Lorenzo later recalled, "for I thought the more we made, the more we would get." This proved a false hope; just before Christmas the family's employer reneged on promises to the share the crops and refused them any more food. Lorenzo's father sought redress from an unsympathetic bureau military officer who "had on Uncle Sam's clothes, but had Uncle Jeff's [Jefferson Davis's] heart." Sadder and wiser, the Ivy family moved to Tennessee. The bureau also acted as an out-of-state employment broker, as in the case of a Michigan railroad that sought four hundred Afro-Virginian workers. Reacting to high black unemployment in the Tidewater area and labor shortages outside the state, white Virginians and bureau officials proposed relocating blacks to Florida.[30]

A Norfolk freedwoman, discovering that her former husband had been forced to remarry, gave vent to bitterness: "White folks got a heap to answer for the way they've done to colored folks! So much they won't never *pray* it away!" Minnie Logan explained about slave marriage: "You see, it's dis way: God made marriage, but de white man made de law." Black men also asserted the right to protect black womanhood. A meeting at Richmond's Second African Baptist Church in August 1865 resulted in a petition against soldiers' deliberate targeting of comely young black women, arresting and jailing them on trumped-up charges and then subjecting them to robbery and rape.[31]

A typical Virginia ex-slave family consisted of husband, wife, and their children. Postbellum marriages and remarriages demonstrated the freedpeople's familial bonds, and in this they were supported by civilian and military authorities. In May 1865 orders were issued promoting their legalized matrimony. Officiants of these ceremonies were excused from the requirement of military-issued professional licenses and couples were exempted from taking loyalty oaths or paying a fee. All marriages were to be registered and the couples given written certificates. At the Freedmen's Village in Arlington, an elderly couple "dropped on their knees together, their eyes streaming with tears of thankfulness as the old man hugged [his wife], saying aloud, 'My dear old woman, I bless God that I can now, for the first time, kiss my own lawful *wife.*'" In Augusta County, 773 couples formalized their wedlock; these registrants comprised 25 percent of the county's 1860 black population. Not until 1866 would Virginia's first postwar General Assembly enact legislation legitimizing former slaves' antebellum marriages.[32]

Freedpeople sought to reunite their families. Nancy Nicolas, hoping to find her husband, placed an advertisement in the *Daily Richmond Whig:* "If this should meet the eye of Oteway Nicolas, of Widow Hall's estate, and sold by William Majors, he can find his wife and two youngest children on 2nd Street between Broad and Marshall Streets, at Mrs. Sophia M. Mallory's." After work and on the weekends freedpeople anxiously searched urban areas for word of long-sold spouses and children. Mrs. Thomas L. Johnson of Richmond sought news of five relatives (her father, grandmother, two sisters, and a brother). Those who were literate hastened to reestablish contact with distant relatives. In Norfolk, Matilda Ward sought information of her sister, while J. W. Elliot informed a female cousin that her relatives were "well and in good health" and hoped she could make a weekend visit. Writing from Liberia, antebellum emigrant William Douglass insisted that his former master locate and return his children: "I have written you four letters . . . inform me Something about my children."[33]

Convinced the freedpeople would "relapse into a state of semi-barbarism" without slavery, whites smugly shared reports of black infanticide. Others, such as Campbell County's Sarah Payne, took callous delight in turning their backs on black children. Though willing to distribute winter clothing to "indolent" former slaves one last time, Payne refused to support them beyond September, "especially the children." Bureau officials apprenticed black children, orphaned or not, to former slaveholders eager to reassume paterfamilias roles. The commander of the bureau's Covington post, deciding "two twin colored children" were not being properly cared for by their family, returned them to their former owner's custody. Several apprentices fled their new masters. Betty Cook, a fifteen-year-old orphan, was apprenticed in September by the bureau against her will to the G. Adolphus White family of Lexington who severely whipped her and treated her like a slave. In October, Cook fled to Mount Crawford where, after she escaped a bounty hunter, sympathetic whites offered her sanctuary, decent wages, and assistance in her appeals to the bureau's Winchester district superintendent. Cook vowed to never return to the Whites alive and in December signed an apprentice contract with Jackson Rhodes, one of her benefactors. After reviewing Cook's contract with White and her statement of complaint attested by six Mount Crawford white men, the bureau revoked her apprenticeship with the Whites.[34]

The slavery experience left some freedpeople physically weakened and unable to afford health care. Jane and Richard Wheeler of Alexandria had barely begun enjoying freedom when two of their daughters, eight-year-old Mary and two-year-old Josephine, died of "Sore Throat" (likely diphtheria) within five days of each other in August. Five years later the Wheelers were bereaved again when a four-day-old son died of "spasms." During antebellum times several slaveholders poisoned, expelled, or deliberately neglected slaves too old or too sick to work. Anticipating this, bureau officials enacted policies in November 1865 requiring local communities to provide for elderly ex-slaves. Those "residing with persons who have received the benefit of their labor during the vigor of life" were to be supported by their erstwhile owners until death. Black communities believed it was their duty to take care of their own by continuing or establishing benevolent societies for seniors and the indigent.[35]

Freedmen's schools had been established during 1861–1864 in the Union-occupied areas of Alexandria, Arlington, City Point, Fort Monroe, Hampton, Harpers Ferry, Newport News, Norfolk, and Portsmouth. Education was a practical way in which the emancipated slaves could assert their independence and build for their future. Considering that most business and personal transactions involved writing and arithmetic, by learning the "three Rs" (reading, writing, and arithmetic) the freedpeople could communicate with relatives, challenge erroneous records, avoid unfair labor contracts and being cheated of wages and rations, secure legal property titles, and prove tax payments. Of 20,000 blacks in Richmond and Manchester, 25 percent were literate and 30 percent were church members; black congregations quickly replaced white clergymen with black and sought to purchase church property.[36]

By the end of April, Richmond blacks had established schools for 1,500 students. The First African Baptist Church housed 500 schoolchildren, who posed at their school as artist Benson Lossing sketched and Mathew Brady photographed them. A Hampton school enrolled 374 pupils, all boys between the ages of six and seventeen who "had accompanied their parents on their escape from the plantations [to Fort Monroe]." There were at least two black schools in the small town (population 2,838) of Charlottesville, both operated by whites. The first was a tuition school established in the spring of 1865 by dry goods store owner named Musgrove who instructed 32 pupils. The Jefferson School, with 50 students, was founded that fall by Massachusetts native Anna Gardner of the New England Freedmen's Aid Society.[37]

At least four newspapers were founded during 1865. The *New Nation,* a weekly, was founded by Richmond blacks and published until 1869; its editor, the Reverend James W. Hunnicut, was a white man. Hampton newspapers included the *True Southerner* and the *American Palladium and Eastern Virginia Gazette*; the latter, founded in August by whites for the freedpeople, received little favor due to its racist paternalism—only one issue ever appeared. Another Hampton newspaper, the *County Journal,* was edited by Sara Banks, a black woman.[38]

On the evening of Richmond's capture a white resident was accosted by two Union soldiers, one black and one white, who demanded to know if he now respected blacks. The Richmonder carefully replied that he respected those who were worthy of respect. "When you are with wolves," he grumbled in the privacy of his diary, "you have to howl." Standards of civility and urban street etiquette changed as social courtesies were initially and grudgingly extended to blacks as "Mr.," "Mrs.," and "Miss," sometimes accompanied by handshakes and bows, hat tipping and polite head nods. More than seventy years after the war, ninety-six-year-old Elizabeth Sparks of Matthews County still relished her memory of the first time a white man (a Union officer seeking directions) took off his hat and bowed while addressing her as "Mrs. Sparks." Clara Shafer, aghast by blacks' refusal to step aside on sidewalks to allow white women to pass, grouched in her diary that "the negro tries to get ahead of the whites when you go in the streets." Freedmen's Bureau commissioner Maj. Gen. Oliver Otis Howard, while conceding "considerable social coldness and prejudice," optimistically believed civility had improved by late September, but this assessment proved short-lived.[39]

The freedpeople's post-emancipation identities continued to be linked with their former owners', as resentful whites cold-shouldered them and belittled their free status by continuing to refer to them by their first names, especially during public and business transactions. A Free Union doctor's ledger evinced this attitude; he denoted black patients with the parenthetical phrase "former slave of." Blacks resisted assaults on their selfhood; in one bureau marriage register of more than 1,500 Augusta County freedpeople, only 13 could or would name their last owner; in Montgomery County, less than half did so.[40]

A mass meeting at Norfolk's Bute Street Baptist Church in May 1865 passed nine resolutions, among them: "That the rights of the colored citizens of Virginia are more directly . . . affected in the restoration of the State to the Federal Union . . . of [our] right and duty to speak and act as freemen. . . . That we will prove ourselves worthy of the elective franchise. . . . That traitors shall not dictate or prescribe to us the terms or conditions of our citizenship, so help us God." A race riot occurred in April 1866 when black Norfolkians attempted to vote in city elections.[41]

Two weeks after Lincoln's assassination, a delegation of black Alexandrians met with President Andrew Johnson, concerned that the city military governor's plans to restore full civil authority to municipal government would again place them "under the authority and control of the unrepealed Slave laws [and with] no guaranty that our rights would be secured to us." For once, Johnson acted swiftly to protect blacks' civil rights, ordering the War Department to take immediate action; two days after the meeting, the request for continued Federal protection was granted. By August, black Alexandrians were again complaining to Federal authorities of "indignities, brutalities and inhumanities" by those who "bore the Negroes an undeserved malice because they were black, and had been freed by the United States Government." They organized Republican political action groups and in March 1867, during Alexandria's municipal elections, cast the majority vote (57 percent). When city officials refused to include black (and white Republican) votes in the final tallies, Union military commanders voided the outcome and suspended further elections until 1870.[42]

After defeat and emancipation, few things maddened Southern whites more than the prospect of black suffrage. Page County sheriff James Robertson despondently admitted to his sister: "We will have to give the negro the same rights that the white man has Politically or be kept out of the Union *So-called.*" King and Queen County farmer and ex–Confederate soldier

Cornelius Carlton could barely contain his sarcastic fury: "All the niggers to vote. Progressive times! All on equality! They were once the slaves—now *Idols* for white folks. 'Top rail now they say.'" A Halifax County tobacco farmer grumbled of the "awful State of Things in our government affairs with the negro Office Seekers."[43]

During a postwar newspaper interview, General Lee remarked, "The Negroes must be disposed of" and suggested they should emigrate to Liberia. If they refused, he opposed their becoming voters and preferred their being taught in schools by white Southerners. Lee's racial deportation idea was shared by congressmen who proposed to exile African Americans to Texas, which would be an exclusively black state. A few disillusioned Afro-Virginians decided to leave in December when a Lynchburg group departed for Liberia via Baltimore. Their spokesman, John McNuckles, "a shrewd, practical man, superior bricklayer and highly esteemed by the citizens of Lynchburg and vicinity," issued a farewell address: "We are all well in fine spirits. . . . We desire you to have this published in remembrance of those that are gone to their father-land. . . . All send their love and respects to their former owners and colored friends." A decade after the war, the American Colonization Society (ACS) reported that of 15,075 African Americans who went to Liberia, 3,739 (25 percent) were Afro-Virginians—the most of any state. The ACS claimed that "many of the intelligent and pious people of color . . . have voluntarily expressed a willingness and readiness to proceed to Liberia," an undertaking "to be measured not by years, but by generations." It was scarcely surprisingly that most Afro-Virginians preferred to stay, such as John Adams, antebellum Richmond's wealthiest free black and a subscriber to the ACS. Lucy Skipwith politely declined to follow her former master's advice: "I have looked over in my mind in regard to going to Liberia but I cannot."[44]

Insurrection anxieties always accompanied the holidays. Despite President Johnson's proclamation of thanksgiving for the end of "the fearful scourge of civil war," Virginians were apprehensive of each other and the future. Shakespeare's words again perhaps best summarize the Old Dominion's mood during that first post-slavery Christmas: "Now is the winter of our discontent . . . to fright the souls of fearful adversaries" (*Richard III,* act 1, scene 1). For a despondent Alexandria County woman, the yuletide was nothing to celebrate: "Christmas has come again, and we are as desolate and lonely and as badly off as at any time during the war." Anticipating that swords would be beaten into plowshares, the freedpeople, who had a deep and abiding bond and respect for the land they had worked so long for others, expected some for their own as Christmas gifts.[45]

Whites were unnerved by rumors and the freedpeople's belief that "the Yanks are going to divide the land at Xmas and give them each a portion of the farms they have been working." They were also alarmed by a rumored uprising of black Jamaicans; Richmond's *Commercial Bulletin* recounted hearsay of conspiracies to bloodily sweep whites from Hampton and Williamsburg and the counties of Gloucester, King and Queen, and Middlesex. So alarming was this erroneous intelligence that Freedmen's Bureau officers launched an investigation and placed military forces on alert. Indignant Afro-Virginians denied any insurrectionary intentions. "We are a peaceable and law-abiding people," declared representatives at a Norfolk mass meeting. "The stories so industriously circulated against us that we are contemplating and preparing for insurrection and riotous proceedings are vile falsehoods designed to provoke acts of unlawful violence against us." They contended that the real threats to public order and safety were unrepentant former slaveholders and ex-Confederates.[46]

A Christmas Day race riot did occur in Alexandria. Anne Frobel worriedly noted, "All think the negroes intend *some* thing" as the day began with a parade of armed blacks led by fife and drums. By late afternoon angry whites, including Confederate veterans, confronted this perceived racial challenge; gunfire was sporadically exchanged until nightfall. (Two months earlier a military judge had revoked a ruling by an Alexandria justice of the peace denying blacks the right to bear arms.) By the time Federal authorities restored order, two whites had been injured and fourteen blacks killed. Christmas scares likewise occurred during 1866–1867. A Princess Anne County resident warned the governor, "The negroes are becoming very insolent . . . if they rise in a body we may be easily murdered and they immediately fall heir to the lands, & indeed such a rumor is now and has been for sometime afloat." Fears of holiday uprisings continued for the remainder of the decade despite an 1866 law threatening punishment of up to ten years' imprisonment for anyone inciting either race to "make insurrection, by acts of violence and war" against the other.[47]

The year ended with both progress and signs of future troubles. Racial hereditary slavery was abolished upon ratification of the Thirteenth Amendment in December, with Virginia among the requisite twenty-seven ratifying states. The First U.S. Colored Cavalry, a Virginia regiment stationed in Texas since June disillusioned by poor treatment, denial of furloughs, concerns about their impoverished families, and being treated like "U.S. Slaves" instead of "U.S. Soldiers," petitioned the War Department for the right to go home and protect their "beloved wives." The regiment was mustered out in early 1866.[48]

The rewards of freedom and citizenship for African Americans' "patient heroism" were squandered by whites' national racial reconciliation. Afro-Virginians' prudent public commemorations of the Union's victory dissociated the South from slavery. In April 1866 a "Colored League" claiming to represent "the Colored People of Richmond" announced a parade for the first anniversary of the city's capture. Anticipating whites' concerns, organizers issued circulars with assurances that blacks were neither "devoid of sense" nor "going to celebrate the fall of the Confederacy, only *their* freedom."[49]

The year 1865 marked the ending of one revolutionary era and the beginning of another. The post-slavery South faced two specters: defeat and emancipation. These dual challenges were experienced differentially, for with defeat came the concomitant struggle to regain autonomy and comity; with emancipation came the struggle to restructure the economic system and reorder society. Caste and class were demarcated in the wake of the Civil War as precursors to Reconstruction's unfulfilled promises.

It is an aphorism that "losers are not inclined to be generous." Like Chesapeake Bay blue crabs in a barrel, each trying to climb out at the expense of the others, the races were beguiled by their own sense of history and victimhood in an unraveling world—blacks by racism and slavery, whites by losing the war and their slaves. Mindful of the symbolism of sitting in Jefferson Davis's chair during a tour of occupied Richmond, Dinwiddie County ex-slave Elizabeth Keckley expressed forgiveness and conciliation: "Dear old Virginia! A birthplace is always dear, no matter under what circumstances you were born."[50] A new generation was coming to the fore in the Old Dominion, and the stakes could not have been higher.

Notes

1. *Richmond Times,* April 25, 1865; Lucy Mae Turner, "The Family of Nat Turner, 1831 to 1954," *Negro History Bulletin* 18 (March 1955): 131.

2. Charles L. Perdue Jr., Thomas E. Barden, and Robert K. Phillips, *Weevils in the Wheat: Interviews with Virginia Ex-Slaves* (Charlottesville: University of Virginia Press, 1976), 128; "Slavery Chain" folder, "Virginia Negro Lore," box A6888, Records of the U.S. Works Project Administration, Library of Congress, Washington, D.C.; mass meeting, "Hall's Hill Va. [Falls Church] August 4th 1865," in Steven Hahn, Steven F. Miller, Susan E. O'Donovan, John C. Rodrigue, and Leslie S. Rowland, eds., *Land and Labor, 1865,* series 3, vol. 1 of *Freedom: A Documentary History of Emancipation, 1861–1867* (Chapel Hill: University of North Carolina Press, 2008), 699. See also *Liberator,* February 24, 1865, 30; and Ervin L. Jordan Jr., *Black Confederates and Afro-Yankees in Civil War Virginia* (Charlottesville: University of Virginia Press, 1995), 305.

3. "From Committee of Richmond Blacks," June 10, 1865, in Andrew Johnson, *The Papers of Andrew Johnson,* 16 vols., ed. Leroy Graf (Knoxville: University of Tennessee Press, 1986), 8:211–12; Annette Gordon-Reed, *The Hemingses of Monticello: An American Family* (New York: Norton, 2008), 719n52.

4. Martha W. Robertson Diary, January 22, 1865, p. 59, accession 36339, Library of Virginia, Richmond (hereafter cited as LVA) ("gloomy" quote); Clara Shafer Civil War Diary, January 10 and February 12, 1865, accession 12456, Special Collections Library, University of Virginia, Charlottesville (hereafter cited as UVA) (food hoarding); Daniel E. Sutherland, *Seasons of War: The Ordeal of a Confederate Community, 1861–1865* (New York: Free Press, 1995), 372, 375, 447n3, 447n9 (Nalle quote); John A. Campbell, "Memoranda of the Conversation at the Conference in Hampton Roads," p. 5 of 9, and "Memoranda of the Conversation at the Conference in Hampton Roads," p. 4 of 8 (both February 1865), in folder "1865 March 13 Memorandum of Lincoln-Stephens Conference at Hampton Roads," box 33, Papers of the Hunter and Garnett Families, accession 38–45, UVA; Keith W. Jennison, *The Humorous Mr. Lincoln* (New York: Bonanza Books, 1965), 133–34; Lerone Bennett Jr., *Forced into Glory: Abraham Lincoln's White Dream* (Chicago: Johnson, 2000), 611–15; Carl Sandburg, *Abraham Lincoln: The Prairie Years and the War Years* (New York: Harcourt, Brace, 1954), 652–53 (Seward quote). For examples of Lincoln and white Northerners as racist would-be emancipators, see Bennett, *Forced into Glory,* 14, 48, 138, 344, 364, 375, 472.

5. *Charlottesville Daily Chronicle,* January 1, 1865, advertisements: "Blacksmiths, Mechanics and Laborers Wanted," "One Hundred Able Bodied Negro Men," "Two Valuable Families of Negroes at Auction" and "For Hire" (slave woman with small children); bill of sale for the slave Jefree, February 10, 1865, accession 13747, UVA; Michael G. Harman (Staunton, Virginia) to Davis, January 12, 1865, in Jefferson Davis, *The Papers of Jefferson Davis,* vol. 11, *September 1864–May 1865,* ed. Lynda Lasswell Crist, Barbara J. Rozek, and Kenneth H. Wil-

liams (Baton Rouge: Louisiana State University Press, 2003), 314–15. Harman was a colonel of the Fifty-second Virginia Infantry, Staunton's quartermaster, and a member of the Virginia Military Institute's board of visitors. Robert J. Driver Jr., *52nd Virginia Infantry* (Lynchburg, Va.: H. E. Howard, 1986), 118.

    6. "Quite a Sensation," *Richmond Daily Whig*, March 25, 1865; "The First Negro Recruits," *Richmond Daily Examiner*, March 18, 1865; "The First Negro Command," *Richmond Daily Examiner*, March 18, 1865; "The Company of Negroes," *Richmond Daily Examiner*, March 27, 1865; Henri Garidel, *Exile in Richmond: The Confederate Journal of Henri Garidel*, ed. Michael Bedout Chesson and Leslie Jean Roberts (Charlottesville: University of Virginia Press, 2001), 357; "The Corps d'Afrique," *Richmond Whig*, March 21, 1865; "20 Negroes at Auction," *Richmond Whig*, March 21, 1865; Theodore P. Savas, *Brady's Civil War Journal: Photographing the War, 1861–65* (New York: Skyhorse, 2008), 128; Jordan, *Black Confederates*, 230–31 (skillet head quote); Thomas S. Gholson, *Speech of Hon. Thos. S. Gholson, of Virginia, on the Policy of Employing Negro Troops, and the Duty of All Classes to Aid in the Prosecution of the War, Delivered in the House of Representatives of the Congress of the Confederate States, on the 1st of February, 1865* (Richmond: George P. Evans, 1865), 4, 8, 13–14. Gholson's congressional district included the counties of Prince George, Nottoway, Amelia, Powhatan, and Cumberland.

    7. "Men of the Month," *Crisis*, August 1921, 166 (obituary notice of Marietta Lilian Chiles); Burke Davis, *To Appomattox: Nine April Days, 1865* (New York: Rinehart, 1959), 95–99; Samuel J. T. Moore Jr., *Moore's Complete Civil War Guide to Richmond*, rev. ed. (Richmond: Privately published, 1978), 39–40, 143; Ann Field Alexander, *Race Man: The Rise and Fall of the "Fighting Editor," John Mitchell Jr.* (Charlottesville: University of Virginia Press, 2002), 18, 26, 32, 201, 216n10; Theresa Guzman-Stokes, "A Flag and a Family: Richard Gill Forrester, 1847–1906," *Virginia Cavalcade* 47 (Spring 1998): 56; Luther Porter Jackson, *Negro Office-holders in Virginia, 1865–1895* (Norfolk, Va.: Guide Quality Press, 1945), 57, 85 (Forrester); "Old Glory Is out of Hiding: Ex-Page—a Unionist—Hoists Flag over Capitol for First Time in 4 Years," *Richmond Times-Dispatch*, October 15, 2000. Chiles may have been the "pompous" sexton mentioned in Nelson Lankford, *Richmond Burning: The Last Days of the Confederate Capital* (New York: Viking, 2002), 62–63. In his massive and tedious reminiscences, Davis mentioned the incident in three brief sentences without details. Jefferson Davis, *The Rise and Fall of the Confederate Government*, 2 vols. (New York: Appleton, 1881), 2:667.

    8. Benjamin Quarles, *The Negro in the Civil War* (Boston: Little, Brown, 1969), 331; Leon F. Litwack, *Been in the Storm So Long: The Aftermath of Slavery* (New York: Knopf, 1979), 167; Thomas Morris Chester, *Thomas Morris Ches-*

ter, *Black Civil War Correspondent: His Dispatches from the Virginia Front,* ed. R. J. M. Blackett (Baton Rouge: Louisiana State University Press, 1989), 41, 196n31, 296, 299, 303; Jordan, *Black Confederates,* 292; David S. Heidler and Jeanne T. Heidler, *Encyclopedia of the American Civil War: A Political, Social, and Military History* (New York: Norton, 2000), 95, 111; Garidel, *Exile in Richmond,* 367–68 (April 3, 1865, entry); "Richmond," *Harper's Weekly,* April 15, 1865, 226; John A. Andrew to Edwin M. Stanton, April 3, 1865, in U.S. War Department, *War of the Rebellion: A Compilation of the Official Records of the Union and Confederate Armies* (Washington, D.C.: Government Printing Office, 1880–1901), series 1, vol. 46, pt. 3, 543 (hereafter cited as *OR*); John W. Blassingame, ed., *Slave Testimony: Two Centuries of Letters, Speeches, Interviews, and Autobiographies* (Baton Rouge: Louisiana State University Press, 1977), 543–47, 546n40 (Ballton).

9. Joseph T. Glatthaar, *Forged in Battle: The Civil War Alliance of Black Soldiers and White Officers* (New York: Free Press, 1990), 209; Lankford, *Richmond Burning,* 45, 126–27, 240; Keith P. Wilson, *Campfires of Freedom: The Camp Life of Black Soldiers during the Civil War* (Kent, Ohio: Kent State University Press, 2002), 111, 113–17, 209; Ira Berlin, Barbara J. Fields, Steven F. Miller, Joseph P. Reidy, and Leslie S. Rowland, eds., *Free at Last: A Documentary History of Slavery, Freedom, and the Civil War* (New York: New Press, 1992), 469–70. Garland White was commissioned as chaplain of the Twenty-eighth U.S. Colored Infantry in 1864. U.S. Adjutant-General's Office, *Official Army Register of the Volunteer Force of the United States Army for the Years 1861, '62, '63, '64, '65,* part 8, *Territories of Washington, New Mexico, Nebraska, Colorado, Dakota; Veteran Reserve Corps, U.S. Veteran Volunteers, U.S. Volunteers, U.S. Colored Troops* (Washington, D.C.: Adjutant-General's Office, 1867; repr., Gaithersburg, Md.: Ron R. Van Sickle Military Books, 1987), 199 (hereafter cited as *Official Army Register*).

10. "Testimony of Major-General Godfrey Weitzel, Commanding 25th Army Corps, before the Congressional Committee on the Conduct of the War, May 18, 1865," in *The Negro in the Military Services of the United States, 1639–1886,* microcopy T-823, roll 4, frames 0143–0145, National Archives Microfilm Publication, Washington, D.C.; Henry Chapin to his father, April 26, 1865 (tearful girl), accession 10310-G, UVA; Lankford, *Richmond Burning,* 236 (Fletcher quote); Shafer Diary, April 4, 5, 7, and 8, 1865.

11. Chester, *Thomas Morris Chester,* 196n31, 299, 303–4; Lankford, *Richmond Burning,* 190–91; *Official Army Register,* 207. Nearly three hundred Virginia State Penitentiary inmates also escaped, "fired the place and rampaged through the city." Chester, *Thomas Morris Chester,* 293, 299; William C. Davis and Bell I. Wiley, eds., *The End of an Era,* vol. 6 of *The Image of War: 1861–1865* (Garden City, N.Y.: Doubleday, 1984), 287.

12. Jordan, *Black Confederates*, 267; Glatthaar, *Forged in Battle*, 168; *Official Army Register*.

13. William C. Davis, *Look Away! A History of the Confederate States of America* (New York: Free Press, 2002); Lankford, *Richmond Burning*, 213 (Goochland), 239 (eviction attempts); Perdue, Barden, and Phillips, *Weevils in the Wheat*, 327–28 (Brunswick County); Mary Randolph, Eastern View, Fauquier County, Virginia, to her daughter, "Dearest Sally," September 9, 1865, Otey Family Papers, Mss1Ot28a, section 3, "Miscellany," folder 4 of 4, Virginia Historical Society, Richmond (hereafter cited as VHS); Jordan, *Black Confederates*, 149–50 (Howard).

14. Chester, *Thomas Morris Chester*, 294–97; Lankford, *Richmond Burning*, 165–67 (Lincoln quotes); Donald C. Pfanz, *The Petersburg Campaign: Abraham Lincoln at City Point, March 20–April 9, 1865* (Lynchburg, Va.: H. E. Howard, 1989), 56, 61–63, 66, 82; "The Truest Mourners," *Harper's Weekly*, May 6, 1865, 274; Ira Berlin, Joseph P. Reidy, and Leslie S. Rowland, eds., *The Black Military Experience*, series 2, vol. 1 of *Freedom: A Documentary History of Emancipation, 1861–1867* (New York: Cambridge University Press, 1982), 652 (Leonard quote); Leonard as a black military chaplain in Glatthaar, *Forged in Battle*, 280, and Jordan, *Black Confederates*, 295–96.

15. Jordan, *Black Confederates*, 301–2, 386n26, 386n27; *OR*, series 1, vol. 46, pt. 3, 1282, 1283, 1293 (Terry orders); Ted Delaney and Phillip Wayne Rhodes, *Free Blacks of Lynchburg, Virginia, 1805–1865* (Lynchburg, Va.: Warwick House, 2001), 85, 183.

16. "What Will He Do with It?" *Charlottesville Semi-weekly Chronicle*, July 19, 1865, 2; June Purcell Guild, *Black Laws of Virginia: A Summary of the Legislative Acts of Virginia concerning Negroes from Earliest Times to the Present* (1936; repr., New York: Negro University Press, 1969), 32–33; Leslie Anderson Morales, ed., *Virginia Slave Births Index, 1853–1865* (Westminster, Md.: Heritage Books, 2007), 1:67, 133, 191; 2:178; 3:277, 326, 519; 4:3, 109, 153, 172; 5:82, 646–47, 695, 703. A May 1865 military order mandated county censuses "of the colored people, each sex" and by age; a month later an estimated 35,000 blacks lived in Richmond. "Circular, Headquarters, Department of Virginia, Army of the James, Richmond, Virginia, May 27, 1865," in *OR*, series 1, vol. 46, pt. 3, 1224–25; Henry Halleck to Alfred H. Terry, June 22, 1865, in *OR*, series 1, vol. 46, pt. 3, 1291.

17. Folder "1869 October 25 List of Slaves of [Robert Thurston Hubard Sr.] and Their Value at Time of Emancipation," box 21, Hubard Family Papers, accession 8039, UVA; John Preston McConnell, *Negroes and Their Treatment in Virginia from 1865 to 1867* (Pulaski, Va.: B. D. Smith and Brothers, 1910), 13 (Petersburg slaveholder); Guy C. Sibley to W. E. Bibb, February 7, 22, April 14, 1896, and William M. Fitch to Bibb, April 1, 1896, folder "1894–1896, Bibb,

W. E.: Political Correspondence," and attached copy of Senate Bill No. 528, "To Incorporate the National Adjustment Society," with letter of Elmer Dovers to Bibb, Louisa, Virginia, February 20, 1903, folder "1898–1904, Bibb, W. E.: Political Correspondence," Papers of W. E. Bibb and Other Louisa County, Virginia, Families, accession 4171, box 14, UVA; Helen Tunnicliff Catterall, *Judicial Cases concerning American Slavery and the Negro,* vol. 1, *Cases from the Courts of England, Virginia, West Virginia, and Kentucky* (Washington, D.C.: Carnegie Institution, 1926), 74.

18. Blassingame, *Slave Testimony,* 559–62 (Coleman); Robertson Diary, April 7, 1865, p. 61 ("ingratitude" quote); [Alice W. Saunders to Louisa M. Davis], December 13, 1865, and Richard T. Davis to "My dear wife" [Laura M. Davis], August 7, 1865, box 5, folder 9, Davis-Preston-Saunders Papers, accession 4951, UVA; John W. Peyton Diary, July 18, August 2, 1865, accession 4944, microfilm 687, UVA.

19. Charles W. White, *The Hidden and the Forgotten: Contributions of Buckingham Blacks to American History* (Marceline, Mo.: Walsworth, 1985), 105, 106; Journals of Robert G. H. Kean, June 1, 1865, vol. 2, 1864–1865, accession 3070, UVA (Gordonsville incident); Edmund Ruffin, *The Diary of Edmund Ruffin,* vol. 3, *A Dream Shattered: June, 1863–June, 1865,* ed. William Kauffman Scarborough (Baton Rouge: Louisiana State University Press, 1989), 871–72 (local patrols entry, May 1, 1865), 880–81 (Amelia freedmen entry, May 6, 1865).

20. "Riot at Smithfield," *Richmond Whig,* July 8, 1865; Garidel, *Exile in Richmond,* 373 (April 6, 1865); Civil War Diary of John Mottram, Thirteenth New Hampshire Volunteers, April 12, 13, 18, 19, 1865, accession 10988, UVA; *Lynchburg Daily Republican,* May 27, 1865; "Statement of Albert Brooks/Statements relating to Abuses of Freedmen in Richmond, June 1865," Records of the Assistant Commissioner for Virginia, Freedmen's Bureau, roll 59, National Archives, Washington, D.C.; "From Committee of Richmond Blacks," June 10, 1865, 8:211–12.

21. White, *Hidden and Forgotten,* 106, 131n13; Stuart Barnes to James P. Wagon, July 31, 1865, in United States Bureau of Refugees, Freedmen, and Abandoned Lands, Records from Buckingham County, Virginia, 1865–1870, accession 10154-A, microfilm 784, UVA; Alrutheus Ambush Taylor, *The Negro in the Reconstruction of Virginia* (Washington, D.C.: Association for the Study of Negro Life and History, 1926), 31; James E. Sefton, *The United States Army and Reconstruction, 1865–1877* (Baton Rouge: Louisiana State University Press, 1967), 9.

22. General Order No. 18, Headquarters, District of the Nottoway, Petersburg, Virginia, July 31, 1865, United States Bureau of Refugees, Freedmen, and Abandoned Lands, Records from Buckingham County, Virginia, 1865–1870,

accession 10154-A, microfilm 784, UVA; Berlin, Reidy, and Rowland, *Freedom*, 721–23.

23. James C. Robertson to Elizabeth M. Lash, April 3, 1866, James Chatham Robertson Letters, accession 32037, LVA; *Lynchburg Daily Republican*, May 25, 1865 (mistreatment of blacks); Garidel, *Exile in Richmond*, 388 (April 27, 1865) and 403 (June 18, 1865); Jackson Martz to Dorilas Martz, August 3, 1866, Miscellaneous Virginia Letters, accession 11176, UVA (sarcastic toast).

24. *Leesburg Washingtonian*, October 6, 1865; "Mother" to "Dear Charlie," May 25, 1865, folder "1865 Letters to Charles Elisha Taylor from Family," Charles Elisha Taylor Papers, accession 3091-A, box 1, UVA ("If the servants" quote); Robertson Diary, May 5, 1865, pp. 61–62 ("poor stupid" quote).

25. Herbert G. Gutman, *The Black Family in Slavery and Freedom, 1750–1925* (New York: Pantheon Books, 1976), 39 (black occupations); in *OR*, series 1, vol. 46, pt. 3, 1086 ("keep negroes on their plantations" quote); Headquarters, Military Sub-district of Lynchburg, General Orders No. 2, May 18, 1865, and General Orders No. 13, May 27, 1865, both in *Lynchburg Daily Republican*, May 25 and 28, 1865. The Lynchburg district issued numerous general orders during May–June 1865; see Hahn et al., *Land and Labor*, 245–51.

26. "Negro Wages," *Richmond Whig*, June 27, 1865; McConnell, *Negroes and Their Treatment*, 33–36.

27. George Long to Henry Tutwiler, August 27, 1868, George Long Letters, accession 1230, UVA ("greater numbers" quote); Lucy M. Cohen, *Chinese in the Post–Civil War South* (Baton Rouge: Louisiana State University Press, 1984), 40–41, 177–79; McConnell, *Negroes and Their Treatment*, 16–17, 32–33; George Long (1800–1879) was among the first University of Virginia faculty, as professor of ancient languages, 1825–1828, before accepting a professorship in Greek at the University of London. Harry Clemons, *Notes on the Professors for Whom the University of Virginia Halls and Residence Houses Are Named* (Charlottesville: University of Virginia Press, 1961), 83–87.

28. [Saunders to Davis], December 13, 1865; Robertson Diary, May 5, 1865, pp. 61–62 (Chesterfield quote); Sarah P. Payne Letterbook, January 2, 1871, pp. 96, 97, Mss2P2936a1, VHS.

29. Taylor, *Negro in the Reconstruction*, 90–91; work agreements between George C. Hannah and freedmen, December 30, 1865, and January 1, 1867, accession 2602, UVA; folders "1865 Sept. 4, List of Negroes & Their Wages at Low Bremo and Their Agreement to Work" and "1865 Sept. 21, JHC's Warrant of Amnesty," box 173, and folder "1865 May 13, Grant of Protection from General E. O. C. Ord, Army of the James, to J. H. Cocke," box 172, John Hartwell Cocke Papers, accession 640, UVA; "John Hartwell Cocke," in Sara B. Bearss et al., eds., *Dictionary of Virginia Biography*, vol. 3, *Caperton-Daniels* (Richmond:

Library of Virginia, 2006), 330–32; John Michael Vlach, *Back of the Big House: The Architecture of Plantation Slavery* (Chapel Hill: University of North Carolina Press, 1993), 159, 177. One of Cocke's mud-walled slave cabins constructed during the 1820s has survived. Calder Loth, ed., *Virginia Landmarks of Black History* (Charlottesville: University of Virginia Press, 1995), 39–43.

30. Charles S. Scheaffer to George W. Hutchinson, August 13, 1866, Hutchinson Family Papers, Mss1H9754a, section 1, VHS; Jordan, *Black Confederates,* 27–29, 46; Blassingame, *Slave Testimony,* 736–38; "Negro Laborers in Demand in Michigan," *Richmond Central Presbyterian,* October 19, 1865, 3; Hahn et al., *Land and Labor,* 61, 410, 459–64, 611–12 (Florida). Lorenzo Ivy's recollections have proven of interest to historians; see Work Projects Administration, *The Negro in Virginia* (Winston-Salem, N.C.: John F. Blair, 1994), 61, 186; Perdue, Barden, and Phillips, *Weevils in the Wheat,* 151–54.

31. Gutman, *Black Family,* 149 (Norfolk freedwoman), 387 (Second African Baptist); Work Projects Administration, *Negro in Virginia,* 95.

32. Gutman, *Black Family,* 10–11; "General Orders No. 8, Headquarters, Military Division of the James, Richmond, May 27, 1865," in *OR,* series 1, vol. 46, pt. 3, 1221; Guild, *Black Laws,* 33; Abigail Mott, *Narratives of Colored Americans* (New York: William Wood, 1877), 269 (Freedmen's Village couple); "Register of Colored Persons of Augusta County, State of Virginia, Cohabiting Together as Husband and Wife on 27th February 1866," accession 36065, LVA; Jordan, *Black Confederates,* 313; J. Tivis Wicker, "Virginia's Legitimization Act of 1866," *Virginia Magazine of History and Biography* 86 (July 1978): 340–41.

33. "Personal" column, *Daily Richmond Whig,* May 23, 1865, 3; "From Committee of Richmond Blacks," June 10, 1865, 8:212; Dorothy Sterling, ed., *We Are Your Sisters: Black Women in the Nineteenth Century* (New York: Norton, 1984), 313; J. W. Elliot to Mrs. Young, November 2, 1865, in Ruth A. Rose, *Norfolk Virginia,* Black America Series (Charleston, S.C.: Arcadia, 2000), 18; William Douglass to Dr. James Minor, August 15, 1865, and January 29, 1866, James Hunter Terrell, letters from former slaves of Terrell settled in Liberia, accession 10460, 10460-A, UVA.

34. "Infanticide," *Richmond Central Presbyterian,* October 19, 1865, 3; Payne Letterbook, September 30, 1865, pp. 3, 7; authorization [Captain Thomas Birmingham] for the return of two slave children to a former master [Christopher Damron], September 15, 1865, accession 11821, UVA; McConnell, *Negroes and Their Treatment,* 97–102; "Virginia Employer to Another White Virginian and Statement by a Virginia Freedwoman," October 15, 1865, in Hahn et al., *Land and Labor,* 562–64. White women, too, committed infanticide, especially when pregnant by black men; see Tommy L. Bogger, *Free Blacks in Norfolk, Virginia,*

1790–1860: The Darker Side of Freedom (Charlottesville: University of Virginia Press, 1997), 136–37.

35. "Death Record" cards for Mary Wheeler, August 11, 1865 (no. 45), Josephine Wheeler, August 16, 1865 (no. 46), and unnamed Wheeler boy, May 15, 1870 (no. 56), Fredericksburg Death Records, 1853–1896, Mss3F8726c, VHS; Jordan, *Black Confederates,* 33; Hahn et al., *Land and Labor,* 668–69; "From Committee of Richmond Blacks," June 10, 1865, 8:210.

36. Jordan, *Black Confederates,* 84, 86, 102–5; "From Committee of Richmond Blacks," June 10, 1865, 8:210–11.

37. Samuel L. Horst, *Education for Manhood: The Education of Blacks in Virginia during the Civil War* (Lanham, Md.: University Press of America, 1987), 254; Diary of Benson J. Lossing, April 19, 1865, p. 8, accession 7857-C, UVA; "Negro Schools in Virginia," *Richmond Whig,* May 31, 1865; Ervin L. Jordan Jr., *Charlottesville and the University of Virginia in the Civil War* (Lynchburg, Va.: H. E. Howard, 1988), 95; Lauranett Lorraine Lee, "Crucible in the Classroom: The Freedpeople and Their Teachers, Charlottesville, Virginia, 1861–1876" (Ph.D. diss., University of Virginia, 2002), 32–33, 40–41; Brady's First African Baptist Church photograph in Davis and Wiley, *End of an Era,* 290; and Bell Irvin Wiley, *Embattled Confederates: An Illustrated History of Southerners at War* (New York: Bonanza Books, 1964), 244.

38. Lester J. Cappon, *Virginia Newspapers, 1821–1935* (New York: Appleton-Century, 1936), 100, 141, 148, 176, 179; Robert F. Engs, *Freedom's First Generation: Black Hampton, Virginia, 1861–1890* (Philadelphia: University of Pennsylvania Press, 1979; repr., New York: Fordham University Press, 2004), 74–75, 167n24–167n27, 168n28; Henry Latham, *Black and White: A Journal of a Three Months' Tour in the United States* (London: Macmillan, 1867), 102; Thomas C. Parramore, Peter C. Stuart, and Tommy L. Bogger, *Norfolk: The First Four Centuries* (Charlottesville: University of Virginia Press, 1994), 227, 236–37, 255.

39. Garidel, *Exile in Richmond,* 368 (two Union soldiers), 401 ("wolves" quote); Shafer Diary, April 8, 1865 ("the negro tries" quote); Lankford, *Richmond Burning,* 238; Work Projects Administration, *Negro in Virginia,* 233–34; Chester, *Thomas Morris Chester,* 196n31, 299, 303; Perdue, Barden, and Phillips, *Weevils in the Wheat,* 277; Jane Dailey, *Before Jim Crow: The Politics of Race in Postemancipation Virginia* (Chapel Hill: University of North Carolina Press, 2000), 104–8, 117–18; Oliver O. Howard to Johnson, September 21, 1865, in *Papers of Andrew Johnson,* 9:108.

40. Entries in 1862–1878 ledger: "Nick Brown Former Slave [of] D. W. Maupin," February 18, 1867, p. 155, "Wesley Michie" [former slave of Winston Wood]," January 2, 1868, p. 182, "Peggy Former Slave of T. M. Douglass," April 3, 1869, p. 216, all in Thomas M. Dunn Medical Records, accession 14266, UVA;

"Register of Colored Persons of Augusta County, State of Virginia, Cohabiting Together as Husband and Wife on 27th February 1866"; Richard B. Dickenson, *Entitled! Free Papers in Appalachia concerning Antebellum Freeborn Negroes and Emancipated Blacks of Montgomery County, Virginia* (Washington, D.C.: National Genealogical Society, 1981), 48–54; Blassingame, *Slave Testimony,* 488; Jordan, *Black Confederates,* 136–39, 204.

41. *Equal Suffrage: Address from the Colored Citizens of Norfolk, Va., to the People of the United States, Also an Account of the Agitation among the Colored People of Virginia for Equal Rights, with An Appendix concerning the Rights of Colored Witnesses before the State Courts* (Bedford, Mass.: E. Anthony and Sons, 1865), 10–11 ("traitors" quote); Parramore, Stuart, and Bogger, *Norfolk,* 224–26; Dailey, *Before Jim Crow,* 16. For a recent study of Civil War traitors, see Edward S. Cooper, *Traitors: The Secession Period, November 1860–July 1861* (Madison, N.J.: Fairleigh Dickinson University Press, 2008), 13–16, 241–46.

42. "Petition from the Colored People of Alexandria," April 29, 1865, in *Papers of Andrew Johnson,* 7:656–58, 658n4; Taylor, *Negro in the Reconstruction,* 14, 84; McConnell, *Negroes and Their Treatment,* 88–89, 112; W. E. B. Du Bois, *Black Reconstruction in America: An Essay toward a History of the Part Which Black Folk Played in the Attempt to Reconstruct Democracy in America, 1860–1880* (New York: Atheneum, 1969), 538; John D. Macoll and George J. Stansfield, eds., *Alexandria: A Town in Transition, 1800–1900* (Alexandria, Va.: Alexandria Bicentennial Commission and Alexandria Historical Society, 1977), 11. The Virginia General Assembly repealed slave codes in February 1866. McConnell, *Negroes and Their Treatment,* 58–62.

43. James C. Robertson to Mrs. Elizabeth M. Lash, May 12, 1867, Robertson Letters; Diary of Cornelius H. Carlton, entry for *ante* July 11, 1867, accession 26882, LVA; unidentified Halifax County resident to "Dear nephew," June 1, 1871, folder "1788–1871 Miscellaneous Correspondence," Papers of the Baker Family, accession 10676, UVA. Carlton enlisted in 1863 as a sergeant in Company F, Twenty-fourth Virginia Cavalry. R. Darryl Holland, *24th Virginia Cavalry Regiment* (Lynchburg, Va.: H. E. Howard, 1997), 163.

44. Elizabeth Brown Pryor, *Reading the Man: A Portrait of Robert E. Lee through His Private Letters* (New York: Viking, 2007), 431, 452–53; Jordan, *Black Confederates,* 305–6, 387n36; Luther Porter Jackson, *Free Negro Labor and Property Holding in Virginia, 1830–1860* (New York: Appleton-Century, 1942), 28–32; Ira Berlin, *Slaves without Masters: The Free Negro in the Antebellum South* (New York: New Press, 1974), 357, 360–64; Bogger, *Free Blacks in Norfolk,* 50–51; "Departure for Liberia," *Richmond Central Presbyterian,* December 14, 1865, 4 (McNuckles); "Africa's Redemption" and "States Which Have Furnished Emigrants," *African Repository* 51 (April 1875): 44–45, 55; "Receipts of the

American Colonization Society, from the 20th of July to the 20th of August, 1857," *African Repository and Colonial Journal,* September 1857, 288 (Adams); folder "1865 Dec. 7, Lucy Skipwith to J. H. Cocke," Cocke Papers, box 173, and reprinted in Sterling, *We Are Your Sisters,* 310.

45. Johnson's October 28, 1865, proclamation declaring December 7 a day of national thanksgiving, in *OR,* series 3, vol. 5, 161; Anne S. Frobel, *The Civil War Diary of Anne S. Frobel,* ed. Mary H. Lancaster and Dallas M. Lancaster (McLean, Va.: EPM, 1992), December 25, 1865, pp. 247–48.

46. Lucy Wallace Courtney to Benie Wallace, October 18, 1865, folder "1865–1900 Wallace and Rogers Family Letters," Wallace Family Papers, accession 2689 (and microfilm 249), UVA ("the Yanks" quote); Dan Carter, "The Anatomy of Fear: The Christmas Day Insurrection Scare of 1865," *Journal of Southern History* 42 (February 1976): 345–64; Chad L. Williams, "Symbols of Freedom and Defeat: African American Soldiers, White Southerners, and the Christmas Insurrection Scare of 1865," in Gregory J. W. Urwin, ed., *Black Flag over Dixie: Racial Atrocities and Reprisals in the Civil War* (Carbondale: Southern Illinois University Press, 2004), 210–30; Armstead L. Robinson, "In the Shadow of Old John Brown: Insurrection Anxiety and Confederate Mobilization, 1861–1863," *Journal of Negro History* 65 (Fall 1980): 279–97; Thomas C. Holt, *The Problem of Freedom: Race, Labor, and Politics in Jamaica and Britain, 1832–1938* (Baltimore, Md.: Johns Hopkins University Press, 1992), chapters 7, 8; Hahn et al., *Land and Labor,* 456–57, 807 (Norfolk quote), 844–47 (*Commercial Bulletin*).

47. Frobel, *Civil War Diary,* entry for December 25, 1865, pp. 247–48; Taylor, *Negro in the Reconstruction,* 83; McConnell, *Negroes and Their Treatment,* 79; Du Bois, *Black Reconstruction,* 538; *Third Edition of the Code of Virginia, Including Legislation to January 1, 1874, Prepared by George W. Munford* (Richmond: James E. Goode, 1873), 1188; Charles B. Foster to the Governor, December 11, 1866, in H. W. Flournoy, *Calendar of Virginia State Papers and Other Manuscripts, from January 1, 1836, to April 15, 1869; Preserved in the Capitol at Richmond* (Richmond: n.p., 1893), 11:471; for 1867 insurrection rumors, see *Papers of Andrew Johnson,* 13:148 (Portsmouth), 201 (Petersburg), 242 (Appomattox County), and 257 (Westmoreland County).

48. Charles H. Wesley and Patricia W. Romero, *Negro Americans in the Civil War: From Slavery to Citizenship* (New York: Publishers Company, 1967), 122; unsigned petition to Dear Sir, December 1865, in Berlin et al., *Free at Last,* 533–35, 548n66; *Official Army Register,* 8:141.

49. "Richmond," *Harper's Weekly,* April 15, 1865, 226 ("patient heroism" quote); "Mary" Richmond, to "My Dear Charlie," April 5, 1866, folder "1866 Jan.–June Letters to Charles Elisha Taylor from Family," Taylor Papers, box 1

("devoid of sense" quote); Michael Kammen, *Mystic Chords of Memory: The Transformation of Tradition in American Culture* (New York: Knopf, 1991), 121–22; Lankford, *Richmond Burning*, 247–48.

50. Suzanne Lebsock, *The Free Women of Petersburg: Status and Culture in a Southern Town, 1784–1860* (New York: Norton, 1984), 248 ("losers" quote); Elizabeth Keckley, *Behind the Scenes; or, Thirty Years a Slave, and Four Years in the White House* (New York: G. W. Carleton, 1868), 165–66.

"So unsettled by the war"

The Aftermath in Virginia, 1865

John M. McClure

When the guns fell silent at Appomattox, only the military battles ended. The fight over the meaning of the Civil War had just begun. African Americans throughout the South celebrated the end of slavery, while most Southern whites bemoaned a bitter defeat. As formerly enslaved blacks, along with white Unionists, endeavored to reform the South, former Confederates not only strove to retain the remnants of antebellum political and social structures but also vehemently rejected the notion that blacks were worthy of the full rights of citizenship. The war ended slavery but produced no consensus on the status of blacks in American society—much less their place in the Southern socioeconomic and political strata. Resolution had yet to fill this deeper chasm of the conflict. The subsequent political controversy, coupled with violence in the South, would soon cause Northerners to debate what the "fruits of victory" should entail.

In Virginia, these debates consumed public and private discourse amid the aftermath of a bitter clash; the war caused destruction that Virginians could have hardly imagined in 1861. Indeed, the Old Dominion was devastated. Virginia had witnessed much of the bloodshed firsthand over the previous four years; many of its localities became synonymous with battlefield carnage. Twenty-six major engagements took place in Virginia, whose farms and factories supplied much of the fodder for the Confederate army.[1] More than 40,000 Virginians died as a result of the war, inflicting an emotional toll on the survivors that is difficult to fathom.[2] The economy essentially collapsed, due to the destruction of railroads, bridges, and farms as well as antebellum debt, abolition, and investments in Confederate currency. African Americans, though free, faced an uncertain future with the advent of a new labor system accompanied by a legal purgatory. As Oliver O.

Howard, the commissioner of the Freedmen's Bureau, put it, "No other State, perhaps, was so unsettled by the war as the State of Virginia . . . it became in part a tract of deserted and broken up farms, and in part an asylum for the thousands of refugees that flocked within [its] lines."[3] Because of its history and its geography, Virginia formed a crucial piece of the puzzle as the tide of secession rose and war ensued. Similarly, its return to the Union generated heated debate and drew close attention. The first months of Reconstruction converted Federal representatives from invaders into occupiers who sought to establish stability before returning the reins of control to local civil leaders.

Virginians' reaction to the end of the war varied with their circumstances. White supporters of secession evinced shock at the fall of the Confederacy, bitterness toward "Federal occupation," and apprehension for the future. Eliza Chew Smith, in Spotsylvania County, confessed to her diary on April 12 that "we no doubt are in Yankee lines . . . hear a thousand rumours, feel sad, sad. Our noble and good Gen'l in Chief surrendered to the enemy the 9th instant—It is hard to believe but I know it to be a *fact* oh, my heart will surely break!"[4] In September Sarah Payne wrote from Campbell County to her Northern cousin Mary Clendenin to describe Virginians' condition after "enduring innumerable privations": "The whole social system [is] suddenly overturned, many persons by that means deprived of every cent of property, . . . every family mourning the loss of one or more friends or seeing them maimed or crippled for life."[5] Others grew weary of the death knells and grimly resigned themselves to difficult times. John Holmes Bocock wrote to Nancy Miller Blanton that he wished to avoid a letter "rehearsing over again the 'heart-death' of the writer," explaining: "We have all suffered. I see no reason to think that our sufferings are yet ended. The abyss of events upon which we are embarked is so immense, and so dark and turbulent."[6]

African Americans, conversely, reveled in the Union victory. In an interview years later Georgianna Preston recalled the night the news reached her. "Us young folks carried on somp'n awful. Ole Marse let us stay up all night, an' didn't seem to mind it at all. Saw de sun sot an' befo' we know it was a-risin' again. Old folks was shoutin' an' singin' songs."[7] Many formerly enslaved blacks immediately took advantage of emancipation to strike out on their own. In Mecklenburg County, Alexander Spotswood Boyd noted that "the negroes are behaving themselves very well. A good many have left their masters & a good many sent off by them."[8] Indeed, the numbers of blacks in urban areas rose dramatically upon the war's close as freedpeople sought work and the chance to reconnect with displaced family members. An estimated 20,000 blacks were in Richmond, with more arriving daily.[9] Alexandria's black population hovered near 6,000 in 1866—nearly tripling from 1860.[10] The Union's occupation of the Norfolk area attracted many thousands throughout much of the war, and the trend only intensified with the end of combat. Robert Francis Engs, a student of the Hampton black community, has noted that "by 1865, 40,000 freedmen were concentrated on the Peninsula; 7,000 were in the village of Hampton alone."[11] The *Staunton Vindicator* observed in an editorial that blacks "do not seem to believe themselves free until they have left their old masters to live with new employers."[12]

As the Old Dominion seemed to turn upside down, the state entered the so-called interregnum period of military rule prior to the reinstitution of civil government. In the days after Lee's surrender, Richmond teemed with freed slaves, paroled Confederate veterans, and refugees who had sought a haven from battle zones. Recently arrived Federal officials faced massive challenges of maintaining order and establishing civil authority across the state within the vacuum that had resulted from the absence of a functioning government. Even as the ashes of Richmond's burned financial district smoldered, the army began raining down orders designed to both stabilize the situation and prepare for military occupation throughout the state.

By the end of May, officials divided the Commonwealth into eleven military districts. The twelfth, the District of Southwestern Virginia, developed in mid-July.[13] In quick succession, Maj. Gen. Edward O. C. Ord and Maj. Gen. Henry W. Halleck commanded what the army referred to as the Department of Virginia. Maj. Gen. Alfred Howe Terry assumed command of the department in June and remained in charge until August 1866. The department extended throughout the Old Dominion, except for Loudoun County, Fairfax County, and Alexandria, which fell into the Washington Department, and six counties in the northwestern corner of the state that were grouped with the Middle Department.[14]

At the close of the war, military leaders set their sights on two basic goals. Assured by field commanders that armed resistance had effectively ended, Ord, Halleck, and Terry deployed troops to maintain order and assist the needy, while headquarters staff demobilized regiments no longer needed in Virginia. Volunteer units tended to be among the first Union troops to depart, though soldiers quickly realized that the army's wheels could turn quite slowly in mustering out troops—especially in comparison to the alacrity commanders had previously displayed in mobilizing regiments for the front lines. Some soldiers found their way home by June, while others remained months longer in the Old Dominion.[15] Indeed, commanders redeployed, rather than repatriated, many units.

Tensions remained high among Virginians as troops passed, and at least occasionally the Federals left bitter memories in their wake. In Boydton, Mecklenburg County, Alexander Spotswood Boyd noted in mid-June that "Sheridan's cavalry & two corps of Sherman's army passed through this place. The Infantry crossed at Taylor's ferry & done considerable damage at Sister Ann's."[16] The recent battles and skirmishes undoubtedly shaded civilians' reactions to encountering Union troops again. Elizabeth Gordon Rennolds wrote in her memoirs of the war years in Fredericksburg that her father's support of "our cause" led to his arrest by Union soldiers when the city fell to the Federals. Soldiers "burned our barns, carried off horses & all cattle" and, before leaving, set the house on fire.[17]

Still, given that the carnage of war had occurred so recently, remarkably few conflicts arose between troops and civilians in other parts of the state. This dynamic undoubtedly pleased Halleck, who was determined that troops on the move should adhere to strict discipline. In an order to General Meade dated April 30, 1865, Halleck advised that private property should not be molested: "The Army of the Potomac has shown Virginians how they were to be treated as enemies. Let them now prove that they know equally well how to treat the same people as friends."[18] Although many Federal units were busily turning in equipment and heading north, some brigades were detached for duty in Virginia. Sizable numbers of troops were already stationed in Fredericksburg, Bowling Green, and Charlottesville—along with the thousands in Richmond and the areas surrounding Alexandria and Norfolk. Halleck ordered the establishment of additional garrisons west of the capital at Lynchburg, Staunton, Gordonsville, and Danville.[19]

In the chaotic aftermath of Lee's surrender, President Lincoln's assassination on April 14 provided another jolt. The news of Lincoln's death prompted many prayers among Afro-Virginians. In Lexington, freedpeople reported, "We nebber eat no breakfast dem mornings, nor carried dinner to our work, but spent the hour for dinner in praying for Mr. Lincoln and de Norf." They also "pray[ed] 'easy'" to avoid whites' notice.[20] At the First African Church hundreds of Richmond blacks reportedly mourned Lincoln's death on the day of his funeral. Norfolk missionary H. C. Percy wrote, "It was exceedingly touching to pass through the narrow lanes, where these people live in all their poverty, and see the expressions of grief in the simple drapery of their almost cheerless homes. Every house and hovel bore the sable badges. Ah, the mourning there was sincere: for if our President had specially endeared himself to any class, it was to these lowly ones, who have found in him their second Savior."[21]

Many white Virginians, meanwhile, reacted to the news of Lincoln's death warily. Though few whites mourned the passing of the president, many worried that Lincoln's death, coming so soon after Appomattox, would exacerbate the tense environment. Newspaper reports detailed angry Yankee suspicions of Southern conspiracies; the anguish of Federal troops stationed in Richmond was palpable. Rumors spread in Richmond that Union army officials would retaliate against Southerners for the assassination—rumors that proved, to some extent, prescient. In Washington, officials suspected that Lincoln's assassins were part of a larger Confederate plot to destabilize the government or even renew the war. Their fears seemed valid in the context of the current climate; Lee and Grant had met at Appomattox just days before, and many Confederate units had yet to surrender. Moreover, as the scholar Emory Thomas has noted, "Lincoln was suddenly a martyr. . . . If in the flush of impending victory anyone had forgotten that treason was a serious matter, Booth certainly recalled attention to the issue."[22] Gen. Ulysses S. Grant acted on his apprehensions on April 15, ordering General Ord, then in command in Richmond, to arrest a number of city officials and ex-Confederates. Grant wanted them remanded to Libby Prison, as long as "assassination remain[ed] the order of the day." Ord managed to convince his superior that such action would only exacerbate an already tense situation, and Grant relented—almost surely averting a dangerous confrontation.[23]

Washington's fears of widespread disorder resulting from Lincoln's assassination did not materialize. Instead, army commanders' most immediate problem proved to be the thousands of refugees that Richmond, Alexandria, and the Norfolk area had attracted during the war. The dire circumstances of overcrowding and poverty prompted army orders that no Northern civilians—or even army officers without orders—would be allowed into Richmond.[24] In the Tidewater area a large number of destitute people threatened to overwhelm officials. As the army demobilized in the summer of 1865, black soldiers were mustered out quickly as army officials sought to defuse a flashpoint of tension among Virginians. Freedwomen previously employed in jobs ancillary to army operations found themselves without work.[25] Embittered landowners frequently dismissed elderly blacks to avoid having to supply them with shelter and sustenance, much less pay them wages. With few options available to them, many older freedpeople turned to local "overseers of the poor" for assistance.[26]

In many parts of the state, Federal officers also contacted local civilian officials in hopes that they would shoulder at least part of the burden. But Richmond administrators quickly realized that the unprecedented need would obliterate the meager means at the disposal of municipal government, even if white officials were inclined to assist Afro-Virginians. Soon after the fall of Richmond, the army helped establish a relief commission there. Between April 8 and April 14, the military issued more than 86,000 rations to African American and white Virginians; by the end of the month officials were distributing some 13,000 rations daily.[27] In other parts of the state, the number of rations disbursed varied widely, depending on both levels of need and the size of the Federal presence. Officials in the area stretching northward from Albemarle, Fluvanna, and Goochland counties to Rappahannock, Culpeper, and Orange counties distributed only 1,643 rations in the month of August. Still, overall, government representatives doled out more than 178,000 rations across the state, at an estimated cost of more than $38,000.[28] Even as the burden grew, the army wanted to curtail its relief efforts drastically. In Richmond, officials attempted to remove refugees by establishing regular departures of trains and military ambulances to ferry civilians back to their homes at points north and south of the city.[29] As Halleck's chief of staff, Brig. Gen. Newton M. Curtis, succinctly commented to the commander in Petersburg, "The policy is to get rid of the women, children, and needy, rather than support them."[30] Still, despite their reluctance to dole out aid and their efforts to disperse large groups of needy freedpeople, Federal officials nonetheless provided critical sustenance for those—both black and white—who were without resources.

Throughout the summer of 1865, these tasks gradually fell to the newly formed Bureau of Refugees, Freedmen, and Abandoned Lands. Congress had organized the Freedmen's Bureau (as it was commonly called) the previous March as part of the War Department, assigning it the arduous task of providing aid to freedpeople, facilitating the establishment of schools for blacks, and overseeing labor relations between landowners and black workers. In its wisdom, however, Congress authorized no budget for the fledgling bureau, while simultaneously charging it with overseeing "all subjects" related to the freedpeople in the South.[31] From its inception, the Freedmen's Bureau thus found itself woefully underfunded and understaffed but nonetheless charged with the Herculean task of refereeing Southern race relations. The bureau charged its agents to conduct censuses of African Americans, "protect the negroes in their rights as free men," oversee labor relations, "cultivate . . . a friendly spirit" among blacks and whites, administer the distribution of rations, and aid the needy.[32] As Eric Foner has asserted, local agents were "expected to win the confidence of blacks and whites alike in a situation where race and labor relations had been poisoned by mutual distrust and conflicting interests."[33]

In Virginia, as elsewhere in the South, the bureau initially struggled to field enough agents. With no salary to offer, bureau officials in Richmond turned to the army for much of the agency's personnel in 1865. Often provost marshals doubled as bureau agents; in some instances Richmond commanders simply ordered officers to fill a bureau assignment on detached duty—a practice that provoked complaints from battle-weary officers anxious to muster out.[34] These dynamics led to frequent personnel turnover and slowed the progress of efforts in the western reaches of Virginia. Indeed, the bureau failed to establish an agent in Montgomery County until June 1866; his subdistrict came to include a large swath of southwestern Virginia.[35] The bureau occasionally employed white Virginians, despite the obvious concern of bias, but many more agents came from the ranks of the Veterans' Reserve Corps (VRC). Previously known as the Invalids' Corps, the VRC consisted of veterans who had been wounded in battle and were thus unfit for combat duty but were still able to contribute their experience in noncombat roles. By virtue of the veterans' attachment to the army, their salaries circumvented Congress's failure to authorize funds for the Freedmen's Bureau, and their experience helped to cement bureau operations in the state.[36]

By the fall of 1865, bureau officials had established eight districts covering the entire state; the boundaries did not coincide with the army's demarcations. For the bulk of the Reconstruction period in Virginia, Col. Orlando Brown filled the role of assistant commissioner as the head of bureau operations in the state. Brown, a physician trained at Yale Medical School, had treated freedpeople during the war when he served as a doctor in Newport News and worked as the superintendent of Negro affairs in Norfolk. Brown's advocacy on the behalf of freedpeople was genuine, as evidenced by Freedmen's Bureau Commissioner O. O. Howard's great faith in him; Generals Ord and Halleck also commended his efforts.[37]

In attempting to implement a free labor system in the vast agricultural areas of the state, Brown and his agents took on a huge task—and engendered the deep enmity of a large majority of white Virginians. While reconciled to military defeat and emancipation, many landowners either failed to understand or refused to concede that blacks' freedom required a fundamental alteration of the labor-capital relationship. Near Lynchburg, John Richard Dennett visited a farmer who openly discussed beating his workers, complaining that "now the bad niggers [will] spoil the rest. Since mine were freed, they have become lazy, stubborn, and impudent." The unnamed landowner expressed surprise that a young woman refused to resume her work after he "boxed her ears."[38] The notion that federal agents would interfere in labor relations—much less take the side of black workers—outraged white Virginians. Alexander Spotswood Boyd's comments typified the sentiments of many whites: "Everything is confusion & a good deal of trouble with the negro population, & yet that infernal Radical party at the North would confiscate the last piece of property & reduce us to degradation."[39]

Boyd hinted at one of the most controversial policies that the federal government attempted during Reconstruction: the redistribution of land in the South. The vagaries of war had forced many landowners to leave their property; in Union-occupied territories, lands designated as abandoned came under the control of the Federal government. Officials in Virginia utilized the property of absentee owners as distribution points for rations, temporary housing, and the establishment of church meetings and schools. Groups like the American Missionary Association (AMA) had been active in the Tidewater area since 1861, and many of their efforts relied upon access to confiscated lands.[40] At the close of the war, some Northern officials called for confiscated lands to be sold or given to the freedpeople. Orlando Brown strongly favored this approach; he commented to his superior, O. O. Howard, that the Freedmen's Bureau should "take possession of all the abandoned and confiscated land we require, and permit the negroes to work it on their own behalf." Over the summer and fall of 1865, however, the momentum of land redistribution halted when President Andrew Johnson pardoned large numbers of ex-Confederate landowners once they took an oath pledging loyalty to the United States; with pardons in hand, the Southerners could reclaim their property.[41] Johnson's actions left Howard little choice but to direct bureau representatives to acquiesce to the demands of the original owners. By September, when Brown heard reports that many Afro-Virginians expected to receive grants of land from the Federal government, he issued a circular ordering bureau agents across the state to encourage blacks to engage in labor contracts and to *take the earliest opportunity to explain to the freedmen that no lands will be given them by the Government.*[42]

With land redistribution cast aside, bureau agents focused on encouraging freedpeople to sign labor contracts with their employers—often the same landowners who had formerly enslaved them. Since the war ended at a critical time in the planting season, many landowners and workers quickly reached verbal agreements, which in turn frequently led to later disputes for local agents to resolve. As bureau agents established operations, written contracts became more common. The agency's printed forms called for workers to receive wages and "proper and suitable food and quarters" in return for "faithfully and diligently" performing the duties assigned to them. The latter phrase is instructive. Bureau officials, while supportive of emancipation, nonetheless echoed the racial bias common to their time. As large numbers of blacks congregated in Virginia's towns and cities, white observers—from North and South—mistook African Americans' desire to leave their former masters for sheer laziness. Many whites assumed that so long as the bureau distributed rations to needy freedpeople, African Americans would refuse to engage in labor. In reaction, army officials throughout the state warned freedpeople that they were expected to work, and some were even forced to work on civil projects.[43] Orlando Brown felt it necessary to lecture freedpeople that it was "his duty" to "teach you how to use that freedom you have so earnestly desired" and to avoid the "mistaken notion that Freedom means liberty to be idle."[44]

The bureau enforced its paternalistic version of free labor by repeatedly warning blacks that they must engage in contracts. For many Afro-Virginians, though, this ethos translated into work conditions that only nominally differed from those of the slavery era. In Amelia County, Lewis Edwin Harvie contracted with his black workers in documents notarized by the local Freedmen's Bureau agent, paying several male employees either $7 or $10 per month—in line with the standard rate for much of the state. Harvie, though, apparently encountered resistance when requiring that work continue after sunset in the harvest season. Bureau agent Alfred Theinhardt wrote a notice warning Harvie's workers that "all Freedmen in [his] employ

. . . are under no circumstances allowed to disobey orders given by said Mr. Harvie" and that if necessary they must "work two to three hours after sunset."[45] Moreover, physical abuse by no means ended with emancipation. Reports of violence against black workers routinely went up the chain of command in the Freedmen's Bureau.[46]

The state's political structure also underwent chaotic change in the early postwar period. As Virginia entered its turbulent summer of 1865, Governor Francis H. Pierpont arrived in Richmond to assume the reins of the state government. Pierpont's political status was unique. A Unionist lawyer from Morgantown, West Virginia (formerly part of Virginia), Pierpont had been instrumental in organizing resistance to Virginia's secession. When the Old Dominion joined the Confederacy, Pierpont led a largely Republican movement that resulted in the formation of a loyal, or "Restored," Virginia state government based in Wheeling in the summer of 1861. The Federal government quickly approved of the proceedings. Within two years, West Virginia became a state, and the Restored government of Virginia was forced to find a new home. Pierpont and his colleagues landed in Alexandria, safely behind Union lines. But despite Federal recognition, the Alexandria government existed largely on paper. With little territory to govern, beset by questions about its legality, and denied participation in Congress because of political wrangling, the Restored government provided an example of one of President Lincoln's various experiments with nominally occupying Confederate regions, but little more.[47]

At the close of the war, Lincoln decided to recognize the Restored government as the legitimate authority in Virginia. President Johnson followed suit after Lincoln's death by issuing an executive order to that effect on May 9, 1865.[48] Virginians wondered what lay in store with Pierpont's arrival in Richmond on May 26, and Pierpont likely shared their anxiety as he took a steamer toward the capital. Many looked forward to his arrival, if only for the ostensible end of military rule. The editors of the *Richmond Whig* somewhat rosily noted, "The interregnum in the civil Government may now be considered at an end, and in a short time the people of this portion of the State will realize all the blessings and advantages which must flow from the restoration of civil authority recognized by the Federal Government."[49] The editors' optimism proved to be misplaced.

Among the challenges awaiting Pierpont was a veritable blizzard of paperwork. In addition to a steady flow of official orders and circulars from the army and the Freedmen's Bureau, Pierpont received "resolutions of loyalty," requests for jobs, and pleas for assistance in myriad matters. Representatives of Albemarle, Augusta, Frederick, and Warren counties asserted in May and June their somewhat superfluous recognition of emancipation and the cessation of hostilities. Numerous letters of introduction called Pierpont's attention to candidates for appointments to state and local government positions, such as postmaster, the board of directors for the Eastern Lunatic Asylum at Williamsburg, and superintendent of the South-Western turnpike in western Virginia.[50] Stephen Fleming wrote from New Orleans to explain that he had been "sold as a Slave from the State of Virginia, Bowling Green Near Fredericksburg, into the State of Louisiana." Fleming requested help in reconnecting with his wife and five children. "I never heard from them Since and I wish her to know (if she is alive) where I am, and for her to write to me in order to determine for the future."[51] Mary Rhodes, of Baltimore, called on Pierpont for aid in caring for Confederate "prisoners . . . too feeble from wounds or sickness to leave with their comrades"; a resolution from Bedford County echoed Rhodes's request, noting that prisoners' families "are suffering for the want of their aid and presence at home."[52]

The war's political aftermath, however, remained Pierpont's paramount trial—and the governor proved unequal to the task of guiding Virginia through the turmoil. Though a dedicated Republican, Pierpont managed to alienate his compatriots and Afro-Virginians, while naïvely expecting white Virginians to commit to a new political and social order. In June 1865, Pierpont encouraged the Restored General Assembly to allow most former Rebels, even ex–Confederate officials, to vote in the upcoming elections—and run for office. The General Assembly's action, combined with blacks' continued exclusion from the polls, unsurprisingly resulted in many former Confederates successfully resuming their political careers after the October elections. The import of Pierpont's blunder is difficult to overstate. In Virginia's first foray into post-emancipation politics, white conservatives won a large majority of the vote and, according to Richard Lowe, "almost every office being contested."[53]

Fellow Republicans and African Americans loudly protested Pierpont's misjudgment of the political atmosphere. While the governor urged the General Assembly to restore ex-Confederates' rights, many warnings arose that should have given him pause. James H. Clements wrote to Pierpont to discuss conservative candidates in Portsmouth, claiming that on a ticket of twelve councilmen, ten were "straight secessionists." Clements wrote that the conservatives played up the issue of race as a means to defeat Unionist Republicans.[54] A Bristol, Tennessee, newspaper ran a political tract facetiously designated as a letter from "Meshack Horner" in Wise County, Virginia; the author espoused the editors' Unionist warning, "I'm sure I could never discover the wisdom of . . . givin the secessioners the chance to wriggle in like a passel of eals tryin to hide themselves in the mud."[55] Pierpont's motivation for his actions toward former Confederates was partly pragmatic; he thought it "folly" that a minority of Republicans should establish a government almost wholly devoid of the electorate's popular support.[56]

Virginia's whites, unsurprisingly, applauded Pierpont's—and President Johnson's—lenient policies toward former Rebels. Mary Blair McCarty of Richmond echoed many when she praised Johnson for putting a "check" on the "course chalked out by the Radicals of the North."[57] Ironically, Southern whites' success in checking Radical Republicans, blacks, and the Freedmen's Bureau in 1865 led to Johnson's bitter struggle with Congress over Reconstruction policy in 1866. Congress refused to seat several Southern delegations—including Virginia's—when faced with the prospect of swearing in members who were associated with the Confederate government only months before. Soon, the nation veered from Presidential Reconstruction to Congressional Reconstruction; the change in direction would be tumultuous.[58]

The governor's actions exposed a fissure among moderate and more radical Republicans that would only deepen in coming years. For their part, Afro-Virginians demanded political agency and, naturally, understood that former Confederates were unlikely partners in that process. Throughout the summer of 1865, Richmond's blacks agitated for the end of the pass system—which required that blacks produce written authorization to be in the city at any time—and the removal of several local and army officials. The *New York Tribune* printed the letter drafted by a group of Richmond African Americans, which in turn prompted action by Governor Pierpont.[59] In the Tidewater area, blacks endured widespread violence from both native whites and Union troops in 1865 and fought back both physically and politically.[60] A meeting held at the Catherine Street Church resulted in a pamphlet that vehemently argued for blacks' right to vote; the pamphlet also made news in New York City.[61] Pierpont's Republican allies also felt betrayed and soon voiced their displeasure with the governor. The Unionist *Alexandria Virginia*

State Journal broke with Pierpont in August, claiming he had "sold himself cheaply to his old, bitter and most deadly enemies."[62]

Pierpont's misreading of events mirrored the failure of Presidential Reconstruction throughout the South. As former Confederates exerted considerable political influence, and landowners resumed labor practices that differed little from the slavery era, Northerners began to question the meaning of their victory. In 1866, as reports of violence against Southern blacks escalated dramatically, African Americans and Radical Republicans demanded a broad revision of Johnson's lenient Reconstruction policy. Congress obliged in early 1867. Virginia found itself designated "Military District Number One," as the army again took charge in the Old Dominion. Ultimately, a new state constitution went into effect in 1869, incorporating the Thirteenth and Fourteenth amendments; African Americans gained the franchise; and the enlarged political arena fostered dynamic change.[63]

In 1865, of course, those developments remained unknown as Virginians coped with a radically altered world. Afro-Virginians, no longer enslaved but not yet citizens, demanded political rights, while most whites struggled to digest the twin shocks of Confederate defeat and emancipation. Some former Confederates contemplated emigration to Mexico; others urged their fellow citizens to buckle down and work hard to restore Virginia to its former glory. Simultaneously, blacks agitated for even greater change in meetings with white officials and in conventions of freedpeople throughout the state.[64] Indeed, upheaval continued in the Old Dominion after the Civil War, and Reconstruction—however traumatic, successful, or ineffective—ushered in a new era.

Notes

1. James I. Robertson Jr., *Civil War Sites in Virginia: A Tour Guide* (Charlottesville: University of Virginia Press, 1982), vii.

2. Ronald L. Heinemann, John G. Kolp, Anthony S. Parent Jr., and William G. Shade, *Old Dominion, New Commonwealth: A History of Virginia, 1607–2007* (Charlottesville: University of Virginia Press, 2007), 241.

3. Gen. Oliver O. Howard, "Report of the Commissioner of the Bureau of Refugees, Freedmen, and Abandoned Lands," November 1, 1867, in *House Executive Documents*, 40th Congress, 2nd sess., no. 1 (serial 1324), 663.

4. Eliza Chew (French) Smith Diary, Wynne Family Papers, Virginia

Historical Society, Richmond. (The Virginia Historical Society is hereafter cited as VHS.)

5. Sarah P. Payne to Mary M. Clendenin, September 30, 1865, Sarah P. Payne Letters, VHS.

6. John Holmes Bocock to Nancy Miller (Armistead) Blanton, December 20, 1865, Armistead, Blanton, and Wallace Family Papers, VHS.

7. Georgianna Preston, quoted in Works Projects Administration, *The Negro in Virginia* (Winston-Salem, N.C.: John F. Blair, 1994), 234.

8. Alexander Spotswood Boyd to John Bennett, June 16, 1865, John Bennett Papers, VHS.

9. Michael B. Chesson, *Richmond After the War, 1865–1890* (Richmond: Virginia State Library, 1981), 74; *Richmond Whig*, May 1, 1865.

10. Joseph P. Reidy, "'Coming from the Shadow of the Past': The Transition from Slavery to Freedom at Freedmen's Village, 1863–1900," *Virginia Magazine of History and Biography* 95 (October 1987): 414.

11. Robert F. Engs, *Freedom's First Generation: Black Hampton, Virginia, 1861–1890* (New York: Fordham University Press, 2004), 67.

12. *Staunton Vindicator,* September 29, 1865.

13. Special Orders No. ——, May 25, 1865, and General Orders No. 89, in U.S. War Department, *War of the Rebellion: A Compilation of the Official Records of the Union and Confederate Armies* (Washington, D.C.: Government Printing Office, 1880–1901), series 1, vol. 46, pt. 3, 1213, 1314 (hereafter cited as *OR*; all references are to series 1).

14. William T. Alderson, "The Influence of Military Rule and the Freedmen's Bureau on Reconstruction in Virginia, 1865–1870" (Ph.D. diss., Vanderbilt University, 1952), 17–19; Richard Lowe, *Republicans and Reconstruction in Virginia, 1856–70* (Charlottesville: University of Virginia Press, 1991), 76.

15. Henry W. Halleck to Ulysses S. Grant, May 14, 1865, in *OR,* vol. 46, pt. 3, 1149; William B. Holberton, *Homeward Bound: The Demobilization of the Union and Confederate Armies, 1865–1866* (Mechanicsburg, Pa.: Stackpole, 2001), 53–63.

16. Alexander Spotswood Boyd to John Bennett, June 16, 1865.

17. Elizabeth Gordon Rennolds Recollections, VHS.

18. Halleck to George G. Meade, April 30, 1865, in *OR,* vol. 46, pt. 3, 1016.

19. Special Orders No. 13, May 12, 1865, in *OR,* vol. 46, pt. 3, 1139; Edward W. Smith to A. H. Markland, May 1, 1865, in *OR,* vol. 46, pt. 3, 1062.

20. Unnamed African American, quoted in W. L. Coan to George Whipple and Michael Strieby, December 12, 1865, document HI-7829, Virginia Field Records, American Missionary Association Archives, Amistad Research Center, New Orleans, Louisiana. The author consulted a microfilmed copy of the

Virginia records of the AMA at the Library of Virginia in Richmond. (Hereafter the Virginia Field Records will be referred to as AMA-VA.)

21. Works Projects Administration, *Negro in Virginia*, 237; H. C. Percy to George Whipple, May 7, 1865, document HI-7112, AMA-VA.

22. James M. McPherson, *Ordeal by Fire: The Civil War and Reconstruction*, 3rd ed. (Boston: McGraw Hill, 2001), 520–22; Elizabeth Brown Pryor, *Reading the Man: A Portrait of Robert E. Lee through His Private Letters* (New York: Viking, 2007), 429–31; Emory M. Thomas, *Robert E. Lee: A Biography* (New York: Norton, 1995), 370.

23. Nelson Lankford, *Richmond Burning: The Last Days of the Confederate Capital* (New York: Penguin Books, 2003), 221–22 (Grant quotation on 221).

24. *Richmond Whig*, April 17, 1865.

25. Engs, *Freedom's First Generation*, 67–69.

26. Christopher J. Tubbs to Captain How, November 11 and December 3, 1865, Letters Sent and Orders Issued, Lexington Office, Records of the Assistant Commissioner for the State of Virginia, Bureau of Refugees, Freedmen, and Abandoned Lands, 1865–1869, Record Group 105, entry 4044, National Archives, Washington, D.C.; Steven Elliott Tripp, *Yankee Town, Southern City: Race and Class Relations in Civil War Lynchburg* (New York: New York University Press, 1997), 165–66; Eric Foner, *Reconstruction: America's Unfinished Revolution, 1863–1877* (New York: HarperCollins, 2005), 131.

27. *Richmond Whig*, April 7, 12, 17, 1865; Chesson, *Richmond After the War*, 73; Halleck to Edwin McM. Stanton, June 26, 1865, in *OR*, vol. 46, pt. 3, 1295. See also Alderson, "Influence of Military Rule," 6. Alderson reports that a "standard ration consisted of 10 ounces of pork or bacon; or, 1 pound of fresh beef; or, 12 ounces of dried fish; or, 16 ounces of pickled fish; or, 1 pound of corn meal, five times a week; with 1 pound of flour or soft bread, or 12 ounces of hard bread twice a week. Coffee, tea, and sugar were authorized for sick women or children, when deemed necessary." At least some local officials refused to aid blacks; see Mary Farmer-Kaiser, "'With a Weight of Circumstances Like Millstones about Their Necks': Freedwomen, Federal Relief, and the Benevolent Guardianship of the Freedmen's Bureau," *Virginia Magazine of History and Biography* 115 (January 2007): 417.

28. Tally of Rations Issued, Summary for Report of August 31, 1865, Records of the Assistant Commissioner for the State of Virginia, Bureau of Refugees, Freedmen, and Abandoned Lands, 1865–1869, Record Group 105, microfilm publication M-1048, roll 55, National Archives, Washington, D.C. (Hereafter, microfilmed Virginia Freedmen's Bureau records will be referred to as BRFAL-VA.)

29. *Richmond Whig*, May 1, 1865.

30. Newton M. Curtis to George L. Hartsuff, May 1, 1865, in *OR*, vol. 46, pt. 3, 1063.

31. George R. Bentley, *A History of the Freedmen's Bureau* (New York: Octagon Books, 1970), 21–25, 46–49; Foner, *Reconstruction,* 68–71.

32. Orlando Brown, Circular Letter to District Superintendents in Virginia, June 15, 1865, roll 41, BRFAL-VA.

33. Foner, *Reconstruction,* 142–48 (quotation on 143); Bentley, *History of the Freedmen's Bureau,* 135–44, 148–61.

34. In Lexington, Virginia, for instance, Lt. Christopher Jerome Tubbs served as a bureau agent in the fall of 1865 on detached duty from the Fifty-eighth Pennsylvania Infantry, but repeatedly requested to be relieved of his duties in order to accompany his unit home when it mustered out. Tubbs left Lexington in early 1866. See Compiled Pension Records for Christopher Jerome Tubbs, Record Group 94, National Archives, Washington, D.C.

35. Bentley, *History of the Freedmen's Bureau,* 71–73; W. L. Coan to George Whipple, October 20, 1865, document HI-7582, AMA-VA; Linda Killen, *"These People Lived in a Pleasant Valley": A History of Slaves and Freedmen in Nineteenth Century Pulaski County, Virginia* (Belspring, Va.: Radford University, 1996), 61.

36. William S. McFeely, *Yankee Stepfather: General O. O. Howard and the Freedmen* (New Haven, Conn.: Yale University Press, 1968), 78–79; Bentley, *History of the Freedmen's Bureau,* 73–75. Examples of white bureau agents in Virginia include Robert Henderson Allen, a landowner in Lunenburg County whose four sons served in the Confederate army; Allen served as a bureau agent and a justice of the peace (see Diary of Robert Henderson Allen, Allen Family Papers, VHS). Dr. Charles E. Davidson of Buckingham County contracted with the medical department of the U.S. Army in September 1865 and began work as a Freedmen's Bureau agent in November of the same year (see Charles E. Davidson Papers, VHS).

37. McFeely, *Yankee Stepfather,* 67; Alderson, "Influence of Military Rule," 29–30; Joe M. Richardson, *Christian Reconstruction: The American Missionary Association and Southern Blacks, 1861–1890* (Athens: University of Georgia Press, 1986), 12.

38. John Richard Dennett, *The South as It Is: 1865–1866,* ed. Henry M. Christman (New York: Viking, 1965), 78–79.

39. Alexander Spotswood Boyd to John Bennett, June 16, 1865.

40. Richardson, *Christian Reconstruction,* 3–9.

41. Foner, *Reconstruction,* 158–64, 183–85 (quotation on 158).

42. Orlando Brown, Circular, September 19, 1865, Orders, Circular Letters, and Letters of Instruction, roll 41, BRFAL-VA.

43. Leon Litwack, *Been in the Storm So Long: The Aftermath of Slavery* (New York: Knopf, 1979), 410–15; Alderson, "Influence of Military Rule," 58 (sample contract); Foner, Reconstruction, 164–70; Farmer-Kaiser, "Freedwomen,"

418–25; *Lynchburg Daily Virginian,* June 2, 12, 1865; *Staunton Vindicator,* June 30, 1865; *Richmond Whig,* May 1, 1865.

44. Circular, July 1, 1865, BRFAL-VA.

45. Alfred Theinhardt Statement, November 1, 1865, Harvie Family Papers, VHS; Litwack, *Been in the Storm So Long,* 411; Alderson, "Influence of Military Rule," 53–55.

46. Examples of agents' reports of violence abound in the "Agents' Monthly Narrative Reports" that commenced in January 1866. See, for instance, Major Carse (in Rockbridge County), March 31, 1866, and J. Arnold Yeckley to James A. Bates, April 19, 1866, BRFAL-VA.

47. Lowe, *Republicans and Reconstruction,* 6–25; Heinemann et al., *Old Dominion, New Commonwealth,* 240–45.

48. Lowe, *Republicans and Reconstruction,* 26.

49. *Richmond Whig,* May 27, 1865.

50. Executive Papers of Governor Francis Harrison Pierpont, 1865–1868, accession 37024, box 1, Library of Virginia, Richmond.

51. Stephen Fleming to Pierpont, May 21, 1865, box 1, Pierpont Executive Papers.

52. Mary Rhodes to Pierpont, July 17, 1865, box 2, and "Resolution," June 10, 1865, box 1, both in Pierpont Executive Papers.

53. Lowe, *Republicans and Reconstruction,* 41–45 (quotation on 43); Heinemann et al., *Old Dominion, New Commonwealth,* 245–48.

54. James H. Clements to Pierpont, June 4, 1865, box 1, Pierpont Executive Papers.

55. *Bristol (Tenn.) News,* September 15, 1865.

56. Lowe, *Republicans and Reconstruction,* 32–33.

57. Mary Blair McCarty to Harriette B. A. Caperton, February 24, 1866, McCarty Family Papers, VHS.

58. Lowe, *Republicans and Reconstruction,* 50–61.

59. Peter J. Rachleff, *Black Labor in Richmond, 1865–1890* (Urbana: University of Illinois Press, 1989), 36–37.

60. Engs, *Freedom's First Generation,* 67–71; Lucy Chase newspaper article (publication unidentified), June 25, 1865, in Henry Lee Swint, ed., *Dear Ones at Home: Letters from Contraband Camps* (Nashville: Vanderbilt University Press, 1966), 165–69.

61. "Equal Suffrage. Address from the Colored Citizens of Norfolk, Va., to the People of the United States. Also an Account of the Agitation of the Agitation among the Colored People of Virginia for Equal Rights," in Philip S. Foner and George E. Walker, eds., *Proceedings of the Black National and State Conventions, 1865–1900* (Philadelphia: Temple University Press, 1979–1980), 1:83–94.

62. Quoted in Lowe, *Republicans and Reconstruction*, 36.

63. For the onset of Congressional Reconstruction, see Foner, *Reconstruction*, 228–80; Lowe, *Republicans and Reconstruction*, 50–96; Heinemann et al., *Old Dominion, New Commonwealth*, 244–50. For post-Reconstruction politics in Virginia, see Jane Dailey, *Before Jim Crow: The Politics of Race in Postemancipation Virginia* (Chapel Hill: University of North Carolina Press, 2000); James Tice Moore, *Two Paths to the New South: The Virginia Debt Controversy, 1870–1883* (Lexington: University Press of Kentucky, 1974).

64. Robert Lewis Dabney to Charles William Dabney, circa 1866, Dabney Family Papers, VHS; John Holmes Bocock to Nancy Miller (Armistead) Blanton, December 20, 1865, Armistead, Blanton, and Wallace Family Papers, VHS; *Rockingham Register and Advertiser*, May 12, 1865; Lowe, *Republicans and Reconstruction*, 112–20.

Diary of a Southern Refugee during the War, August 1864–May 1865

Judith Brockenbrough McGuire

Edited by James I. Robertson Jr.

A feeling of helplessness slowly enveloped Judith McGuire in the last year of the Civil War. Her faith in God remained unbendable; her support for the Confederacy was unwavering. Yet she was powerless to stem the inexorable wave of Union might that swept slowly and destructively over her beloved Virginia.

In the latter part of 1864, the McGuires once again had to find living quarters in Richmond. The search was long and, in the face of galloping inflation, painful. Mrs. McGuire remained steadfast to her clerical and nursing duties. But, as the war worsened, her emotions seemed to become sharper.

She penned a long, heavily biased account of an August 20 incident in the Shenandoah Valley. One of Gen. George Custer's Union cavalry regiments had wantonly burned three estates and left the residents literally empty-handed. The Union troopers were moving to the next point of vandalism when Col. John Mosby's Confederate rangers galloped upon the scene and exacted a no-prisoner vengeance. Mrs. McGuire was satisfied with the result. "I want the North to feel the war to its core," she wrote, "and then it will end, and not before."

Negative voices from Richmond citizens likewise stirred Mrs. McGuire's anger. She called such doomsayers and second-guessers "croakers," declaring sarcastically that "were I a credulous woman, and ready to believe all that I hear in the office, in the hospital, in my visits and on the streets, I should think that Richmond is now filled with the most accomplished military geniuses on which the sun shines."

Reduced to two meals a day, and hearing weekly of the deaths of friends and acquaintances in service, the diarist continued recording her observations. The 1865 entries read like a long obituary for the Southern Confederacy. Her descriptions of the evacuation and destruction of Richmond in April rank among the most detailed in Civil War history. The end of the struggle found Rev. and Mrs. McGuire marooned among the ruins of the capital, with no home, no funds, no jobs, and no future.

Diary of a Southern Refugee

August 11—Sheridan's and Early's troops are fighting in the Valley. We suffered a disaster near Martinsburg,[1] and our troops fell back to Strasburg; had a fight on the old battle-ground at Kernstown, and we drove the enemy through Winchester to Martinsburg, which our troops took possession of.[2] Poor Winchester, how checkered its history throughout the war! Abounding in patriotism as it is, what a blessing it must be to have a breath of free air, even though it be for a short time! Their welcome of our soldiers is always so joyous, so bounding, so generous! How they must enjoy the blessed privilege of speaking their own sentiments without having their servants listening and acting as spies in their houses, and of being able to hear from or write to their friends! Oh, I would that there was a prospect of their being disenthralled forever.[3]

12th—I am sorry to record a defeat near Moorfield, in Hardy County.[4] These disasters are very distressing to us all, except to the croakers, who find in them so much food for their gloom, that I am afraid they are rather pleased than otherwise. They always, on such occasions, elongate their mournful countenances, prophesy evil. And chew the cud of discontent with a better show of reason than they can generally produce. The signal failure of Grant's mine to blow up our army,[5] and its recoil upon his own devoted troops, amply repay us for our failure in Hardy. God's hand was in it, and to Him be the praise.

One of my friends in the office is a victim of Millroy's reign in Winchester. She wrote to a friend of hers at the North, expressing her feelings rather imprudently. The letter was intercepted, and she was immediately arrested, and brought in an ambulance through the enemy' lines to our picket-post, where she was deposited by the roadside. She says she was terribly distressed at leaving her mother and sisters, but when she got into Confederate lines the air seemed wonderfully fresh, pure and free, and she soon found friends. She came to Richmond and entered our office. About the same time a mother and daughters who lived perhaps in the handsomest house in the town, were arrested, for some alleged imprudence of one of the daughters.[6] An ambulance was driven to the door, and the mother was taken from her sick-bed and put into it, together with the daughters. Time was not allowed them to prepare a lunch for the journey. Before Mrs. [Logan] was taken from her house Mrs. Millroy had entered it, the General having taken it for his head-quarters; and before the ambulance had been driven off, one of their own officers was heard to say to Mrs. M[ilroy], seeing her so entirely at home in the house, "For goodness' sake, madam, wait until the poor woman gets off."[7] Is it wonderful, then, that the Winchester ladies welcome our troops with gladness? That they rush out and join the band, singing "The bonnie blue flag" and "Dixie," as the troops enter the streets, until their enthusiasm and melody melt all hearts? Was it strange that even the great and glorious, though grave and thoughtful, Stonewall Jackson should, when pursuing Banks [in 1862] through its streets, have been excited until he waved his cap with tears of enthusiasm, as they broke forth in harmonious songs of welcome? Or that the ladies, not being satisfied by saluting them with their voices, waving their handkerchiefs, and shouting for joy, should follow them with more substantial offerings, filling their haversacks with all that their depleted pantries could afford? Or is it wonderful that our soldiers should love Winchester so dearly and fight for it so valiantly? No, it is beautiful to contemplate the long-suffering, the firmness under oppression, the patience, the generosity, the patriotism of Winchester. Other towns, I dare say, have borne their tyranny as well, and when their history is known they will call forth our admiration as much; but we *know* of no such instance. The "Valley" throughout shows the same devotion to our cause, and the sufferings of the country people are even greater than those in town.

Some amusing incidents sometimes occur, showing the eagerness of the ladies to serve our troops after a long separation. A lady living near Berryville, but a little remote from the main road, says that when our troops are passing through the country, she sometimes feels sick with anxiety to do something for them. She, one morning, stood in her porch, and could see them turn in crowds to neighbouring houses which happened to be on the road, but no one turned out of the way far enough to come to her house. At last one man came along, and finding that he was passing her gate, she ran out with the greatest alacrity to invite him to come in and get his breakfast. He turned to her with an amused expression and replied: "I am much obliged to you, madam; I wish I could breakfast with you, but as I have already eaten *four* breakfasts to please the ladies, I must beg you to excuse me."

14th—Norfolk, poor Norfolk![8] Nothing can exceed its long-suffering, its nights of gloom and darkness. Unlike Winchester, it has no bright spots—no oasis in its blank desert of wretchedness. Like Alexandria, it has no relief, but must submit, and drag on its chain of servility, till the final cry of victory bursts its bonds, and makes it free. I have no time to write of all I hear and know of the indignities offered to our countrymen and countrywomen in Alexandria, Norfolk, Portsmouth, and other places which remain incarcerated in the sloughs of Federal tyranny. God help them, and give us strength speedily to break the chain that binds them.

August 15—An account from my relatives, of the raid of the 19th of June into the village of Tappahannock,[9] has lately reached me. The village had been frequently visited and pillaged before, and both sides of the beautiful Rappahannock, above and below, had been sadly devastated; but the last visit seems to carry with it more of the spirit of revenge than any before. My aunt[10] writes:

> About daybreak on that peaceful Sabbath morn six gun-boats were seen returning down the river. A rumour that [Gen. Wade] Hampton was after them, had driven them from their work of devastation in the country above us to their boats for safety. By six o'clock six hundred negroes and four hundred cavalry and marines were let loose upon the defenceless town. The first visit I received was from six cavalrymen; the pantry-door was unceremoniously broken open, and a search made for wine and plate; but all such things had been removed to a place of safety, and when I called loudly for an officer to be sent for, the ruffians quietly went to their horses and departed. Next came a surgeon from Point Lookout, to search the house, and deliver the key to Dr. R's[11] store, which he had sent for as soon as he

landed—making a great virtue of his not breaking open the door, and of his honesty in only taking a few pills. This dignitary walked through the rooms, talking and murdering the "king's English" most ludicrously. However, he behaved quite well through the day, and was, under Heaven, the means of protecting us from aggression by his frequent visits. In a short time every unoccupied house in the village was forcibly entered, and every thing taken from them or destroyed. Dr. R's house was completely sacked. I had made all necessary preparations for returning home, but all was swept by the Vandals. Dr. R's surgical instruments, books, medicines, his own and his sister's clothes, as well as those of their dead parents, were taken, the officers sharing the plunder with the soldiers. The furniture, such as was not broken up, was carried off in dray-loads to the boats, and these two young people were as destitute of domestic comforts as though a consuming fire had passed over their pleasant residence. My lot was filled with the creatures going in and out at pleasure, unless the cry, "The Johnnies are coming," sent them running like scared beasts to their rendezvous, and gave us a few moments of quiet. The poor negroes belonging to the town seemed to lose all power over themselves, and to be bereft of reason. Some seemed completely brutalized by the suggestions that were constantly whispered in their ears; others so frightened by the threats made, that reason deserted them; others so stupefied that they lost all power to direct themselves, and gave up to the control of others. It is impossible to describe the madness that possessed them. For myself, I had but one care left—to keep them from polluting my house any farther by keeping them out; and this I was enabled to do after shutting and locking the door in the face of one of them. The most painful event of the day was when a little coloured girl, a great pet with us, was dragged from the house. The aunt of the child was determined to take her with her, but she resisted all her aunt's efforts, and came to the house for protection. An officer came for her, and after talking with her, and telling her that he would not "trouble her, but she was not old enough to know what was good for her," he went off. About night a white man and the most fiendish-looking negro I ever saw came for her in the name of the aunt, and vowed they would have her at all risks.

The officers had all gone to the boats, and it was in vain to resist them, and with feelings of anguish we saw the poor child dragged from us. I cannot think of this event without pain. But night now set in, and our apprehensions increased as the light disappeared; we knew not what was before us, or what we should be called on to encounter during the hours of darkness. We only knew that we were surrounded by lawless banditti, from whom we had no reason to expect mercy, much less kindness; but above all, there was an eye that never slumbered, and an arm mighty to defend those who trusted in it, so we made the house as secure as we could, and kept ready a parcel of *sharp case-knives* (don't laugh at our weapons) for our defence, if needed, and went up-stairs, determined to keep close vigils all night. Our two faithful servants, Jacob and Anthony, kept watch in the kitchen. Among the many faithless, those two stood as examples of the comfort that good servants can give in time of distress. About nine o'clock we heard the sound of horses' feet, and Jacob's voice under the window. Upon demanding to know what was the matter, I was answered by the voice of a gun-boat captain, in broken German, that they were going to fire over my house at the "Rebs" on the hill, and that we had better leave the house, and seek protection in the streets. I quietly told our counsellor that I preferred remaining in my own house, and should go to the basement, where we should be safe. So we hastily snatched up blankets and comforts, and repaired to the basement, where pallets were spread, and G's little baby laid down to sleep, sweetly unconscious of our fears and troubles. We went to apprise the Misses G.[12] of the danger, and urge them to come to us. They came, accompanied by an ensign, who had warded off danger from them several times during the day. He was a grave, middle-aged man, and was very kind. At the request of the ladies, he came into the rooms with us and remained until twelve o'clock. He was then obliged to return to the gun-boat, but gave us an efficient guard until daybreak. He pronounced Captain Schultz's[13] communication false, as they had no idea of firing. We knew at once that the object had been to rob the house, as all unoccupied houses were robbed with impunity. This gentleman's name was Nelson. I can never forget his kindness. During the night our relative, Mrs. B——m,[14] came to us in great agitation; she had attempted to stay at home, though entirely alone, to protect her property. She had been driven from her house at midnight, and chased across several lots to the adjoining one, where she had fallen from exhaustion. Jacob, hearing cries for help, went to her, and brought her to us. Our party now consisted of twelve females of all ages. As soon as the guard left us at daybreak, they came in streams to the hen-yard, and woe to the luckless chicken who thought itself safe from robbers! At one o'clock on Monday the fleet of now eighteen steamers took its departure. Two of the steamers were filled with the deluded negroes who were leaving their homes. We felt that the incubus which had pressed so heavily upon us for thirty hours had been removed, and we once more breathed freely, but the village was left desolate and destitute.

18th—For several days our whole time has been occupied nursing the dear little grandchild, whose life was despaired of for two days. We are most thankful for his recovery. The army is now on the north side of James River, and this evening at this moment, we hear heavy cannonading, and musketry is distinctly heard from the hills around the city.[15] Oh, Heavenly Father! Guide our generals and troops, and cause this sanguinary conflict to end by a desirable, an honourable peace!

20th—A friend from the Valley has described a successful attack made by Mosby on a Federal wagon-train near Berryville.[16] It was on its way to the army at Strasburg, and Mosby was on the other side of the Shenandoah [River]. He crossed in the night with one cannon and about seventy-five men, and at daylight surprised the drivers and guard as they were beginning to hitch their mules, by a salute from the cannon and seventy-five pistols. There was a general stampede in an instant of all who were unhurt. As quick as thought, 600 mules were turned towards the river, and driven to the command in Loudoun [County]. In the mean time, the wagons were set on fire, and most of them and their contents were consumed before the luckless drivers could return to their charge.

It is said that our new steamer, the "Tallahassee," has been within sixty miles of the city of New York, very much to the terror of the citizens.[17] It also destroyed six large vessels. I bid it God-speed with all my heart; I want the North to feel the war to its core, and then it will end, and not before.

22d—Just been on a shopping expedition for my sister and niece, and spent $1,500 in about an hour. I gave $110 for ladies' morocco boots; $22 per yard for linen; $5 apiece for spools of cotton; $5 for a paper of pins, etc. It would be utterly absurd, except that it is melancholy, to see our currency depreciating so rapidly.

31st—The last day of this exciting, troubled summer of 1864. How many young spirits have fled—how many bleeding, breaking hearts have been left upon earth, from the sanguinary work of this summer! Grant still remains near Petersburg; still by that means is he besieging Richmond. He has been baffled at all points, and yet his indomitable perseverance knows no bounds. Sherman still besieges Atlanta. God help us!

We are again troubled in mind and body about engaging rooms; we find we must give up these by the 1st of October, and have begun the usual refugee occupation of room-hunting.

Letters from our friends in the Valley, describing the horrors now going on there. A relative witnessed the burning of three very large residences on the 20th of August.[18] General Custar was stationed with his brigade of Michigan Cavalry near Berryville. He had thrown out pickets on all the roads, some of which were fired on by Mosby's men. This so exasperated the Federals, that an order was at once issued that whenever a picket-post was fired on the nearest house should be burned. On the morning of the 20th this dreadful order was put into execution, and three large houses were burnt to the ground, together with barns, wheat-stacks, and outhouses. The house of Mr. [Ware] was near a picket-post, and about midnight on the 19th a messenger arrived with a note announcing the sudden death of Mr. [Ware]'s sister, on a plantation not many miles distant. A lamp was lighted to read the note, and, unfortunately, a little while afterwards the picket-post was fired on and one man wounded. The lighting of the lamp was regarded as a signal to Colonel Mosby. During the same night the pickets near two other large houses were fired on. This being reported at head-quarters, the order was at once issued to burn all three houses. Two companies of the Fifth Michigan Cavalry, commanded by Captain Drake, executed the fearful order. They drew up in front of Mr. [Ware]'s house and asked for him. "Are you Mr. [Ware]?" demanded the Captain. "I have orders to burn your house." In vain Mr. [Ware] remonstrated. He begged for one hour, that he might see General Custar and explain the circumstances of the night before; he also pleaded the illness of his son-in-law,[19] then in the house. No reply was vouchsafed to the old gentleman, but with a look of hardened ferocity, he turned to the soldiers. With the order: "Men, to our work, and do it thoroughly!" In an instant the torch was applied to that home of domestic elegance and comfort. One soldier seized the sick son-in-law, who is a surgeon in our service, threatening to carry him to head-quarters, and was with difficulty prevented by the kind interposition of Dr. Sinclair,[20] the surgeon of the regiment. They allowed the family to save as much furniture as they could, but the servants were all gone, and there was no one near to help them. The soldiers at once went to Mr. [Ware]'s secretary, containing $40,000 in bonds, destroyed it, and scattered the mutilated papers to the winds. Matches were applied to window and bed curtains; burning coals were sprinkled in the linen-closet, containing every variety of house and table linen. Mrs. [Brown], the daughter, opened a drawer, and taking her jewelry, embracing an elegant diamond ring and other valuables, was escaping with them to the yard, when she was seized by two ruffians on the stair-steps, held by the arms by one, while the other forcibly took the jewels; they then, as she is a very small woman, lifted her over the banister and let her drop into the passage below; fortunately it was not very far and she was not at all injured. Nothing daunted, she rushed up-stairs, to rescue a box containing her bridal presents of silver, which was concealed in the wall above a closet. She climbed up to the highest shelf of the closet, seized the box, and, with unnatural strength, threw it through the window into the yard below. While still on the shelf, securing other things from their hiding-place, all unconscious of danger, a soldier set fire to some dresses hanging on the pegs below the shelf on which she stood. The first intimation she had of it was feeling the heat; she then leaped over the flames to the floor; her stockings were scorched, but she was not injured. She next saw a man with the sign of the Cross on his coat; she asked him if he was a chaplain? He replied that he was.[21] She said, "Then in mercy come, and help me to save some of my mother's things." They went into her mother's chamber, and she hurriedly opened the bureau drawer, and began taking out the clothes, the chaplain assisting, but what was to her horror to see him putting whatever he fancied into his pocket—among other things a paper of pins. She says she could not help saying, as she turned to him, "A minister of Christ stealing pins!!" In a moment the chaplain was gone, but the pins were returned to the bureau. Mrs. [Brown] is the only daughter of Mr. [Ware], and was the only lady on the spot. Her first care, when she saw the house burning, was to secure her baby, which was sleeping in its cradle up-stairs. A guard was at the foot of the steps, and refused to let her pass; she told him that she was going to rescue her child from the flames. "Let the little d——d rebel burn!" was the brutal reply. But his bayonet could not stop her; she ran by, and soon returned, bearing her child to a place of safety. When the house had become a heap of ruins, the mother returned from the bedside of her dead sister, whither she had gone at daylight that morning, on horseback (for her harness had been destroyed by the enemy, making her carriage useless). She was, of course, overwhelmed with grief and with horror at the scene before her. As soon as she dismounted, a soldier leaped on the horse, and rode off with it. Their work of destruction in one place being now over, they left it for another scene of vengeance.

The same ceremony of Captain Drake's announcing his orders to the mistress of the mansion (the master was a prisoner) being over, the torch was applied. The men had dismounted; the work of pillage was going on merrily; the house was burning in every part, to insure total destruction. The hurried tramp of horses' feet could not be heard amidst the crackling of flames and falling of rafters, but the sudden shout and cry of "No quarter! no quarter!" from many voices, resounded in the ears of the unsuspecting marauders as a death-knell.[22] A company of Mosby's men rushed up the hill and charged them furiously; they were aroused by the sound of danger, and fled hither and thither. Terrified and helpless, they were utterly unprepared for resistance. The cry of "No quarter! no quarter!" still continued. They hid behind the burning ruins; they crouched in the corners of fences; they begged for life; but their day of grace was past. The defenceless women, children, and old men of the neighbourhood had borne their tortures too long; something must be done, and all that this one company of braves could do, was done. Thirty were killed on the spot, and others, wounded and bleeding, sought refuge, and asked pity of those whom they were endeavouring to ruin. —— writes:

> Two came to us, the most pitiable objects you ever beheld, and we did what we could for them; for, after all, the men are not to blame half so much as the officers. Whether these things have been ordered by Sheridan or Custar, we do not know. These two wounded men, and all who took refuge among Secessionists, were removed that night, contrary to our wishes, for we knew that their tortures

in the ambulances would be unbearable; but they were unwilling to trust them, and unable to believe that persons who were suffering so severely from them could return good for evil.[23]

One man gruffly remarked: "If we leave any of them with you all, Mosby will come and kill them over again." We have since heard that those two men died that night. The pickets were then drawn in nearer to head-quarters. All was quiet for the rest of the day, and as Colonel Mosby had but one company in that section of the country, it had of course retired. That night, two regiments (for they could not trust themselves in smaller numbers) were seen passing along the road; their course was marked by the torches which they carried. They rode to the third devoted house and burned it to the ground. No one knows whose house will be the next object of revenge. Some fancied wrong may make us all homeless. We keep clothes, house-linen, and every thing compressible, tied up in bundles, so that they can be easily removed.

Such are some of the horrors that are being enacted in Virginia at this time. These instances, among many, many others, I note in my diary, that my children's children may know what we suffer during this unnatural war. Sheridan does not mean that [Gen. David] Hunter and [Gen. Benjamin] Butler shall bear the palm of cruelty—honours will at least be divided. I fear, from appearances , that he will exceed them, before his reign of terror is over. —— says she feels as if she were nightly encircled by fire—camp-fires, picket-fires, with here and there stacks of wheat burning, and a large fire now and then in the distance, denote the destruction of something—it may be a dwelling, or it may be a barn.

September 1—[Grace McGuire] has this day entered on her duties as clerk in the "Surgeon-General's Department," which she obtained with very little trouble on her part.[24] We had always objected to her applying for an office, because we were afraid of the effect of sedentary employment on her health; but now it seems necessary to us, as the prices of provisions and house-rent have become so very high. Providence has dealt most mercifully with us from the beginning of the war; at first it seemed to be the pleasure of our friends as well as ourselves that we should be with them; then, when it became evident that the war would continue, Mr. [McGuire] obtained an office, which gave us a limited, but independent support. Then, when prices became high, and we could not live on the salary, the chaplaincy came, with a little better income. As provisions continued to increase in price, and our prospect seemed very poor for the winter, my office was obtained without the least effort on my part, though I had often sought one in the Treasury without success; and now, when difficulties seem to be increasing with great scarcity of provisions, the way is again made comparatively easy. So it seems that the Lord intends us to work for our daily bread, and to be independent, but not to abound.

10th—We must give up our rooms by the last of this month, and the question now arises about our future abode. We are searching hither and thither. We had thought for a week past that our arrangements were most delightfully made, and that we had procured, together with Dr. M. and Colonel G,[25] six rooms in a house on Franklin Street. The arrangement had been made, and the proprietor gone from town. The M[ason]s and ourselves were to take four rooms in the third story; the back parlour on the first floor was to be used by all parties; and Colonel G[arnett] would take the large front basement room as his chamber, and at his request, as our dining-room, as we could not be allowed to use the upper chambers as eating-rooms. Our large screen was to be transferred to the Colonel's bedstead and washing apparatus, and the rest of the room furnished in dining-room style. These rooms are all furnished and carpeted. Nothing could have suited us better, and we have been for some days anticipating our comfortable winter-quarters. The M[ason]s have left town with the blissful assurance of a nice home; to add to it all, the family of the proprietor is all that we could desire as friends and companions. Last night I met with a friend, who asked me where we had obtained rooms. I described them with great alacrity and pleasure. She looked surprised, and said, "Are you not mistaken? Those rooms are already occupied." "Impossible," said I; "we have engaged them." She shook her head, saying, "There was some mistake; they have been occupied for some days by a family, who say that they have rented them." None but persons situated exactly in the same way can imagine our disappointment. The Colonel looked aghast; Mr. [McGuire] pronounced it a mistake; the girls were indignant, and I went a little farther, and pronounced it bad treatment. This morning I went up before breakfast to hear the truth of the story—the family is still absent, but the servants confirmed the statement by saying that a family had been in the rooms that we looked at for a week, and that a gentleman, a third party, had been up the day before to claim the rooms, and said that the party occupying them had no right to them, and must be turned out. The servant added that this third gentleman had sent up a dray with flour which was now in the house, and had put his coal in the coal-cellar. All this seems passing strange. Thus have we but three weeks before us in which to provide ourselves with an almost impossible shelter. The "Colonel" has written to Mr. [Powell][26] for an explanation, and the M[ason]s have been apprised of their dashed hopes. I often think how little the possessors of the luxurious homes of Richmond know of the difficulties with which refugees are surrounded, and how little we ever appreciated the secure home-feeling which we had all enjoyed before the war began. We have this evening been out again in pursuit of quarters. The advertisements of "Rooms to let" were sprinkled over the morning papers, so that one could scarcely believe that there would be any difficulty in our being supplied. A small house that would accommodate our whole party, five or six rooms in a large house, or two rooms for ourselves, if it were impossible to do better, would answer out purpose—any thing for a comfortable home. The first advertisement alluded to basement rooms—damp, and redolent of rheumatism. The next was more attractive—good rooms, well furnished, and up *but two* flights of stairs; but the price was enormous, far beyond the means of any of the party, and so evidently an extortion designed to take all that could be extracted from the necessity of others, that we turned from our hard-featured proprietor with disgust. The rooms of the third advertisement had already been rented, and the fourth seemed more like answering our purpose than we had seen. There were only two rooms, and though small, and rather dark, yet persons whose shelter was likely to be the "blue vault of heaven"[27] could not be very particular. The price, too, was exorbitant, but with a little more self-denial it might be paid. The next inquiry was about kitchen, servant's room and coal-house; but we got no further than the answer about the kitchen. The lady said there was no kitchen that we could possibly use; her stove was small, and she required it all; we must either be supplied from a restaurant, or do our own cooking in one of the rooms. As neither plan was to be thought of, we ended the parley. A *part of a kitchen* is indispensable, though perhaps the most annoying thing to which refugees are subjected. The mistress is generally polite enough, but save me from the self-sufficient cook. "I would like to oblige you, madam, but you can't have loaf-bread to-morrow morning, because my mistress has ordered loaf-bread and rolls, and our stove is small;" or, "No, madam, you can't '*bile*' a ham, nor anything else to-day, because it is our washing-day," or, "No, ma'am, you can't have biscuits for tea, because the stove is cold, and I've got no time to heat it." So that we must either submit, or go to mistress for redress, and probably find none, both of whom have us very much in their power. As I walked home from this unsuccessful effort, it was nearly dark; the gas was being lighted in hall, parlour, and chamber. I looked in as I passed, and saw cheerful countenances collecting around centre-tables, or sitting here and there on handsome porticos or marble steps, to enjoy the cool evening breeze—countenances of those whose families I had known from infancy, and who were still numbered among my friends and acquaintances. I felt sad, and asked myself, if those persons could realize the wants of others, would they not cheerfully rent some of their extra rooms? Rooms once opened on grand occasions, and now, as such occasions are few and far between, not opened at all for weeks and months together.

Would they not cheerfully remove some of their showy and fragile furniture for a time, and allow those who had once been accustomed to as large rooms of their own to occupy and take care of them? The *rent* would perhaps be no object with them, but their kindness might be twice blessed—the refugees would be made comfortable and happy, and the money might be applied to the wants of the soldiers or the city poor. And yet a third blessing might be added—the luxury of doing good. Ah, they would then find that the "quality of mercy is not strained," but that it would indeed, like the "gentle dew from heaven,"[28] fall into their very souls, and diffuse a happiness of which they know not. These thoughts filled my mind until I reached the present home of a refugee friend from Washington.[29] It was very late, but I thought I would run in, and see if she could throw any light upon our difficulties. I was sorry to find that she was in a similar situation, her husband having that day been notified that their rooms would be required on the first of October. We compared notes of our room-hunting experiences, and soon found ourselves laughing heartily over occurrences and conversations which were both provoking and ridiculous. I then wended my way home, amid brilliantly lighted houses and badly lighted streets. Squads of soldiers were sauntering along, impregnating the air with tobacco-smoke; men were standing at every corner, lamenting the fall of Atlanta or the untimely end of General Morgan.[30] I too often caught a word, conveying blame of the President for having removed General Johnston.[31] This blame always irritates me, because the public became so impatient at General Johnston's want of action, that they were clamorous for his removal. For weeks the President was abused without measure because he was not removed, and now the same people are using the same terms towards him because the course which they absolutely required at his hands has disappointed them. The same people who a month ago curled the lip in scorn at General Johnston's sloth and want of energy, and praised General Hood's course from the beginning of the war, now shrug their unmilitary shoulders, whose straps have never graced a battle-field, and pronounce the change "unfortunate and uncalled for." General Hood, they say, was an "admirable Brigadier," but his "promotion was most unfortunate;" while General Johnston's "Fabian policy"[32] is now pronounced the very thing for the situation—the course which would have saved Atlanta, and have made all right. This may all be true, but it is very distressing to hear it harped upon now; quite as much so as it was six weeks ago to hear the President called obstinate, because he was ruining the country by not removing General J[ohnston]. But I will no longer make myself uneasy about what I hear, for I have implicit confidence in our leaders, both in the Cabinet and on the field. Were I a credulous woman, and ready to believe all that I hear in the office, in the hospital, in my visits and on the streets, I should think that Richmond is now filled with the most accomplished military geniuses on which the sun shines. Each man expresses himself, as an old friend would say, with the most "dogmatic infallibility" of the conduct of the President, General Lee, General Johnston, General Hampton, General Beauregard, General Wise, together with all the other lights of every degree. It is true that there are as many varieties of opinion as there are men expressing them, or I should profoundly regret that so much military light should be obscured among the shades of the Richmond Departments; but I do wish that some of them would refrain from condemning the acts of our leaders, and from uttering such awful prophesies, provided the President or General Lee does not do so and so. Although I do not believe their forebodings, yet the reiteration of such opinions, in the most assured tones, makes me nervous and uneasy. I would that all such men could be sent to the field; I think at least a regiment could be spared from Richmond, for then the women of the city at least would be more peaceful.

12th—After holding a consultation with a particular friend of Dr. M[ason], together with Mr. [McGuire] and the "Colonel," we have determined to await the decision of Mr. [Powell] about the rooms on Franklin Street, and not to attempt to get others, hoping that as there are so many competitors for them, we may be considered the rightful claimants. There can be no doubt that they were promised to us.

The morning papers report "all quiet" at Petersburg, except that shells are daily thrown into the city, and that many of the women and children are living in tents in the country, so as to be out of reach of shells.

The death of the bold and dashing General Morgan is deeply regretted. He has done us great service throughout the war, but particularly since his wonderful escape from his incarceration in the Ohio Penitentiary. It seems so short a time since he was here, all classes delighting to do him reverence. It is hard for us to give up such good men.

General Hood telegraphs that the inhabitants of Atlanta have been ordered to leave their homes, to go they know not whither.[33] Lord, how long must we suffer such things? I pray that the enemy's hands may be stayed, and that they may be driven from our fair borders to their own land. I ask not vengeance upon them, but that they may be driven to their own homes, and that we may be henceforward and forever a separate people.

16th—A visit to-day from my brother Dr. [William S. R.] B[rockenbrough], who bears the utter desolation of his home quietly, though so sudden a change of circumstances is of course very depressing. He tells me that he has lately had a visit from a very interesting young South Carolinian, who came to look for the body of his brother. The two brothers were being educated in Germany when the war broke out; and as soon as they were of military age, with the consent of their parents, they hastened home to take part in their country's struggle. In one of the cavalry fights in Hanover [County], in May last, one brother was killed and the other, "not being able to find the body at the time, was now seeking it." His mother was on the ocean returning to her home, and he could not meet her with the information that her son's body could not be found. He had heard that some of the fallen had been buried at S[ummer] H[ill] or W[estwood]. He mentioned that their intimate friend, young Middleton, had fallen in the same fight. Mr. Middleton had been buried at S[ummer] H[ill], and his grave had been marked by Mrs. N[ewton]; but young Pringle (the name of the brothers) had been carried to neither place. Mr. Pringle had seen in a New York paper an account given by a Yankee officer of several wounded Confederates who had been captured, and having died on their way to the "White House,"[34] they were buried by the roadside, and he had some reason to believe that his brother was among them. It was then remembered that there were three graves on the opposite side of the Pamunky River, and one was marked with the name "*Tingle.*" It was an excessively warm Sunday morning; but as the young soldier's furlough only extended to the following day, there was no time to be lost. Dr. B[rockenbrough] and the brother set out upon their melancholy mission, having obtained a cart, one or two men, and given an order at a neighbouring carpenter's shop for a coffin. After crossing the river they found the three graves, at the place designated, in the county of King William. The one marked "Tingle" contained the body of a Federal and one of a Confederate soldier, but not the brother. The next one opened was not the right one; but the third contained the much-loved remains, which were easily recognized by the anxious brother. Tenderly and gently, all wrapped in his blanket, he was transferred from his shallow grave to his soldier's coffin, and then conveyed to S[ummer] H[ill], to be placed by his friend Middleton. It was now night, the moon shone brightly, and all was ready. The families from both houses gathered around the grave. "Slowly and sadly they laid him down." No minister of the Gospel was near to perform the services. Dr. B[rockenbrough] stood at the head with a Prayer-Book for the purpose, but his defective sight obliged him to yield the book to Mrs. N[ewton], who, with a clear, calm voice read by the light of a single lantern the beautiful ritual of the Episcopal Church. The grave was filled in solemn silence, the brother standing at the foot.[35] When all was over, the young ladies and children of the families advanced with wreaths and bouquets, and in an instant the soldier's grave was a mound of fresh flowers. The brother could no longer restrain his feelings; he was completely overwhelmed, and was obliged to retire to his room, where he could indulge them freely. Next morning he returned to his command, after a leave-taking in which the feelings expressed by all parties evinced more of the friendship of years than the acquaintance of hours. It seems strange indeed that this scene, so similar to that of the burial of the lamented Captain Latane, should have occurred at the same place. But who could relate, who could number the sad scenes of this war? Many such have probably occurred in various parts of the country.

18th—Nothing yet from Mr. [Powell] about our rooms. All the furnished rooms that I have seen, except those, would cost us from $100 to $110 per month for each room, which, of course, we cannot pay; but we will try and not be anxious overmuch, for the Lord has never let us want comforts since we left our own dear home, and if we use the means which He has given us properly and in His fear, He will not desert us now.

I went with Mr. [McGuire] as usual this morning to the "Officers' Hospital," where he read a part of the service and delivered an address to such patients among the soldiers as were well enough to attend. I acted as his chorister, and when the services were over, and he went around to the bedsides of the patients, I crossed the street, as I have done several times before, to the cemetery—the old "Shockoe Hill Cemetery."[36] It is, to me, the most interesting spot in the city. It is a melancholy thought, that, after an absence of thirty years, I am almost a stranger in my native place. In this cemetery I go from spot to spot, and find the names that were the household words of my childhood and youth; the names of my father's and mother's friends; of the friends of my sisters, and of my own school-days. The first that struck me was that of the venerable and venerated Bishop [Richard Channing] Moore, on the monument erected by the church; then, that of his daughter, the admirable Miss Christian; then the monument to Colonel [Jacquelin] Ambler, erected by his children. Mrs. Ambler lies by him. Mr. and Mrs. Chapman Johnson, Judge and Mrs. [William] Cabell, Mr. and Mrs. John Wickham, surrounded by their children, who were the companions of my youth; also, their lovely grand-daughter, Mrs. W. H. F. Lee, who passed away last winter, at an early age, while her husband was prisoner of war. Near them is the grave of the Hon. Benjamin Watkins Leigh; of Judge and Mrs. [Robert Conway] Stanard, and of their gifted son; of dear Mrs. Henningham Lyons and her son James, from whose untimely end she never recovered; of our sweet friend, Mrs. Lucy Green. Then there is the handsome monument of Mrs. Abram Warwick and the grave of her son, dear Clarence, who died so nobly at Gaines's Mill in 1862.[37] His grave seems to be always covered with fresh flowers, a beautiful offering to one whose young life was so freely given to his country. Again I stood beside the tombs of two friends, whom I dearly loved, Mrs. Virginia Heth and Mrs. Mary Ann Barney, whose graves are also there. Then the tomb of our old friend, Mr. James Rawlings, and those of Mr. and Mrs. Herbert A. Claiborne and their daughter, Mary Burnet. Just by them is the newly-made grave of our sweet niece, Mary Anna, the wife of H. Augustine Claiborne, freshly turfed and decked with the flowers she loved so dearly. A little farther on lies my young cousin, Virginia, wife of Major J[ohn] H[ayes] Clairborne, and her two little daughters. But why should I go on? Time would fail me to enumerate all the loved and lost. Their graves look so peaceful in that lovely spot. Most of them died before war came to distress them. The names of two persons I cannot omit, before whose tombs I pause with a feeling of veneration for their many virtues. One was that of Mrs. [Elizabeth] Sully, my music-teacher, a lady who was known and respected by the whole community for her admirable character, accompanied by the most quiet and gentle manner. The other was that of Mr. Joseph Danforth, the humble but excellent friend of my precious father. The cemetery at Hollywood is of later date, though many very dear to me repose amid its beautiful shades.

But enough of the past and of sadness. I must now turn to busy life again, and note a little victory, of which General Lee telegraphed yesterday, by which we gained some four hundred prisoners, many horses and wagons, and 2,500 beeves.[38] These last are most acceptable to our commissariat!

The Southern Army are having an armistice of ten days, for the inhabitants of Atlanta to get off from their homes. Exiled by Sherman, my heart bleeds for them. May the good Lord have mercy upon them, and have them in His holy keeping!

21st—Bad news this morning.[39] General Early has had a defeat in the Valley near Winchester, and has fallen back to Strasburg. Our loss reported heavy. Major-General Rodes killed, and Brigadier-General Godwin and General Fitz Lee wounded. No other casualties heard of; and I dread to hear more.

28th—Mr. P[owell] came home, and at once decided that we were entitled to the rooms. By this arrangement we are greatly relieved. The family who occupies them have moved off, and Mr. P[owell] having convinced the third party of his mistake, has taken off his hands the coal and flour which he had stowed away, and now all is straight. The "Colonel" and ourselves moved our goods and chattels to these rooms yesterday. The M[ason]s will be here in a day or two. We have a long walk to our offices, but it is very near my hospital. Mr. [McGuire]'s hospital is very far from every point, as it is on the outskirts of the city; but he thinks the walk is conducive to his health, so that we are, upon the whole, very comfortable.

October 10—I am cast down by hearing that J. P.[40] has been captured; he was caught while scouting in the enemy's lines, on James River. Poor child! I feel very, very anxious about him.

Our army in the Valley has regained its foothold, the enemy having retreated. E. C.[41] had his horse killed under him near Waynesborough, but he escaped unhurt.

The Federal Army below Richmond advanced a few days ago, and took "Fort Harrison."[42] We live now amid perpetual firing of cannon. The loss of Fort Harrison is, I am afraid, a very serious loss to us. The enemy made a second advance, which has been handsomely repulsed. They seem to be putting forth their utmost efforts against us. I pray that our armies may be able to resist them and drive them to their own land.

12th—The armies around Richmond remain quiet. Butler is digging the canal at "Dutch Gap,"[43] and Grant is fortifying "Fort Harrison" most vigorously. General Rosser has had a little reverse in the Valley, losing some guns.[44] He had a cavalry fight, overcame the enemy, and drove them for miles; but encountering a body of infantry which was too much for him, he had to retreat, leaving his guns to the enemy.

The hospitals are full of the wounded; my afternoons are very much engaged nursing them. I was very sorry yesterday to find R. S. painfully wounded.

13th—The day has passed as usual—six hours in the Commissary Department, and the remainder occupied in various ways. Rumours of fighting below Richmond; we hear the cannon, but it is said to be merely a skirmish.

20th—Nothing new in the field. Armies quiet; perhaps preparing for dreadful work. I got a note last night from J[efferson] P[helps], written with a pencil. He and other prisoners are working ten hours a day on "Dutch Gap Canal." They work under the fire of our own batteries. Poor fellow! My heart yearns over him.

26th—The armies around Richmond continue quiet. General Early's second misfortune was very depressing to us all.[45] We are now recovering from it. I trust that God will turn it all to our good. A striking and admirable address from him to his soldiers was in the morning papers.[46] Oh, I trust they will retrieve their fortunes hereafter.

28th—Very much interested lately in the hospitals; not only in our own, "the Robertson hospital," but in Mr. [McGuire]'s "the officers' hospital."

He has just told me of a case which had interested me deeply. An officer from the far South was brought in mortally wounded. He had lost both legs in a fight below Petersburg. The poor fellow suffered excessively; could not be still a moment; and was evidently near his end. His brother, who was with him, exhibited the bitterest grief, watching and waiting on him with silent tenderness and flowing tears. Mr. [McGuire] was glad to find that he was not unprepared to die. He had been a professor of religion for some years, and told him that he was suffering too much to think on that or any other subject, but he constantly tried to look to God for mercy. Mr. [McGuire] then recognized him, for the first time, as a patient who had been in the hospital last spring, and whose admirable character had then much impressed him. He was a gallant and brave officer, yet so kind and gentle to those under his control that his men were deeply attached to him, and the soldier who nursed him showed his love by his anxious care of his beloved captain. After saying to him a few words about Christ and his free salvation, offering up a fervent prayer in which he seemed to join, and watching the sad scene for a short time, Mr. [McGuire] left him for the night. The surgeons apprehended that he would die before morning, and so it turned out; at the chaplain's early call there was nothing in his room but the chilling signal of the empty "hospital bunk." He was buried that day, and we trust will be found among the redeemed in the day of the Lord. This, it was thought, would be the last of this good man; but in the dead of night came hurriedly a single carriage to the gate of the hospital. A lone woman, tall, straight, and dressed in deep mourning, got quickly out, and moved rapidly up the steps into the large hall, where, meeting the guard, she asked anxiously: "Where's Captain T?" Taken by surprise, the man answered hesitatingly, "Captain T. is dead, madam, and was buried to-day." This terrible announcement was as a thunderbolt at the very feet of the poor lady, who fell to the floor as one dead. Starting up, oh, how she made that immense building ring with her bitter lamentations! Worn down with apprehension and weary with travelling over a thousand miles by day and night, without stopping for a moment's rest, and wild with grief, she could hear no voice of sympathy—she regarded not the presence of one or many; she told the story of her married life, as if she were alone—how her husband was the best man that ever lived; how everybody loved him; how kind he was to all; how devoted to herself; how he loved his children, took care of, and did every thing for them; how, from her earliest years almost, she had loved him as herself; how tender he was of her, watching over her in sickness, never seeming to weary of it, never to be unwilling to make any sacrifice for her comfort and happiness; how that, when the telegraph brought the dreadful news that he was dangerously wounded, she never waited an instant nor stopped a moment by the way, day nor night, and now "I drove as fast as the horses could come from the depot to this place, and he is dead and buried!—I never shall see his face again! What *shall* I do?—But where is he buried?" They told her where. "I must go there; he must be taken up; I must see him!" "But, madam, you can't see him; he has been buried some hours." "But I must see him; I can't live without seeing him; I must hire some one to go and take him up; can't you get some one to take him up? I'll pay him well; just get some men to take him up. I *must* take him home; he must go home with me. The last thing I said to his children was, that they must be good children, and I would bring their father home, and they are waiting for him now! He must go; I can't go without him; I can't meet his children without him!" and so, with her woman's heart, she could not be turned aside—nothing could alter her purpose. The next day she had his body taken up and embalmed. She watched by it until every thing was ready, and then carried him back to his own house and his children, only to seek a grave for the dead father close by those he loved, among kindred and friends in the fair sunny land he died to defend.

Many painfully interesting scenes occur, which I would like so much to write in my diary, but time fails me at night, and my hours of daylight are very closely occupied.

November 13—The "military situation" seems very much the same. Some cheering intimations from Georgia. Hood has made movements on Sherman's flank,[47] and Forrest upon his rear, which it is thought promise most valuable results, but nothing final has been yet accomplished, and we may be too sanguine.

General Price is still successful in Missouri.[48]

In the Valley of Virginia an immense amount of private property has been destroyed.[49] Sheridan, glorying in his shame, boasts of, and probably magnifies, what has been done in that way. He telegraphs to Grant that he has burned 2,000 barns. The Lord shorten his dreadful work, and have mercy upon the sufferers!

Nothing new about Richmond. A few days ago the enemy made several attempts to advance upon the Darbytown road, and were handsomely repulsed. The firing of cannon is so common a sound that it is rather remarkable when we do not hear it.

Mr. [McGuire] has been telling us of some other interesting cases in his hospital; among them, that of Captain Brown,[50] of North Carolina, has awakened our sympathies. He came into the hospital bright and cheerful, with every appearance of speedy recovery. He talked a great deal of his wife and six children at home, one of whom he had never seen. Knowing that his wife would be sick, he had obtained a furlough, and made arrangements to go home, but the recent battles coming on, he would not leave his post. Through many a hard-fought action God had kept him unharmed; he had never been touched by a solitary weapon, until he began to feel that here was not the slightest danger to him, even amid the harvest of death. He wrote that he should be at home as soon as this fight was over; but it was not to be so, and he soon came into the hospital severely wounded. As he lay upon his bed of suffering, the image of his dear wife in her sickness and sorrow, and then with her new-born infant, seemed constantly before him. "I intended to be there," he would say dreamily; "I made all my arrangements to be there; I know she wants me; she wrote to me to come to her; oh, I wish I was there, but no I can't go, but I hope I did right; I hope it is all right." A letter from her, speaking of herself and infant as doing well, relieved his anxiety, and he tried to bear the disappointment with patience, still hoping soon to be at home. God, however, had ordered it otherwise. The word had gone forth, "He shall not return to his house, neither shall his place know him any more."[51] Gangrene appeared, and it was melancholy to see his strength giving way, his hopes fading, and death coming steadily on. He was a professor of religion, and Mr. [McGuire] says he was always ready to hear the word of God, and, though anxious to live, yet he put himself into the Lord's hand, with humble faith and hope, such as may give his friends assurance that death was a gain to him.

The war news seems encouraging. Many persons are very despondent, but I do not feel so—perhaps I do not understand the military signs. Our men below Richmond have certainly had many successes of late. Sheridan, instead of capturing Lynchburg, as he promised, is retreating down the Valley.[52] In the South, the army of Tennessee is in Sherman's rear, and Forrest still carries every thing before him. General Price seems to be doing well in

Missouri; Arkansas and Texas seem to be all right. Kentucky, too, (poor Kentucky!) seems more hopeful. Then why should we despond? Maryland, alas for Maryland! The tyrant's heel appears too heavy for her, and we grievously fear that the prospect of her union with the South is rapidly passing away. If we must give her up, it will not be without sorrow and mortification. We shall mournfully bewail her dishonor and shame. If her noble sons who have come to the South must return, they will take with them our gratitude and admiration for their gallant bearing in many a hard-fought battle. Readily will we receive those who choose to remain among us; and in holy ground take care of her honoured dead, who so freely gave their lives for Southern rights. The Potomac may seem to some the natural boundary between North and South; but it is hard to make up one's mind yet to the entire surrender of our sister State; and if we could, gladly would we hope for Maryland, even as we hope for the Southern Confederacy herself.

21st—We attended hospital services yesterday as usual. There are few patients, and none are very ill. On Friday night a most unexpected death took place, under very painful circumstances. A young adjutant lost his life by jumping out of a window at the head of his bed, about ten feet from the ground. His attendants were a sister, brother, and two servants. His suffering with a wound in his foot had been so intense that he would not allow any one to touch it except the ward-master, who handled it with the greatest tenderness. Yet while his attendants were asleep (for they thought it unnecessary to be up with him all night) he managed to get up, raise the window, and throw himself out, without disturbing any of them. His mind was no doubt unsettled, as it had been before. He lived almost an hour after being found. His poor sister was wild with grief and horror, and his other attendants dreadfully shocked.

23d—Military movements are kept very much in the dark. Nothing going on about Richmond, except cannonading, particularly at Dutch Gap.

Sherman is moving across Georgia,[53] in direction of Milledgeville, looking towards Savannah, or perhaps Charleston, or to some intermediate point on the coast, where he may, if necessary, meet with reinforcements and supplies from Federal shipping already there, or on their way down the Atlantic coast for that very purpose. Efforts are being made by the Governors of South Carolina and Georgia to arrest him. Beauregard, too, has made a short, stirring address,[54] assuring them that he was hastening down to their aid, and that with proper exertions which might be made on their part, the destruction of the enemy would be certain. Nothing equal to the demands of these trying times has yet been done by any of the authorities. Oh that they would strain every nerve to put a stop to this bold and desolating invader! It would require united effort, made without delay. No hesitation, no doubting and holding back must there be; every human being capable of bearing arms must fly to the rescue; all the stores of every kind should be destroyed or removed; bridges burned, roads torn up or obstructed; every difficulty should be thrown in the way. He should be harassed day and night, that he might be delayed, and entrapped, and ruined. Oh that these things could be done! It may be a woman's thought, but I believe that had Georgia one tithe of the experience of the ruined, homeless, Virginians, she would exert every fibre of her frame to destroy the enemy; she would have no delusive hope of escape. I trust that the doctrines of [Joseph E.] Brown, [Alexander H.] Stephens, and such like,[55] are not now bearing their bitter fruits! That the people of patriotic Georgia have not been rendered unfit for the sacrifices and dangers of this fearful day, when every man is required to stand in the deadly breach, and every earthly interest, even life itself, must be surrendered rather than yield to the barbarous foe, by their treasonable doctrines of reconstruction, reunion, etc. Oh, I trust not; and I hope that our now uncertain mails may bring information that all Georgia and South Carolina are aroused to their awful condition.

December 4, Sunday—We attended this evening the funeral of Colonel Angus W. McDonald,[56] the relative of Mr. [McGuire]. His is a sad story. He was educated at West Point, but in early life resigned his position in the regular army and joined a company of fur traders, went with them to the Rocky Mountains, where he led an adventurous life, well suited to his excitable temper. For years his life was full of adventure, with the broad heavens for his roof and the cold earth for his couch. With a bold spirit and great muscular power, he soon acquired extensive influence with the Indian tribes among which he moved, and was chosen as chief of one of them, where he was known as the "Big Warrior." As such he led his braves to many a hard-fought battle, and taught surrounding tribes to fear him and them, by such courage and prowess as always so deeply impress the savage mind. Many incidents of his life among the Indians are full of interest. On one occasion, having received an injury from a neighbouring tribe, he sent [word] to them that he was coming to settle with them for it, and that they must meet him for the purpose, at a certain time and place. Accordingly, all the warriors were assembled and seated in due form, at the proper distance from and around a central post, ready and waiting for the conference. At the appointed time, the "Big Warrior," in full dress, made his appearance, and striding through to the centre of the dark, silent circle, he struck his tomahawk deep into the "post." And looking quietly but sternly around from one gloomy warrior to another, he in a few words told them why he was there, and what he required of them. "You have insulted me," said he; "you robbed some of my men, and you killed two of them; you must restore the goods and give up the murderers, or you must *fight* it out, and I am here for that purpose." His imposing appearance, his boldness, the justice of his cause, and his steady purpose of retaliating to the full, so awed them, that his terms were promptly assented to, and he quickly returned to his people with the most ample satisfaction for the injuries they had received. He grew weary of his life after some years, and determined to return to his early home and associations. Acting upon this impulse, we next find him in Romney, Hampshire County, among his kindred, where he quietly resumed the duties of civilized life, was married, and practised law for years. Still restless and different from other men, he was constantly speculating in one thing and another—politics, property, etc. At one time he was in the Virginia Legislature, and controlled the vote of his county in a way new to our republican experience. For this purpose he got possession of a large mountain region, filling it with a population whom he ruled very much as a Scottish chief would have done in his ancestral Highlands, and using their votes to decide any public controversy in which he chose to engage. This, of course, did not last long; it was too much opposed to the public views and feelings, and under the consequent changes around him, he found it expedient to return to private life. From this retirement, however, his native State soon recalled him, as one of the three commissioners to settle the boundary line between Maryland and Virginia. In his capacity as such, the Virginia Legislature sent him to England to examine the public records bearing upon this subject. He discharged the duties of his mission with ability and success, as his voluminous report will show. The present war found him residing with his large family near Winchester, his native place. The Confederate Government having given him the commission of a colonel, it was hoped that he would be of great use in the bloody contest; but a discipline better suited in its severity to Indian warriors than to our high-minded volunteers, together with advanced years and declining health, disappointed the expectations of himself and his friends. He found, indeed, that bodily infirmity alone rendered him unfit for active service, and this, with other difficulties, made it proper to break up his command. Thus it happened that when that brute, [Gen. David] Hunter, marched through Lexington, spreading desolation in his path, Colonel McDonald, then a resident of the town, believing that the enemy, who had manifested great harshness towards him, injuring his property near Winchester, etc., would arrest him, determined to keep out of their way, and with others took refuge in a neighbouring forest. Here, unfortunately, the enemy found him, with his son Harry, a youth of some sixteen years, and took them prisoners. It is somewhat singular that the presence of this devoted son caused the father's arrest. He had always determined that he would never surrender, never be taken alive. But when he looked at this boy, who had fought so nobly by his side, and who would surely be sacrificed if he refused to surrender, he could fight no longer; it seemed to him, as he afterwards said, as the voice from Heaven which stayed the armed hand of Abraham, and he could not fire another shot. Father and son were thus captured. Harry escaped in a day or two; but the father was tied and dragged along at a rapid pace towards the Maryland line. When he could no longer walk a step, they allowed him to get into a wagon with nothing to rest upon but some old iron, rough tools, etc. Thus they hastened him to Cumberland, Maryland, where they hand-cuffed him and put him into solitary confinement; thence he was hurried to Wheeling, where he was again, with his manacles on, shut up in a dungeon, seven feet by ten, with nothing to relieve the sufferings incident to such a fate, nothing to expect or hope for, but the bitterest cruelty. From this dreadful captivity he was released two or three weeks ago, and reached the house of his daughter, in this city, with health, bad for years, now worse than ever, and constitution entirely broken by hard and cruel bondage. Cheered by freedom, and the society of his children who were here, he flattered himself that he would be enabled to return to his home of refuge in Lexington. This hope proved delusive. It soon appeared that his whole nervous system was shattered, and his end rapidly approaching; his wife was sent for, but did not arrive until the day after he died.[57] Not dreaming of what awaited her, she came full of hope and joy at the anticipated meeting. But who may describe the grief which overwhelmed her on her arrival? His checkered life was closed in his sixty-sixth year. The funeral took place this evening at St. Paul's Church. He was buried with military honors at Hollywood Cemetery. While manacled in the horrid dungeon, his only petition was to be allowed to keep a Bible, from which he professed to have derived great peace and comfort. His family think that he returned from prison a changed man. His spirit, which was naturally stern, had become gentle and loving, and strangely grateful to every being who showed him the least kindness. The Bible was still his daily companion; from it he seemed to derive great comfort and an abiding faith in Christ his Saviour.

17th—The military movements are important, but to what they tend we know not. More troops have been added from Sheridan to Grant, and Early to Lee, and Sherman has crossed Georgia with little opposition or loss. Our last news is, that he has taken Fort McAllister,[58] some miles below Savannah. What fate awaits that city we tremble to think of. A raid on Bristol and up the railroad, towards Saltville, has alarmed us for the salt-works;[59] but General Breckinridge having turned up in the right place, suddenly appeared in their front and drove them off, to the great relief of the public mind.

24th—Savannah has been evacuated, without loss to us, except of some stores, which could not be removed. The city was surrendered by its mayor, Arnold by name, and he seems to be worthy of the traitorous name.[60] Our troops marched towards Charleston. Savannah was of little use to us for a year past, it has been so closely blockaded, and its surrender relieves troops which were there for its defence, which may be more useful elsewhere; but the moral effect of its fall is dreadful. The enemy are encouraged, and our people depressed. I never saw them more so.

On the 22d General Rosser beat a division of the enemy near Harrisonburg,[61] and on the 23d General Lomax repulsed and severely punished another, near Gordonsville.[62]

To-morrow is Christmas day.[63] Our girls and B[etty][64] have gone to Cedar Hill to spend a week. Our office has suspended its labours, and I am anticipating very quiet holidays. A Christmas present has just been handed me from my sweet young friend S. W.[65]—a box filled with all manner of working materials, which are now so scarce and expensive, with a beautiful mat for my toilet at the bottom of it. Christmas will come on the Sabbath. The "Colonel" is gone, but J[ames McGuire] and G[race McGuire] will take their usual Sunday dinner, and I have gotten up a little dessert, because Christmas would not be Christmas without something better than usual; but it is a sad season to me. On last Christmas our dear R. T. C[olston] was buried; and yesterday I saw my sweet young cousin E. M.[66] die, and to-morrow expect to attend her funeral. Full of brightness and animation, full of Christian hope and charity, she was the life of her father's house, the solace and comfort of her already afflicted mother, one of the many mothers whose first-born has fallen a sacrifice to the war. This interesting girl, with scarcely a warning, has passed into heaven, leaving a blank in the hearts of her family never to be filled.

26th—The sad Christmas has passed away. J[ames] and G[race] were with us, and very cheerful. We exerted ourselves to be so too. The Church services in the morning were sweet and comforting. St. Paul's was dressed most elaborately and beautifully with evergreens; all looked as usual; but there is much sadness on account of the failure of the South to keep Sherman back. When we got home our family circle was small, but pleasant. The Christmas turkey and ham were not. We had aspired to a turkey, but finding the prices range from $50 to $100 in the market on Saturday, we contented ourselves with roast-beef and the various little dishes which Confederate times have made us believe are tolerable substitutes for the viands of better days. At night I treated our little party to tea and ginger cakes—two very rare indulgences; and but for the sorghum, grown in our own fields, the cakes would be an impossible indulgence. Nothing but the well-ascertained fact that Christmas comes but once a year would make such extravagance at all excusable. We propose to have a family gathering when the girls come home, on the day before or after New Year's day, (as that day will come on Sunday,) to enjoy together, and with one or two refugee friends, the contents of a box sent the girls by a young officer who captured it from the enemy, consisting of white sugar, raisins, preserves, pickles, spices, etc. They threaten to give us a plum-cake, and I hope they will carry it out, particularly if we have any of our army friends with us. Poor fellows, how they enjoy our plain dinners when they come, and how we love to see them enjoy them! Two meals a day has become the universal system among refugees, and many citizens, from necessity. The want of our accustomed tea or coffee is very much felt by the elders. The rule with us is only to have tea when sickness makes it necessary, and the headaches gotten up about dark have become the joke of the family.

A country lady, from one of the few spots in all Virginia where the enemy has never been, and consequently where they retain their comforts, asked me gravely why we did not substitute milk for tea. She could scarcely believe me when I told her that we had not milk more than twice in eighteen months, and then it was sent by a country friend. It is now $4 a quart.

28th—A bright spot in our military horizon. The enemy's fleet of more than thirty gun-boats made a furious attack on Fort Fisher, near Wilmington, N. C., on the 24th (last Saturday);[67] they kept up an average fire of thirty shots per minute until night. On the 25th the attack was renewed, and on the 27th, after being three times repulsed, the enemy abandoned his position above Fort Fisher, and re-embarked. The damage done to us was very slight—only two guns disabled, and but few other casualties. Thus failed utterly this great expedition of land and sea forces, from which the Federal authorities and the whole North confidently expected such grand results. And so may it ever be; the Lord help us, and deliver us in every such hour of need.

Yesterday we had a pleasant little dinner-party at Dr. G[ibson]'s—so rare a thing now, that I must note it in my diary. Many nice things on the table were sent by country friends. What would we do without our country friends?[68] Their hearts seem warm and generous to those who are not so well off as themselves. They set a good example, which I trust will not be lost on us. Our relatives and friends, though they have been preyed upon by the enemy almost to exhaustion, never seem to forget us. Sausage from one, a piece of beef from another, a bushel of dried fruit, a turkey, etc., come ever and anon to our assistance. One can scarcely restrain tears of affection when it is remembered that these things are evidences of self-denial, and not given from their abundance, as at the beginning of the war. The soldiers are not forgotten by these country friends—those who remember the refugees are never forgetful of the soldiers. Take our people as a whole, they are full of generosity and patriotism. The speculators and money-makers of these trying times are a peculiar class, of which I neither like to speak, think, nor write; they are objects of my implacable disgust. They do not belong to our noble Southern patriots. They are with us, but not of us! I should think that a man who had made a fortune during the war would, when the war is over, wish to hide it, and not own his ill-gotten gains. I trust there are not many such. The year 1864 has almost passed away. Oh, what a fearful account it has rendered to Heaven! What calamities and sorrows crowd into its history, in this afflicted country of ours! God help us, and guide us onward and upward, for the Saviour's sake!

January 1st, 1865—At St. James's Church this morning. Our children came over from Union Hill[69] yesterday, to take their dinner from the contents of the captured box, and were detained by snow and rain. We were too much pleased to have them with us not to make it convenient to accommodate them, which we did with the assistance of our kind friend Mrs. [Elizabeth] P[aine]. To-morrow G[race] and myself will return to our offices, after a good rest, for which we are very thankful.

2d—This bitter cold morning, when we entered the office, we found that our good "Major" had provided us a New Year's treat of hot coffee. Of course we all enjoyed it highly, and were very grateful to him; and when I returned home, the first thing that met my eye was a box sent from the express office. We opened it, and found it a Christmas box, filled with nice and substantial things from a friend now staying in Buckingham County, for whom I once had an opportunity of doing some trifling kindness. The Lord is certainly taking care of us through His people. The refugees in some of the villages are much worse off than we are. We hear amusing stories of a friend in an inland place, where nothing can possibly be bought, hiring a skillet from a servant for one dollar per month, and other cooking utensils, which are absolutely necessary, at the same rate; another in the same village, whose health seems to require that she should drink something hot at night, has been obliged to resort to hot water, as she has neither tea, coffee, sugar, nor milk. These ladies belong to wealthy Virginia families. Many persons have no meat on their tables for months at a time; and they are the real patriots, who submit patiently, and without murmuring, to any privation, provided the country is doing well. The flesh-pots of Egypt have no charm for them; they look forward hopefully to the time when their country shall be disenthralled, never caring for the trials of the past or the present, provided they can hope for the future.

8th—Some persons in this beleaguered city seem crazed on the subject of gayety. In the midst of the wounded and dying, the low state of the commissariat, the anxiety of the whole country, the troubles of every kind by which we are surrounded, I am mortified to say that there are gay parties given in the city.[70] There are those denominated "starvation parties," where young persons meet for innocent enjoyment, and retire at a reasonable hour; but there are others where the most elegant suppers are served—cakes, jellies, ices in profusion, and meats of the finest kinds in abundance, such as might furnish a meal for a regiment of General Lee's army. I wish these things were not so, and that every extra pound of meat could be sent to the army. When returning from the hospital, after witnessing the dying scene of a brother whose young sister hung over him in agony, with my heart full of the sorrows of hospital-life, I passed a house where there were music and dancing. The revulsion of feeling was sickening. I thought of the gayety of Paris during the French Revolution, of the "cholera ball" in Paris, the ball at Brussels the night before the battle of Waterloo, and felt shocked that our own Virginians, at such a time, should remind me of scenes which we were wont to think only belonged to the lightness of foreign society. It seems to me that the army, when it hears of the gayety of Richmond, must think it heartless, particularly while it is suffering such hardships in her defence. The weddings, of which there are many, seem to be conducted with great quietness. We were all very much interested in a marriage which took place in this house a short time ago. Our sweet young friend, Miss A. P.,[71] was married to a Confederate States' surgeon from South Carolina. We assembled in the parlour, which was brilliantly lighted, before the dawn of day. The bride appeared in travelling costume; as soon as the solemn ceremony was done the folding-doors were thrown open, revealing a beautifully spread breakfast-table in the adjoining room. Breakfast being over, the bride and groom were hurried off to the cars, which were to bear them South. But, as usual in these war-times, the honeymoon was not to be uninterrupted. The furlough of the groom was of short continuance—the bright young bride will remain in the country with a sister, while he returns to his duty in the field. As soon as the wedding was over and the bridal party had gone, the excitement of the week had passed with us, leaving a blank in the house; but the times were too unquiet for a long calm—the gap was closed, and we returned to busy life. There seems to be a perfect mania on the subject of matrimony.[72] Some of the churches may be seen open and lighted almost every night for bridals, and wherever I turn I hear of marriages in prospect.

In peace Love tones the shepherd's reed;
In war he mounts the warrior's steed,[73]

sings the "Last Minstrel" of the Scottish days of romance; and I do not think that our modern warriors are a whit behind them either in love or war. My only wonder is, that they find the time for the love-making amid the storms of warfare. Just at this time, however, I suppose our valiant knights and ladies fair are taking advantage of the short respite, caused by the alternate snows and sunshine of our variable climate having made the roads impassable to Grant's artillery and baggage-wagons. A soldier in our hospital called to me as I passed his bed the other day. "I say, Mrs. [McGuire], when do you think my wound will be well enough for me to go to the country?" "Before very long, I hope." "But what does the doctor say, for I am mighty anxious to go?" I looked at his disabled limb, and talked to him hopefully of his being able to enjoy country air in a short time. "Well, try to get me up, for, you see, it ain't the country air I am after, but I wants to get married, and the lady don't know that I am wounded, and maybe she'll think I don't want to come." "Ah," said I, "but you must show her your scars, and if she is a girl worth having she will love you all the better for having bled for your country; and you must tell her that

> It is always the heart that is bravest in war,
> That is fondest and truest in love."[74]

He looked perfectly delighted with the idea; and as I passed him again he called out, "Lady, please stop a minute and tell me the verse over again, for, you see, when I do get there, if she is affronted, I wants to give her the prettiest excuse I can, and I think that verse is beautiful."

11th—Every thing seems unchanging in the outer world during the past few days. We were most delightfully surprised last night. While sitting quietly in the Colonel's room, (in the basement,) the window was suddenly thrown up, and in sprang our son J[ames], just returned from Northern captivity. Finding that we had changed our quarters since he was here, he walked up the street in search of us, and while stopping to ascertain the right house, he espied us through the half-open window shutter, and was too impatient for the preliminaries of ringing a bell and waiting for servants to open the door. He was in exuberant spirits, but much disappointed that his wife was not with us. So, after a short sojourn and a cup of tea, he went off to join her on "Union Hill." They both dined with us to-day. His confinement has not been so bad as we feared, from the treatment which many other prisoners had received, but it was disagreeable enough. He was among the surgeons in Winchester in charge of the sick and wounded; and when we retreated before Sheridan after the battle of the 19th of August, it fell to his lot, among eighteen or twenty other surgeons, to be left there to take care of our captured wounded. When those duties were at an end, instead of sending them under flag of truce to our own army, they were taken first to the old Capitol, where they remained ten days, thence to Fort Delaware, for one night, and thence to Fort Hamilton, near Fortress Monroe,[75] where they were detained four weeks. They there met with much kindness from Southern ladies, and also from a Federal officer, Captain Blake.[76]

16th—Fort Fisher has fallen; Wilmington will of course follow.[77] This was our last port into which blockade-runners were successful in entering, and which furnished us with an immense amount of stores. What will be the effect of this disaster we known not; we can only hope and pray.

21st—We hear nothing cheering except in the proceedings of Congress and the Virginia Legislature, particularly the latter.[78] Both bodies look to stern resistance to Federal authority. The city and country are full of rumours and evil surmising; and while we do not believe one word of the croaking, it makes us feel restless and unhappy.

29th—As usual, we attended Mr. Peterkin's church and enjoyed his sermon. Every thing looks so dark without that our only comfort is in looking to God for His blessing. The Union Prayer-Meetings are great comforts to us. They are attended by crowds; ministers of all denominations officiate at them. Prayers for the country, hymns of praise, and exhortation, fill up the time. Some of the addresses are very stirring, urging the laity to work and to give, and to every branch of the Christian Church to do its duty to the country. Our brave old Bishop Meade, on his dying bed, admonished one of his presbyters to speak boldly to the people in behalf of the country; and I am glad to hear the ministers do it. They speak cheerfully, too, on the subject; they are sanguine of our success, depending upon the Lord and on the bravery of our troops—on the "sword of the Lord and of Gideon."[79]

February 8—I feel more and more anxious about Richmond. I can't believe that it will be given up; yet so many persons are doubtful that it makes me very unhappy. I can't keep a regular diary now, because I do not like to write all that I feel and hear. I am constantly expecting the blessing of God in a way that we know not. I believe that all of our difficulties are to be overruled for good. A croaker accuses me of expecting a miracle to be wrought in our favour, which I do not; but we have been so often led on in a manner so wonderful, that we have no right to doubt the mercy of God towards us. Our troops, too, are standing up under such hardships and trials, which require the most sublime moral as well as personal courage to endure, that I cannot avoid expecting a blessing upon them!

Sherman moves on in his desolating path.[80] Oh for men to oppose and crush him!

In the midst of our trials, *Hymen*[81] still comes in to assert his claims, and to amuse and interest us. We have lately seen our beautiful young friend, M. G.,[82] led to his altar; and two of our young office associates are bidding us farewell for the same *sacrifice*. One of them, Miss T. W.,[83] has sat by my side for more than a year, with her bright face and sweet manners. She will be a real loss to me, but I cannot find it in my heart to regret that she will bless with her sweetness one of our brave Confederate officers.

28th—Our new Commissary-General is giving us brighter hopes for Richmond by his energy.[84] Not a stone is left unturned to collect all the provisions from the country. Ministers of the Gospel and others have gone out to the various county towns and court-houses, to urge the people to send in every extra bushel of corn or pound of meat for the army. The people only want enlightening on the subject; it is no want of patriotism which makes them keep any portion of their provisions. Circulars are sent out to the various civil and military officers in all disenthralled counties in the State—which, alas! when compared with the whole, are very few—to ask for their superfluities. All will answer promptly, I know, and generously.

Since I last wrote in my diary, our Essex friends have again most liberally replenished our larder just as they did this time last year—if possible, more generously. The Lord reward them!

March 10—Still we go on as heretofore, hoping and praying that Richmond may be safe. Before Mr. Hunter (Hon. R. M. T. Hunter)[85] left Richmond, I watched his countenance whenever I heard the subject mentioned before him, and though he said nothing, I thought he looked sad. I know that he understands the situation of affairs perfectly, and I may have fancied the sad look, but I think not; and whenever it arises before my mind's eye, it makes me unhappy. I imagine, too, from a conversation which I had with Mr. Secretary Mallory,[86] that he fears much for Richmond. Though it was an unexpressed opinion, yet I fear that I understood it rightly. I know that we ought to feel that whatever General Lee and the President deem right for the cause must be right, and that we should be satisfied that all will be well; but it would almost break my heart to see this dear old city, with its hallowed associations, given over to the Federals. Fearful orders have been given in the offices to keep the papers packed, except such as we are working on. The packed boxes remain in the front room, as if uncertainty still existed about moving them. As we walk in every morning, all eyes are turned to the boxes to see if any have been removed, and we breathe more freely when we find them still there.

To-day I have spent in the hospital, and was very much interested in our old Irishman. He has been there for more than two years; first as a patient sent from Drury's Bluff, with ague and fever. Though apparently long past the military age, he had enlisted as a soldier in a Georgia regiment, but it was soon discovered that he was physically unable to stand camp-life; he was therefore detailed to work in the gardens, which supplied the soldiers at the Bluff with vegetables. He got well, and returned to his post, but was soon sent back again, too sick for service. The climate did not suit him, and when he again recovered, Miss T[ompkins] employed him as a gardener and marketman to her hospital. We all became interested in him, because of his quiet, subdued manner, faithfulness to his duty, and respectful bearing. Some months ago his health began to decline, and day after day he has been watched and cared for by the surgeons and ladies with deep interest; but he steadily declines in strength, and is now confined to his cot, and it is but too evident that his end is approaching. We had all remarked that he never alluded to his early history, and was singularly reserved with regard to his religious faith; yet, as long as he was able to go out, he might be seen every Sunday seated alone in a corner of the gallery of St. James's Church. This evening, as I was walking around the room in which he lies, and had just administered to him some nourishment, he said to me: "When you get through with the men won't you come back and let me talk to ye?" When I returned and took my seat by him, he looked earnestly in my face, and said: "Mrs. [McGuire], you have an Irish name—have you friends there?" "No, my husband's grandfather was from Ireland, but we have no relatives there now." "Yes," was his reply, "it is a good name in Ireland, and you have been kind to me, and I want to talk to you a bit before I die. You know that I am a Protestant, and I have been constantly to Mr. Peterkin's church since I came here, because I like the church, and I like him; and I hope that now I am prepared to die. But I was not brought up an Episcopalian in the old country—our house was divided, like. My father was a Catholic, and my mother was a Protestant; neither went to the church of the other, but they were a loving couple for all that. He said to her, when we were but wee things: 'Mary,' said he, 'the children must go to your church sometimes, and to mine sometimes; you may teach them the Bible; but when they are old enough, they must judge for themselves.' And so it was; we were obliged every Sunday to go to one church or the other, but we determined for ourselves. I most always went with mother, because she was so good and gentle, and I loved her so much. We grew up a cheerful, happy family. My father was a gardener, three-quarters of a mile from Londonderry; he had a good little farm, and sold his fruit and vegetables in Derry, and had made a great deal of money; and we had a good house, and were so comfortable. We all went to school, and kept on so until I, the eldest child, was grown. In the neighbourhood was a man that my father hated. Oh, how he hated that man! But I loved that man's daughter; with my whole heart I loved that girl."

Here his voice became excited, his eyes were suffused with tears, and his emaciated, pock-marked face almost glowed with animation. The room had become still; the sick and wounded and visitors in the room were all listening with deep attention to the old man's story. "I knew," he continued, "that my father would see me dead before he would agree to my marrying into that family, and he was a stern man, and I was afraid to let him know; and I tried to get over my love; but I saw her whenever I went to church, and at last I told her that I loved her, and she said she would marry me, and then, Mrs. [McGuire]," he said with energy, "no mortal man could have made me give her up. After awhile my father said to me, 'Johnny,' said he, 'you are of age, and must work for yourself now; I will give you ten acres of my farm; begin early in spring, break it up, and make a garden; in a few years you will be an independent man.' Said I, 'Father, may I put a house on it?' 'No, my son; when I die you will have this house; can't you live now with your mother and me?' 'But, father,' said I, 'suppose I get married, where can

I live then?' 'If I like the match,' said he, 'you may live here.' I said no more then, but I saw Mary Dare" (he added, in a subdued voice, "her name was Mary Dare"), "and I told her I would try my father again, and if he would not agree to what I said, I would go to America and make a home for her. She was distressed, and I was in misery. Towards the spring my father said to me every now and then, 'Johnny, why don't you break up your ground? I have seeds for ye; it is time to begin.' But I could not begin; and I could not tell him why, I had such a dread of him. At last he said, 'Johnny, you are behindhand; why don't you go to work?' I knew from his look that I must speak now, and my mother looked so tender-like into my face, that I said, 'Father, I can't live here, unless I can bring my wife here, or build a house for her. I am going to marry Mary Dare, and if you object to it, I will go to America.' My father looked sternly at me, and said, 'I will not have you in my house or on my land, if you marry that girl; think about it; if you will give her up, you may live here and be well off; if not, you can go to America at once, and I will bear your expenses. Let me know to-morrow morning.' My mother looked heart-broken, but she did not speak. She never opposed my father. This was Sunday. Next morning he asked me if I had made up my mind. I said, 'Yes, sir; to go to America.' 'Then, Johnny, on Wednesday morning I will go to Derry and get you ready.' On Wednesday he called me to get his pony, and to walk to town, and meet him at a tailor's. He was there before me, and selected cloth to make me two good suits of clothes. We then went to a draper's and got linen (for we wear linen in Ireland, not cotton) to make me twelve shirts, and other clothes besides. Then we went to the packet office, where we were told that a packet would sail on that day week for Liverpool, to meet an emigrant ship just ready to sail for New York. He paid my passage without saying a word to me, though his manner was kind to me all the time. As we turned to go home he said, 'I have four pounds to give you for pocket-money, and I shall deposit fifty pounds in New York for you, which you can draw if you are in want; but I advise you not to draw it unless you are in want, for it is all I shall give you.' When we got home my mother collected her friends and neighbours to make my clothes. She and my sisters looked sorry enough, but not a word did they say about it. I knew that my father had told them not to do it, and my heart was too full to speak to anybody except to Mary Dare—she knew that as soon as I could come for her I would come. When I took leave of my mother she almost died, like. I told her, 'Mother,' said I, 'I am coming back when I am independent, and can do as I please. Write to me, mother dear; I will write to you and my sisters when I get to New York, and tell you where I am;' and I did write to Mary and my mother. I could not write to my father; I could not forgive him, when I thought how he had grieved Mary and me; and I could not be deceitful. As soon as I got to New York, I engaged with a gentleman at Williamsburg, on Long Island, to work his garden. For two years I worked, and laid up my wages; and not a single letter came for me. I grieved and sorrowed, and thought about Mary—I thought maybe her letters were stopped by somebody. I knew she would not forget me. Sometimes I thought I would go home to Ireland, and see what was the matter. At last, one day, my employer came into the garden with a newspaper in his hand. 'Mr. Crumley,' says he, 'here is something for you;' and sure enough there was a line to John Crumley, asking me to meet an old friend that had just come from Derry. I could not work another stroke, but went to the city, and there he was. I asked him first about my mother. 'All well; I have a letter from her for you.' 'And haven't you another letter? Didn't Mary Dare write to me?' 'Mary Dare,' he said; 'don't you know that Mary Dare died soon after you left the old country?'"

The old man stopped for a moment to recover himself. Then, striking the side of his cot with his hard, sunburnt hand, he added, "Yes, she was dead, and I was then left the lone man that you see me now, Mrs. [McGuire]. My mother had not written before, because she hated to distress me, but she wrote to beg that I could come home; my father's health was failing, and he wanted me, his first-born, to come and take the homestead. But Ireland and home were nothing to me now. I wrote to her that my next brother must take the homestead, and take care of my father and her, God bless her! I should never see Ireland again, but I loved her and my sisters all the same. The next letter was long after that. My mother wrote, 'Your father is dead; come back, Johnny, and take your own home.' I could not go; and then I went to Georgia, and never heard from home again. I tried to fight for the South, because the Southern people were good to me, and I thought if I got killed there was nobody to care for me."

His story was done. He looked at me, and said, "You have all been so good to me, particularly Miss T[ompkins]. God bless you all for it! I am now almost at my journey's end." When I looked up I found the man subdued and sorrowful. The story, and the weak, sad tones with which it was told, had touched them all, and brought tears from some.

11th—Sheridan's raid through the country is perfectly awful,[87] and he has joined Grant, without being caught. Oh, how we listened to hear that he had been arrested in his direful career! It was, I suppose, the most cruel and desolating raid upon record—more lawless, if possible, than Hunter's.[88] He had an overwhelming force, spreading ruin through the Upper Valley, the Piedmont country, the tide-water country, until he reached Grant. His soldiers were allowed to commit any cruelty on non-combatants that suited their rapacious tempers—stealing every thing they could find; ear-rings, breastpins, and finger-rings were taken from the first ladies of the land; nothing escaped them which was worth carrying off from the already desolated country. And can we feel patient at the idea of such soldiers coming to Richmond, the target at which their whole nation, from their President to the meanest soldier upon their army-rolls, has been aiming for four years? Oh, I would that I could see Richmond burnt to the ground by its own people, with not one brick left upon another, before its defenceless inhabitants should be subjected to such degradation.

Fighting is still going on; so near the city, that the sound of cannon is ever in our ears.[89] Farmers are sending in produce which they cannot spare, but which they give with a spirit of self-denial rarely equaled. Ladies are offering their jewelry, their plate, any thing which can be converted into money, for the country. I have heard some of them declare, that, if necessary, they will cut off their long suits of hair, and send them to Paris to be sold for bread for the soldiers; and there is not a woman, worthy of the name of Southerner, who would not do it, if we could get it out of the country, and bread or meat in return. Some gentlemen are giving up their watches, when every thing else has been given. A colonel of our army[90] was seen the other night, after a stirring appeal had been made for food for the soldiers, to approach the speaker's stand with his watch in his hand, saying: "I have no money, nor provisions; my property was ruined by Hunter's raid last summer; my watch is very dear to me from association, but it must be sold for bread." Remembering, as he put it down, that it had been long worn by his wife, now dead, though not a man who liked or approved *of scenes,* he obeyed the affectionate impulse of his heart, took it up quickly, kissed it, and replaced it on the table.

12th—A deep gloom has just been thrown over the city by the untimely death of one of its own heroic sons. General John Pegram fell while nobly leading his brigade against the enemy in the neighbourhood of Petersburg.[91] But two weeks before he had been married in St. Paul's Church, in the presence of a crowd of relatives and friends, to the celebrated Miss H[ettie] C[ary], of Baltimore. All was bright and beautiful. Happiness beamed from every eye. Again has St. Paul's, his own beloved church, been opened to receive the soldier and his bride—the one coffined for a hero's grave, the other, pale and trembling, though still by his side, in widow's garb.

31st—A long pause in my diary. Every thing seems so dark and uncertain that I have no heart for keeping records. The croakers croak about Richmond being evacuated, but I can't and won't believe it.

There is hard fighting about Petersburg, and General A. P. Hill has been killed.[92] Dreadful to think of losing such a man at such a time; but yet it comes nearer home when we hear of the young soldiers whom we have loved, and whose youth we have watched with anxiety and hope as those on whom our country must depend in days to come, being cut down when their country most needs them. We have just heard of the death of Barksdale Warwick,[93] another of our E[piscopal] H[igh] S[chool] boys—another one of the parents who yielded up their noble first-born son on the field of battle three years ago. He fell a day or two ago; I did not hear precisely when or where; I only know that he has passed away, as myriads of our young countrymen have done before him, and in the way in which our men would prefer to die.

A week ago we made a furious attack upon the enemy's fortifications near Petersburg,[94] and several were taken before daylight, but we could not hold them against overwhelming numbers, and batteries vastly too strong for any thing we could command; and so it is still—the enemy is far too strong in numbers and military resources. The Lord save us, or we perish! Many persons think that Richmond is in the greatest possible danger, and may be evacuated at any time. Perhaps we are apathetic or too hopeful, but none of us are desponding at all, and I find myself planning for the future, and feeling excessively annoyed when I find persons less sanguine than myself.

April 3—Agitated and nervous, I turn to my diary to-night as the means of soothing my feelings. We have passed through a fatal thirty-six hours. Yesterday morning (it seems a week ago) we went, as usual, to St. James's Church, hoping for a day of peace and quietness, as well as of religious improvement and enjoyment. How short-sighted we are, and how little do we know of what is coming, either of judgment or mercy! The sermon being over, as it was the first Sunday of the month, the sacrament of the Lord's Supper was administered. The day was bright, beautiful. And peaceful, and a general quietness and repose seemed to rest upon the congregation, undisturbed by rumours and apprehensions. While the sacred elements were being administered, the sexton came in with a note to General Cooper,[95] which was handed him as he walked from the chancel, and he immediately left the church. It made me anxious; but such things are not uncommon, and caused no excitement in the congregation. The services being over, we left the church, and as the congregations from the various churches were being mingled on Grace Street, our children, who had been at St. Paul's, joined us, on their way to the usual family gathering in our room on Sunday. After the salutations of the morning, J[ames] remarked, in an agitated voice, to his father, that he had just returned from the War Department, and that there was sad news—General Lee's lines had been broken, and the city would probably be evacuated within twenty-four hours. Not until then did I observe that every countenance was wild with excitement. The inquiry, "What is the matter?" ran from lip to lip. Nobody seemed to hear or to answer. An old friend ran across the street, pale with excitement, repeating what J[ames] had just told us, that unless we heard better news from General Lee the city would be evacuated. We could do nothing; no one suggested any thing to be done. We reached home with a strange, unrealizing feeling. In an hour J. (who is now Professor of Mathematics in the Naval School) received orders to accompany Captain Parker to the South with the Corps of Midshipmen.[96] Then we began to understand that the Government was moving, and that the evacuation was indeed going on. The office-holders were now making arrangements to get off. Every car was ordered to be ready to take them south. Baggage-wagons, carts, drays, and ambulances were driving about the streets; every one was going off that could go, and now there were all the indications of alarm and excitement of every kind which could attend such an awful scene. The people were rushing up and down the streets, vehicles of all kinds were flying along, bearing goods of all sorts and people of all ages and classes who could go beyond the corporation lines. We tried to keep ourselves quiet. We could not go south, nor could we leave the city at all in this hurried way. J[ames] and his wife had gone. The "Colonel," with B., intended going in the northern train this morning—he to his home in Hanover County, and she to her father's house in Clarke County, as soon as she could get there. Last night, when we went out to hire a servant to go to Camp Jackson[97] for our sister, we for the first time realized that our money was worthless here, and that we are in fact penniless. About midnight she walked in, escorted by two of the convalescent soldiers. Poor fellows! All the soldiers will go who can, but the sick and wounded must be captured. We collected in one room, and tried to comfort one another; we made large pockets and filled them with as many of our valuables as we could suspend from our waists. The gentlemen walked down to the War Office in the night to see what was going on. Alas! every sight and sound was grievous and heavy.

A telegram just received from General Lee hastened the evacuation.[98] The public offices were all forsaken. They said that by three o'clock in the morning the work must be completed, and the city ready for the enemy to take possession. Oh, who shall tell the horror of the past night! Hope seemed to fade; none but despairing words were heard, except from a few brave hearts. Union men began to show themselves; treason walked abroad.[99] A gloomy pall seemed to hang over us; but I do not think that any of us felt keenly, or have yet realized our overwhelming calamity. The suddenness and extent of it is too great for us to feel its poignancy at once. About two o'clock in the morning we were startled by a loud sound like thunder; the house shook and the windows rattled; it seemed like an earthquake in our midst. We knew not what it was, nor did we care. It was soon understood to be the blowing up of a magazine below the city.[100] In a few hours another exploded on the outskirts of the city, much louder than the first, and shivering innumerable plate-glass windows all over Shockoe Hill.[101] It was then daylight, and we were standing out upon the pavement. The Colonel and B. had just gone. Shall we ever meet again? Many ladies were now upon the streets. The lower part of the city was burning. About seven o'clock I set off to go to the central depot to see if the cars would go out. As I went from Franklin to Broad Street, and on Broad, the pavements were covered with broken glass; women, both white and coloured, were walking in multitudes from the Commissary offices and burning stores with bags of flour, meal, coffee, sugar, rolls of cotton cloth, etc.; coloured men were rolling wheelbarrows filled in the same way. I went on and on towards the depot, and as I proceeded shouts and screams became louder. The rabble rushed by me in one stream. At last I exclaimed, "Who are those shouting? What is the matter?" I seemed to be answered by a hundred voices, "The Yankees have come." I turned to come home, but what was my horror, when I reached Ninth

Street, to see a regiment of Yankee cavalry come dashing up, yelling, shouting hallooing, screaming! All Bedlam[102] let loose could not have vied with them in diabolical roarings. I stood riveted to the spot; I could not move nor speak. Then I saw the iron gates of our time-honoured and beautiful Capitol Square, on the walks and greensward of which no hoof had been allowed to tread, thrown open and the cavalry dash in. I could see no more; I must go on with a mighty effort, or faint where I stood. I came home amid what I thought was the firing of cannon. I thought that they were thundering forth a salute that they had reached the goal of their ardent desires; but I afterwards found that the Armory was on fire,[103] and that the flames having reached the shells deposited there for our army, they were exploding. Those explosions were kept up until a late hour this evening; I am rejoiced they are gone; they, at least, can never be turned against us. I found the family collected around the breakfast-table, and was glad to see Captain M[ason]'s family with them. The captain has gone, and the ladies have left their home on "Union Hill" to stay here among friends, Colonel P.[104] having kindly given them rooms. An hour or two after breakfast we all retired to our rooms exhausted. No one had slept; no one had sought repose or thought of their own comfort. The Federal soldiers were roaming about the streets; either whiskey or the excess of joy had given some of them the appearance of being beside themselves. We had hoped that very little whiskey would be found in the city, as, by order of the Mayor, casks were emptied yesterday evening in the streets, and it flowed like water through the gutters; but the rabble had managed to find it secreted in the burning shops, and bore it away in pitchers and buckets. It soon became evident that protection would be necessary for the residences, and at the request of Colonel P[eyton] I went to the Provost Marshal's office to ask for it. Mrs. P[eyton] was unfortunately in the country, and only ladies were allied to apply for guards. Of course this was a very unpleasant duty, but I must undertake it. Mrs. D.[105] agreed to accompany me, and as we proceeded to the City Hall—the City Hall, which from my childhood I had regarded with respect and reverence, as the place where my father had for years held his courts, and in which our lawyers, whose names stand among the highest in the Temple of Fame, for fifty years expounded the Constitution and the laws, which must now be trodden under foot. We reached it. After passing through crowds of negro soldiers there, we found on the steps some of the elderly gentlemen of the city seeking admittance, which was denied them. I stopped to speak to Mr.

——, in whose commission house I was two days ago, and saw him surrounded by all the stores which usually make up the establishment of such
a merchant; it was now a mass of blackened ruins. He had come to ask
protection for his residence, but was not allowed to enter. We passed the
sentinel, and an officer escorted us to the room in which we were to ask our
country's foe to allow us to remain undisturbed in our own houses. Mrs.
D[ickins] leant on me tremblingly; she shrank from the humiliating duty.
For my own part, though my heart beat loudly and my blood boiled, I
never felt more high-spirited or lofty than at that moment. A large table was
surrounded by officials, writing or talking to the ladies, who came on the
same mission that brought us. I approached the officer who sat at the head
of the table, and asked him politely if he was the Provost Marshal. "I am the
Commandant, madam," was the respectful reply. "Then to whom am I to
apply for protection for our residence?" "You need none, madam; our troops
are perfectly disciplined, and dare not enter your premises." "I am sorry to
be obliged to undeceive you, sir, but when I left home seven of your soldiers
were in the yard of the residence opposite to us, and one has already been
into our kitchen." He looked surprised, and said, "Then, madam, you are
entitled to a guard. Captain, write a protection for the residence on the
corner of First and Franklin Streets, and give these ladies a guard." This was
quickly done, and as I turned to go out, I saw standing near me our old
friend, Mrs. [Rutherford].[106] Oh! how my heart sank when I looked into her
calm, sad face, and remembered that she and her venerable and highly esteemed husband must ask leave to remain in peace in their home of many
years. The next person who attracted my attention was that sweet young
girl, S. W. Having no mother, she of course must go and ask that her father's
beautiful mansion may be allowed to stand uninjured.[107] Tears rolled down
her cheeks as she pressed my hand in passing. Other friends were there; we
did not speak, we could not; we sadly looked at each other and passed on.
Mrs. D[ickins] and myself came out, accompanied by our guard. The fire
was progressing rapidly, and the crashing sound of falling timbers was distinctly heard. Dr. Read's church was blazing.[108] Yankee citizens, and negroes
were attempting to arrest the flames. The War Department was falling in;
burning papers were being wafted about the streets. The Commissary Department, with out desks and papers, was consumed already. Warwick &
Barksdale's mill[109] was sending its flames to the sky. Cary and Main Streets
seemed doomed throughout; Bank Street was beginning to burn, and now

it had reached Franklin. At any other moment it would have distracted me, but I had ceased to feel any thing. We brought our guard to Colonel P[eyton], who posted him; about three o'clock he came to tell me that the guard was drunk, and threatening to shoot the servants in the yard. Again I went to the City Hall to procure another. I approached the Commandant and told him why I came. He immediately ordered another guard, and a corporal to be sent for the arrest of the drunken man. The flames had decreased, but the business part of the town was in ruins. The second guard was soon posted, and the first carried off by the collar. Almost every house is guarded; and the streets are now (ten o'clock) perfectly quiet. The moon is shining brightly on our captivity. God guide and watch over us!

April 5—I feel as if we were groping in the dark; no one knows what to do. The Yankees, so far, have behaved humanely. As usual, they begin with professions of kindness to those whom they have ruined without justifiable cause, without reasonable motive, without right to be there, or anywhere else within the Southern boundary. General Ord[110] is said to be polite and gentlemanly, and seems to do every thing in his power to lessen the horrors of this dire calamity. Other officers are kind in their departments, and the negro regiments look quite subdued. No one can tell how long this will last. Norfolk had its day of grace, and even New Orleans was not down-trodden at once. There are already apprehensions of evil. Is the Church to pray for the Northern President? How is it possible, except as we pray for all other sinners? But I pause for further developments.

6th—Mr. Lincoln has visited our devoted city to-day.[111] His reception was any thing but complimentary. Our people were in nothing rude or disrespectful; they only kept themselves away from a scene so painful. There are very few Unionists of the least respectability here; these met them (he was attended by Stanton and others) with cringing loyalty, I hear, but the rest of the small collection were of the low, lower, lowest of creation.[112] They drove through several streets, but the greeting was so feeble from the motley crew of vulgar men and women, that the Federal officers themselves, I suppose, were ashamed of it, for they very soon escaped from the disgraceful association. It is said that they took a collation at General Ord's—our President's house!! Ah! it is a bitter pill. I would that dear old house, with all its associations, so sacred to the Southerners, so sweet to us as a family, had shared in the general conflagration. Then its history would have been unsullied, though sad. Oh, how gladly would I have seen it burn! I have been nowhere since Monday, except to see my dear old friend, Mrs. R[owland], and to the hospital. There I am not much subjected to the harrowing sights and sounds by which we are surrounded. The wounded must be nursed; poor fellows, they are so sorrowful! Our poor old Irishman died on Sunday. The son of a very old acquaintance was brought to our hospital a few days ago, most severely wounded—Colonel Charles Richardson, of the artillery. We feared at first that he must die, but now there is a little more hope.[113] It is so sad that after four years of bravery and devotion to the cause, he should be brought to his native city, for the defence of which he would have gladly given his life, dangerously if not mortally wounded, when its sad fate is just decided. I love to sit by his bedside and try to cheer him; his friends seem to vie with each other in kind attention to him.

We hear rumours of battles, and of victories gained by our troops, but we have no certain information beyond the city limits.

10th—Another gloomy Sabbath-day and harrowing night. We went to St. Paul's in the morning, and heard a very fine sermon from Dr. Minnegerode—at least so said my companions. My attention, which is generally riveted by his sermons, wandered continually. I could not listen; I felt so strangely, as if in a vivid, horrible dream. Neither President was prayed for; in compliance with some arrangement with the Federal authorities, the prayer was used as for all in authority! How fervently did we all pray for our own President![114] Thank God, our silent prayers are free from Federal authority. "The oppressor keeps the body bound, but knows not what a range the spirit takes."[115] Last night, (it seems strange that we have lived to speak or write of it), between nine and ten o'clock, as some of the ladies of the house were collected in our room, we were startled by the rapid firing of cannon. At first we thought that there must be an attack upon the city; bright thoughts of the return of our army darted through my brain; but the firing was too regular. We began to think it must be a salute for some great event. We threw up the windows, and saw the flashes and smoke of cannon towards Camp Jackson. Some one present counted one hundred guns. What could it be? We called to passers-by: "What do those guns mean?" Sad voices answered several times: "I do not know." At last a voice pertly, wickedly replied: "General Lee has surrendered, thank God!" Of course we did not believe him, though the very sound was a knell. Again we called out: "What is the matter?" A voice answered, as if from a broken heart: "They say General Lee has surrendered." We cannot believe it, but my heart became dull and heavy, and every nerve and muscle of my frame seems heavy too. I cannot even now shake it off. We passed the night, I cannot tell how—I know not how we live at all. At daybreak the dreadful salute commenced again. Another hundred guns at twelve to-day. Another hundred—can it be so? No, we do not believe it, but how can we bear such a doubt? Where are all our dear ones, our beloved soldiers, and out noble chief to-night, while the rain falls pitilessly? Are they lying on the cold, hard ground, sleeping for sorrow? Or are they moving southward triumphantly, to join General Johnston,[116] still able and willing—ah, far more than willing—to avenge their country's wrongs? God help us!—we must take refuge in unbelief.[117]

Tuesday Night—No light on our sorrow—still gloomy, dark, and uncertain.

I went to-day to the hospital, as was my duty. My dear friend S[ally] T[ompkins] cheers me, by being utterly incredulous about the reported surrender. As usual, she is cheerfully devoting her powers of mind and body to her hospital. For four years she has never thought of her own comfort, when by sacrificing it she would alleviate a soldier's sorrow. Miss E. D.,[118] who has shared with her every duty, every self-sacrificing effort in behalf of our sick and wounded soldiers, is now enduring the keenest pangs of sorrow from the untimely death of her venerable father. On the day of the evacuation, while walking too near a burning house, he was struck by a piece of falling timber, and the blow soon closed his long life. Alas! the devoted daughter, who had done so much for other wounded, could do nothing for the restoration of one so dear to her.

Wednesday Night—We have heard nothing new to-day confirming the report of the surrender, which is perhaps the reason my spirit feels a little more light. We must *hope,* though our prospects should be as dark as the sky of this stormy night. Our wounded are doing well—those who remain in our hospital and the convalescents have been ordered to "Camp Jackson." Indeed, all of the patients were included in the same order; but Miss T[ompkins] having represented that several of them were not in a condition to be removed, they have been allowed to remain where they are.

Colonel R[ichardson] is improving, for which we are most thankful.

Thursday Night—Fearful rumours are reaching us from sources which it is hard to doubt, that it is all too true, and that General Lee surrendered on Sunday last, the 9th of April. The news came to the enemy by telegram during the day, and to us at night by the hoarse and pitiless voice of the cannon. We know, of course, that circumstances forced it upon our great commander and his gallant army. How all this happened—how Grant's hundreds of thousands overcame our little band, history, not I, must tell my children's children. It is enough for me to tell them that all that bravery and self-denial could do has been done. We do not yet give up all hope. General Johnston is in the field, but there are thousands of the enemy to his tens. The citizens are quiet. The calmness of despair is written on every countenance. Private sorrows are now coming upon us. We *know* of but few casualties.

Good Friday—As usual, I went to the hospital, and found Miss T[ompkins] in much trouble. A peremptory order has been given by the Surgeon-General to remove *all* patients. In the opinion of our surgeon, to five of them it would be certain death. The ambulances were at the door. Miss T[ompkins] and myself decided to go at once to the Medical Director and ask him to recall the order. We were conducted to his office, and, for the first time since the entrance of the Federal army, were impolitely treated. On two occasions we had been obliged to make application to officials, and had been received with great respect and consideration, and we believe it has been uniformly the case; and we were, therefore, very much surprised when a request which seemed to us so reasonable was at first refused most decidedly. We could not give up our application, as it seemed to be a matter of life and death; so we told him what our surgeon had said, and that we hoped he would reconsider his order. He replied, that he should send a surgeon with the ambulances, and if in *his* judgment they could be removed, it should be done without hesitation, as he was determined to break up the mall hospitals *which you have all about town,* (ours is the only hospital in town,) and that he had ordered neither rations nor medicines to be issued to them. Miss T[ompkins] told him that nothing of the sort was necessary; she had never asked nor received rations from the Federal Government; that she had now but five men under her care, and they were desperately wounded, and she would greatly prefer that the hospital should be considered in the light of a private establishment, which we could take care of without asking help. A change came over his countenance, but not his manner; he brusquely told us that he would "see about it." In an hour afterwards the surgeon and the ambulance came, but after what seemed to me rather a pompous display of surgical examination and learned medical terms, addressed to the lady-nurses, he determined to leave our dear mangled soldiers to our care. One of them is in a dying condition; he cannot survive many hours.

We had no service in our churches to-day. An order came out in this morning's papers that the prayers for the President of the United States must be used. How could we do it? Mr. [McGuire] went to the hospital by the request of Colonel Richardson, and had prayers in his room. Ambulances are constantly passing with horses in the finest possible condition—even finer than ours were in the beginning of the war. It seems to me passing strange that, with all their advantages, we kept them at bay so long, and conquered them so often. Had one port been left open to us—only one, by which we might have received food and clothing—Richmond would not now be in their hands; our men were starved into submission.[119]

Sunday Night—The Episcopal churches being closed, we went to the Rev. Dr. Hoge's church.[120] The rector was absent; he went off, to be in the Confederate lines; but the Rev. Dr. Read, whose church is in ruins, occupied the pulpit.

Strange rumours are afloat to-night. It is said, and believed, that Lincoln is dead, and Seward much injured.[121] As I passed the house of a friend this evening, she raised the window and told me of the report. Of course I treated it as a Sunday rumour; but the story is strengthened by the way which the Yankees treat it. They, of course, know all about it, and to-morrow's papers will reveal the particulars. I trust that, if true, it may not be by the hand of an assassin, though it would seem to fulfil the warnings of Scripture. His efforts to carry out his abolitionist theories have caused the shedding of oceans of Southern blood, and by man it now seems has his blood been shed. But what effect will it have on the South? We may have much to fear.[122] Future events will show. This event has made us wild with excitement and speculation.

General Lee has returned. He came unattended, save by his staff—came without notice, and without parade;[123] but he could not come unobserved; as soon as his approach was whispered, a crowd gathered in his path, not boisterously, but respectfully, and increasing rapidly as he advanced to his home on Franklin Street, between 8th and 9th, where, with a courtly bow to the multitude, he at once retired to the bosom of his beloved family. When I called in to see his high-minded and patriotic wife, a day or two after the evacuation, she was busily engaged in her invalid's chair, and very cheerful and hopeful. "The end is not yet," she said, as if to cheer those around her; "Richmond is not the Confederacy." To this we all most willingly assented, and felt very much gratified and buoyed by her brightness. I have not had the heart to visit her since the surrender, but hear that she still is sanguine, saying that "General Lee is not the Confederacy," and that there is "life in the old land yet." He is not the Confederacy; but our hearts sink within us when we remember that he and his noble army are now idle, and that we can no longer look upon them as the bulwark of our land. He has returned from defeat and disaster with the universal and profound admiration of the world, having done all that skill and valour could accomplish. The scenes at the surrender were noble and touching. General Grant's bearing was profoundly respectful; General Lee's as courtly and lofty as the purest chivalry could require. The terms, so honourable to all parties, being complied with to the letter, our arms were laid down with breaking hearts, and tears such as stoutest warriors may shed. "Woe worth the day!"[124]

Tuesday Night—I try to dwell as little as possible on public events. I only feel that we have no country, no government, no future. I cannot, like some others, look with hope on Johnston's army. He will do what he can; but ah, what can he do? Our anxiety now is that our President and other public men may get off in safety. O God! have mercy upon them and help them! For ourselves, like the rest of the refugees, we are striving to get from the city. The stereotyped question when we meet is, "When and where are you going?" Our country relatives have been very kind. My brother offers us an asylum in his devastated home at W[estwood]. While there we must look around for some other place, in which to build up a home for our declining years. Property we have none—all gone. Thank God, we have our faculties; the girls and myself, at least, have health. Mr. [McGuire] bears up under our difficulties with the same hopeful spirit which he has ever manifested. "The Lord will provide," is still his answer to any doubt on our part. The Northern officials offer free tickets to persons returning to their homes—alas! to their homes! How few of us have homes! Some are confiscated; others destroyed. The families of the army and navy officers are here. The husbands and sons are absent, and they remain with nothing to anticipate and nothing to enjoy. To-day I met a friend, the wife of a high official, whose hospitality I have often enjoyed in one of the most elegant residences in Virginia, which has been confiscated and used as a hospital for "contrabands."[125] Hearing where we were going, she replied, "I have no brother, but when I hear from my husband and son, I shall accept the whole-souled invitation of a relative in the country, who has invited me to make his house my home;" but, she added, as her beautiful eyes filled with tears, "when are our visits to end? We can't live with our ruined relatives, and when our visits are over, what then? And how long must our visits of charity last?" The question was too sad; neither of us could command our voices, and we parted in silence and tears.

20th—The cars on the Central Railroad will run tomorrow, for the first time, under Federal rule, and the day after we will use our passports and free tickets to leave the city—dearer than ever, in its captivity and ruin. It is almost impossible to get current money. A whole-hearted friend from Alexandria met me the other day, and with the straightforward simplicity due to friendship in these trying times, asked me at once, "Has your husband any money?" I told him I thought not. He replied, "Tell him I have between twenty-five and thirty dollars—that's all—and he shall have half of it; tell him I say so." Ten dollars were accepted, for the circumstances of want which pressed so hard, and for the kindly spirit in which it was offered. Two other friends came forward to share with us their little all. God help the warm hearts of our conquered but precious country! I know they will be blessed, and that light will yet shine through the blackness of darkness which now surrounds them.

W[estwood], 24th—On Saturday evening my brother's wagon met us at the depot and brought us to this place, beautiful in its ruins. We have not been here since the besom of destruction swept over it, and to us, who have been in the habit of enjoying the hospitality when all was bright and cheerful, the change is very depressing. We miss the respectful and respectable servants, born in the family and brought up with an affection for the household which seemed a part of their nature, and which so largely contributed to the happiness both of master and servant. Even the nurse of our precious little S[arah], the sole child of the house, whose heart seemed bound up in her happiness, has gone. It is touching to hear the sweet child's account of the shock she experienced when she found that her "mammy," deceived and misled by the minions who followed Grant's army, had left her; and to see how her affection still clings to her, showing itself in the ardent hope that her "mammy" has found a comfortable home. The army has respected the interior of the house, because of the protection of the officers. Only one ornament was missing, and that was the likeness of this dear child. Since the fall of Richmond, a servant of the estate, who had been living in Washington, told me that it was in the possession of a maid-servant of the house, who showed it to him, saying that she "looked at it every day." We all try to be cheerful and to find a bright side; and we occupy the time as cheerfully as we can. The governess having returned to her home in Norfolk, I shall enjoy myself in teaching my bright little niece here and the dear children at S[ummer] H[ill], and feel blessed to have so pleasant a duty.

25th—J. P.[126] arrived to-day direct from Mosby's command, which is disbanded, but has not surrendered. He is full of enthusiasm and visions of coming success, and is bent on joining Johnston. Dear boy, his hopeful spirit has infected me, and aroused a hope which I am afraid to indulge.

28th—We have no mail communication, and can hear nothing from General Johnston. We go on as usual, but are almost despairing. Dear M[ary],[127] in her sadness, has put some Confederate money and postage stamps into a Confederate envelope, sealed it up, and endorsed it "In memory of our beloved Confederacy." I feel like doing the same, and treasuring up the buttons, and the stars, and the dear gray coats, faded and worn as they are, with the soiled and tattered banner, which has no dishonouring blot, the untarnished sword, and other arms, though defeated, still crowned with glory. But not yet—I cannot feel that all is over yet.

May 4—General Johnston surrendered on the 26th of April. "My native land, good-night!"[128]

How empty Judith McGuire must have felt at war's end. She had no home to which she could return, no family heirlooms still left. In 1861 the middle-aged lady had been driven from a secure and pleasant way of life in Alexandria to a rambling existence of uncertainty, despair, and impoverishment in and around Richmond.

Faith in God and her fellow Southerners sustained her during the war years. She attended church regularly, cared for an ailing husband, walked the streets in search of temporary shelter, agonized over family and friends, became one of history's first female nurses, and worked as a government clerk to bolster the family's limited funds. Only when all of these tasks had been done did Mrs. McGuire sit down to relate her misfortunes to her diary.

She and her husband remained but a short time at the Westwood estate in Hanover County. A cousin, Benjamin Blake Brockenbrough, and his wife, Ann Mason, invited the McGuires to move into the ancestral family home at Tappahannock. This would be the final home of the longtime refugees.

Rev. McGuire gave small parishes in Essex County as much priestly assistance as his declining health would permit. Judith McGuire spent much of late 1865 and early 1866 editing her diary for publication. She claimed that she was releasing the record to the public at the insistence of her family. That was only partially true. It is highly likely that she ventured into the literary world for the first time because the family was in dire financial straits.

The easy flow of grammar and transition in the journal reflects how intently Mrs. McGuire labored on her entries. She expanded some passages into mini-homilies; personal incidents appeared with lengthy conversations included; hindsight is visible here and there. Rarely was her memory guilty of factual error, in spite of her haste to submit the diary to a publisher.

The first two printings appeared in 1867 and 1868 from E. J. Hale and Son in New York. In 1889 the Richmond firm of E. J. Randolph and English printed a third edition without any changes. Matthew Page Andrews lifted large blocs of the diary for inclusion in his 1920 work, *Women of the South in War Time*. Andrews identified a few of the people identified by initials or blanks with "the assistance of the relatives of Mrs. McGuire."[129] A 1995 reprint by the University of Nebraska Press contained a brief commentary on the diary.

Shortly after settling in Tappahannock, the McGuires turned their home into a girls' school. The husband-wife teaching team was short-lived. Rev. McGuire died in 1869, remembered as "Apostle to the Rappahannock" for his Episcopalian labors.[130] Mrs. McGuire continued to maintain the school with local help. She published a second book, *General Robert E. Lee: The Christian Soldier,* for use by her students. Royalties were donated to her parish, St. John's Church.

Mrs. McGuire died March 21, 1897, two days after her eighty-fourth birthday. For years thereafter, Mrs. McGuire's remains lay in St. John's cemetery inside an "iron-railed, vine-covered, but unmarked" grave.[131] In the 1970s, the gravesite underwent complete renovation. Two large, flat, engraved stones now mark the final resting places of Rev. McGuire and—on his right hand—Judith McGuire, a woman "of a stock noted for strength of character . . . intellectual power [and] sterling honesty and worth."[132]

Notes

1. This report was untrue. After the raid on Washington, Gen. Jubal Early's Confederate army fell back to a defensive line along Cedar Creek north of Strasburg. There Early rested his men and awaited an opportunity to strike the larger Federal host arrayed against him.

2. On July 23, Early learned that half of the Union force in the Valley had returned to Washington. He immediately moved forward and attacked the Federals in his front. After two days of fighting and 1,200 casualties, the Union corps retreated down the Valley. This defeat led to a reorganization of Federal forces in the Shenandoah under a new commander, Gen. Philip H. Sheridan.

3. Winchester's location as the northern gateway to the Valley made it a prime target for both sides during the Civil War. Eight major engagements occurred in and around the city. In four years, Winchester changed hands an estimated seventy times.

4. On Sunday morning, August 7, Union cavalry surprised an encamped Confederate force at Moorefield, West Virginia. Federals captured 27 officers, 400 enlisted men, 400 horses, and a large quantity of small arms in what one historian has classified as "the most thorough fiasco suffered by any Confederate cavalry force in the Virginia theater during the entire war." Gary W. Gallagher, ed., *Struggle for the Shenandoah: Essays on the 1864 Valley Campaign* (Kent, Ohio: Kent State University Press, 1991), 87.

5. The most spectacular of Grant's attempts at Petersburg to break Lee's lines came on July 30. Union coal miners dug a 511-foot tunnel to a point beneath the Confederate entrenchments, then detonated four tons of gunpowder, blowing a huge crater in the lines. Yet the Union attack that followed was poorly coordinated and badly led. It cost Grant 4,000 losses.

6. When Mrs. Milroy arrived in Winchester, she took an instant liking to the Lloyd home at North Braddock and West Piccadilly streets. The occupants, Mrs. Ann Logan and her five children, were thereupon turned out into the street. One resident who came to their relief was Betty Taylor Dandrige, daughter of President Zachary Taylor. Ben Ritter, Winchester, Va., to editor, July 18, 2004; 1860 Virginia Census—Frederick County.

7. Mary Armitage was the daughter of one of the contractors of the Erie

Canal. In 1849 she had married Robert Milroy. Naturally, the citizenry of Winchester never took warmly to her. Mrs. Milroy was even accused of blowing her nose through her fingers in public. Sheila R. Phipps, *Genteel Rebel: The Life of Mary Greenhow Lee* (Baton Rouge: Louisiana State University Press, 2004), 197.

8. Virginia's principal seaport suffered wear, tear, and damage from the moment the state seceded. In 1864 Union general Benjamin F. Butler took command of the city and submitted Norfolk to its worst indignities. See Hans L. Trefouse, *Ben Butler: The South Called Him Beast* (New York: Twayne, 1957), 166–69, 176–77.

9. The most detailed account of the Union raid on Tappahannock and nearby environs is in James B. Slaughter, *Settlers, Southerners, Americans: The History of Essex County, Virginia, 1608–1984* (Salem, W.Va.: Walsworth, 1985), 195–98.

10. Frances Blake Brockenbrough, widow of Dr. Austin Brockenbrough, lived on Walter Lane in the center of Tappahannock.

11. The 1860 Essex County census listed Lawrence Roane as a widower with two teenage sons and almost $80,000 in personal assets—a princely sum in those days.

12. Mrs. Brockenbrough was likely referring to Adeline, Jane, Mary, and Lucy Gray, spinster daughters of well-to-do widow Susan W. Gray. 1860 Virginia Census—Essex County.

13. Gerhard C. Schulze was acting master of the Union gunboat *Jacob Bell.* Union reports of the raid on Tappahannock are in U.S. Naval War Records Office, ed., *Official Records of the Union and Confederate Navies in the War of the Rebellion* (Washington, D.C.: Government Printing Office, 1894–1922), series 1, 5:445–50.

14. Lucy A. Branham, according to the 1860 Essex County census, was a widow in her fifties with personal assets close to $60,000.

15. "Brisk artillery firing" began in late afternoon on the 18th as Grant and Lee dueled southeast of Richmond. J. B. Jones, *A Rebel War Clerk's Diary at the Confederate States Capital* (Philadelphia: Lippincott, 1866), 2:266.

16. On August 13, Col. John S. Mosby with 250 partisan rangers and two small cannon surprised a Union wagon train encamped three miles from Berryville. Mosby's men killed or wounded 15 Federals while taking 200 prisoners. Some 420 mules, 36 horses, and 200 cattle were seized, while more than 40 wagons were burned. James A. Ramage, *Gray Ghost: The Life of John Singleton Mosby* (Lexington: University Press of Kentucky, 1999), 190–91.

17. The Confederate privateer *Tallahassee* was originally christened the *Atlanta* and ultimately bore the name *Olustee*. In August 1864, the vessel raided shipping along the New England coast and captured twenty-six ves-

sels. Panic raged until the *Tallahassee* returned to its Wilmington, North Carolina, base.

18. In retaliation for military raids by Mosby, Union general George Custer issued orders to burn five homes along the Leesburg-Berryville Turnpike near the Shenandoah River. A detachment of the Fifth Michigan Cavalry, under Capt. George Drake, destroyed the properties of Josiah Ware, Province McCormick, and Mrs. William Sowers. Federals were in the act of setting fire to the Benjamin Morgan residence when Mosby's command attacked with a vengeance. See Hugh C. Keen and Horace Mewborn, *43rd Battalion Virginia Cavalry: Mosby's Command* (Lynchburg, Va.: H. E. Howard, 1993), 162–64; J. H. Kidd, *Personal Recollections of a Cavalryman* (Ionia, Mich.: Sentinel, 1908), 378.

19. Judith Brockenbrough McGuire's annotated copy of *Diary of a Southern Refugee* belonging to Mrs. Margaret Dickins (hereafter cited as Dickins Copy) identified the son-in-law as Dr. Brown. The possibility is strong of this being James Conway Brown, who resigned as surgeon of the Eighth Virginia in 1862 and died in 1864. John E. Divine, *8th Virginia Infantry* (Lynchburg, Va.: H. E. Howard, 1983), 57.

20. Arthur K. St. Clair was then surgeon of the Fifth Michigan Cavalry. *Roster of Regimental Surgeons and Assistant Surgeons in the U.S. Army Medical Department during the Civil War* (Gaithersburg, Md.: Old Soldier Books, 1989), 88.

21. Episcopal priest Oliver Taylor was chaplain of the Fifth Michigan Cavalry. A Baptist cleric, John Gunderman Jr., had served a brief term in the regiment's first organization. John W. Brinsfield et al., eds., *Faith in the Fight: Civil War Chaplains* (Mechanicsburg, Pa.: Stackpole, 2003), 158, 200.

22. Three weeks after the affair, a still-angry Mosby reported to Robert E. Lee: "Such was the indignation of our men in witnessing some of the finest residences in that portion of the State enveloped in flames that no quarter was shown, and about 25 of them were shot to death for their villainy. About 30 horses were brought off, but no prisoners." U.S. War Department, *War of the Rebellion: A Compilation of the Official Records of the Union and Confederate Armies* (Washington, D.C.: Government Printing Office, 1880–1901), series 1, vol. 43, pt. 1, 634 (hereafter cited as *OR*).

23. While applauding Mosby for showing no mercy to Union marauders, Mrs. McGuire nevertheless felt sympathy for captives who pled for mercy. Many Southern women shared her feeling. Hospital nurse Kate Cumming once commented: "Seeing an enemy wounded and helpless is a different thing from seeing him in health and power." Kate Cumming, *A Journal of Hospital Life in the Confederate Army of Tennessee* (Louisville, Ky.: John P. Morton, 1866), 14.

24. Grace Fenton McGuire, Mrs. McGuire's stepdaughter, later married Rev. Kinloch Nelson of the Virginia Theological Seminary.

25. Augustine Smith Mason served at hospitals in Richmond, Fredericksburg, and Atlanta before becoming medical director of the Department of Richmond. Dickins Copy; Wyndham B. Blanton, *Medicine in Virginia* (Richmond: William Byrd, 1930), 408; Joseph Jones, "Roster of the Medical Officers of the Army of Tennessee, during the Civil War between the Northern and Southern States," *Southern Historical Society Papers* 22 (1894): 239. John Jameson Garnett was a Westmoreland County native and graduate of West Point. He spent most of the war as an "inspector of ordnance and artillery." Dickins Copy; Robert K. Krick, *Lee's Colonels: A Biographical Register of the Field Officers of the Army of Northern Virginia* (Dayton, Ohio: Morningside Bookshop, 1979), 130.

26. Listed in the 1860 Richmond census as a teacher, D. Lee Powell operated the Southern Female Institute on Franklin Street. The building still stands and is today the Linden Row Inn. Michael D. Gorman, Richmond, to editor, March 19, 2005.

27. Mrs. McGuire was referring to the open sky. She probably lifted the phrase from Washington Irving's 1832 book, *The Alhambra*: "The words were scarcely from his lips, when the carpet rose in the air, bearing off the prince and princess. . . . It became a little speck on the white bosom of a cloud, and then disappeared in the blue vault of heaven."

28. The two quotations are lines from Shakespeare's *The Merchant of Venice*: "The quality of mercy is not strain'd, / It droppeth as the gentle rain from heaven."

29. Mary Wise Garnett was the oldest daughter of Governor-General Henry A. Wise and the wife of prominent surgeon A. Y. P. Garnett. Dickins Copy; Craig M. Simpson, *A Good Southerner: The Life of Henry A. Wise of Virginia* (Chapel Hill: University of North Carolina Press, 1985), 276, 294.

30. On September 2, after a four-month campaign that began at Chattanooga, the city of Atlanta fell to Union forces under Gen. William T. Sherman. Two days later, Confederate general John Hunt Morgan was killed in a cavalry action at Greeneville, Tenn.

31. In mid-July, after Gen. Joseph E. Johnston had retired all the way to the Atlanta defenses, President Davis removed him from command and replaced him with headstrong Gen. John B. Hood. The result, one writer asserted, was "the blunder to crown the sad series of blunders in the West." Clifford Dowdey, *The Land They Fought For* (Garden City, N.Y.: Doubleday, 1955), 346.

32. A "Fabian policy," named after the Roman general who defeated Hannibal, refers to a strategy of caution and delay rather than battle.

33. On September 8, Sherman directed that Atlanta, "being exclusively required for warlike purposes, will at once be vacated by all except the armies of the United States and such civilian employees as may be retained." The Union commander informed Washington authorities: "I am not willing to have Atlanta

encumbered by the families of our enemies. I want it a pure Gibraltar." *OR*, series 1, vol. 38, pt. 5, 837, 839.

34. White House was then the highest navigable point on the Pamunkey River. McClellan had used it as a supply base during the 1862 Peninsula campaign. Grant likewise made White House a major river port in his offensive against Lee.

35. Mrs. McGuire related that Middleton and Pringle were buried at Summer Hill. If so, family or friends later removed the remains to other locations. Helen Kay Yates, ed., *Family Graveyards in Hanover County, Virginia, 1995* (Mechanicsville, Va.: privately published, 1995), 37, 107.

36. Shockoe Hill Burying Ground had opened early in the nineteenth century. In 1864 it remained the most prestigious cemetery in Richmond, though it was no longer the largest.

37. Lt. Col. Warwick first appeared in the June 28, 1862, entry of Mrs. McGuire's diary.

38. On September 14, Gen. Wade Hampton led 4,000 Confederate cavalry on a raid to secure at least part of a 2,500-cattle herd south of City Point inside Union lines. Union forces outnumbered Hampton by 20 to 1; nevertheless, the "Beefsteak Raid" netted 2,486 cattle plus 300 prisoners at a cost of 61 Southerners. The affair remains the largest cattle-rustling operation in American history.

39. The third battle of Winchester occurred September 19 between Gen. Philip Sheridan's 43,000 troops and Gen. Jubal Early's 12,500 ill-equipped soldiers. Superior Union numbers eventually carried the day. Federal casualties were 5,000; Early's 3,500 losses represented almost one-third of his command. Among those killed were Confederate generals Robert E. Rodes and Archibald C. Godwin. Gen. Fitzhugh Lee suffered a thigh wound that would incapacitate him from duty for four months.

40. Jefferson Phelps of the Ninth Virginia Cavalry was captured September 24 and exchanged in January 1865. Robert K. Krick, *9th Virginia Cavalry* (Lynchburg, Va.: H. E. Howard, 1982), 92.

41. Pvt. Edward H. Colston of the Second Virginia Cavalry emerged unharmed from the September 29 action at Waynesboro. He later was promoted to corporal and lost an arm in the April 6, 1865, battle at High Bridge, Virginia. Robert J. Driver Jr. and H. E. Howard, *2nd Virginia Cavalry* (Lynchburg, Va.: H. E. Howard, 1995), 208.

42. Fort Harrison was a key stronghold in the Confederate defenses north of the James River. Federals attacked and captured the works on the 29th, then withstood counterattacks the following day. Grant was unable to proceed beyond Fort Harrison to the inner defenses of Richmond.

43. Failing to take Richmond by land, Union general Benjamin Butler tried

another scheme. On August 10, Butler's Army of the James began digging a canal across a 174-yard neck of land called Dutch Gap. If successful, the canal would bypass nearly five miles of the meandering James River. The canal was completed by year's end, but it was not until April 1865—too late to be of value—that the canal opened to river traffic.

44. An October 9 attack on Gen. Thomas Rosser's outmanned cavalry division resulted in the first defeat that Rosser had suffered in the war. Federals seized three hundred prisoners at a loss of seventeen men. Millard K. and Dean M. Bushong, *Fightin' Tom Rosser, C.S.A.* (Shippensburg, Pa.: Beidel, 1983), 118–21.

45. On October 19, Early's army delivered a surprise attack on encamped Federals at Cedar Creek. Fighting extended for several miles until Union general Sheridan rallied his army. Weight of numbers drove Early from the field in what was to be the last major engagement in the Shenandoah Valley.

46. The October 22 "Address from General Early to His Troops" is in *Richmond Daily Dispatch,* October 27, 1864.

47. While Hood and his battered Army of Tennessee were preparing to drive into Tennessee in a desperate hope of pulling Sherman from Georgia, the Union general was finalizing plans for his own offensive: an eastward march to the Atlantic Ocean.

48. In the autumn of 1864, with a force of about 12,000 men, Gen. Sterling Price invaded Missouri and made for St. Louis. A bloody engagement followed at Pilot Knob. Prince then advanced west along the Missouri River with a larger Union army in pursuit. Defeated at Westport on October 23, Price retired all the way to Texas.

49. In Rockingham County alone, Sheridan's men burned 30 dwellings, 31 mills, 450 barns, and 3 factories. Over 100 miles of fencing were destroyed, as were 100,000 bushels of wheat, 50,000 bushels of corn, and 6,232 tons of hay. Federals also killed or seized 1,750 cattle, 1,750 horses, 4,200 sheep, and 3,350 hogs. John L. Heatwole, *The Burning: Sheridan in the Shenandoah Valley* (Charlottesville, Va.: Howell, 1998), 192–93.

50. John W. Brown was a captain in the Forty-seventh North Carolina. On August 25, he was wounded in the right thigh at Reams's Station. He died there on October 5. Weymouth T. Jordan Jr., *North Carolina Troops, 1861–1865: A Roster,* XI (Raleigh: North Carolina Office of Archives and History, 2004), 340.

51. *Job* 7:10.

52. On November 13, a defeated Early retired to New Market. Some of the Confederates rejoined Lee's command at Petersburg. Sheridan drew back his forces to guard the more strategic points in the lower Valley.

53. Sherman and 60,000 veteran soldiers left Atlanta in flames on November 16 and headed east on what would become the "March to the Sea." This offensive

would demonstrate conclusively that the Confederacy was no longer capable of protecting its interior.

54. Although Gen. P. G. T. Beauregard was a departmental commander and outranked Hood, the latter made no effort to utilize his services or even to keep him informed of army movements. Beauregard thereupon left his Mississippi headquarters and went to Georgia to assist in the defense against Sherman. "Arise for the defense of your native soil!" he told the Georgia people in a November 19 proclamation. "Obstruct and destroy all roads in Sherman's front, flank, and rear, and his army will soon starve in your midst! . . . I hasten to join you in defense of your homes and firesides." *OR*, series 1, vol. 44, 867.

55. Georgia governor Joseph E. Brown and Vice President Stephens were leading spokesmen for the growing anti-Davis faction in the South.

56. Angus William McDonald Sr., born in 1799, had prospered in the lower Shenandoah Valley as a lawyer. He was first colonel of the Seventh Virginia Cavalry but resigned late in 1861 because of crippling rheumatism. In July 1864, Federals captured McDonald in Rockbridge County. He died in Richmond on December 1, "after having [suffered] a succession of indecencies at the hands of his captors, notably Gen. David Hunter." Krick, *Lee's Colonels*, 214–15.

57. For Mrs. Cornelia Peake McDonald's account of her husband's death and funeral, see her *A Diary with Reminiscences of the War and Refugee Life in the Shenandoah Valley, 1860–1865,* ed. Hunter McDonald (Nashville: Cullom and Ghertner, 1934), 236–43.

58. On December 13, elements of Sherman's army captured Fort McAllister on the Ogeechee River south of Savannah. This action reopened Sherman's communications with the outside world via the U.S. Navy.

59. Some 4,000 Union horsemen under Gen. George Stoneman conducted a mid-December raid on the lead mines near Wytheville and the saltworks at Saltville. Confederate general John C. Breckinridge, outnumbered four to one, could offer only minimum resistance. On December 21, Federals captured and destroyed the ponds at Saltville.

60. Mayor Richard D. Arnold surrendered Savannah to Union forces on December 20. In a telegram two days later, Sherman presented the city to President Lincoln as a Christmas gift.

61. For details of the December 10 nighttime attack by Gen. Thomas Rosser's cavalrymen against a portion of Union general George Custer's division, see Bushong, *Fightin' Tom Rosser*, 155.

62. On December 19, Union general A. T. A. Torbert and 8,000 cavalry conducted a raid on the railroad junction of Gordonsville. Several small actions took place in bitterly cold weather. Troopers under Lunsford Lomax eventually repulsed the Federal probe. See *OR*, series 1, vol. 43, pt. 1, 678, 942–44.

63. Never in the war years did Mrs. McGuire become gay and carefree about Christmas. Being devout and sensitive to the tragedy of the period, she opted for religious dedication. One commentator noted that Mrs. McGuire "regretted the excessive extravaganza and frivolity which so many people insisted on at this season, but Mrs. McGuire never caustically criticized them, for such was not her nature. She was only saddened by their conduct which she felt hurt rather than helped the Confederacy." Mary Elizabeth Massey, *Refugee Life in the Confederacy* (Baton Rouge: Louisiana State University Press, 1964), 199.

64. Betty McGuire was Mrs. McGuire's stepdaughter-in-law.

65. Fifteen years old in 1860, Sallie M. Warwick was the youngest of five children of Abram Warwick. He co-owned Gallego Flour Mills and was one of Richmond's wealthiest residents. 1860 Virginia Census—Henrico County.

66. Mary Elizabeth Meredith, daughter of John A. Meredith, died December 23 of typhoid fever. *Richmond Daily Dispatch*, December 24, 1864.

67. Fifty-six Union vessels—the largest American armada ever assembled to that time—converged on Fort Fisher, which guarded the river entrance to Wilmington, North Carolina. The heaviest naval bombardment of the Civil War followed on December 23–24, but little damage was done to the sand-built installation.

68. Of all Southern cities, Richmond felt the privations of war most keenly. Its resources and citizen cooperation were all but exhausted by late 1864.

69. Union Hill was a residential section of Richmond east of Shockoe Valley and near Church Hill.

70. Since Mrs. McGuire was from an old and respected Richmond family, she had every right to attend these social functions. Yet she thought the war too heartbreaking for such revelry. Other Southern residents compared the partygoers to Nero fiddling while Rome burned. See Cumming, *Journal*, 86.

71. In the Dickins Copy, Mrs. McGuire identified this person as Annette Powell. She may have been Sally A. Powell, listed in the 1860 Virginia Census—Henrico County as the twenty-three-year-old daughter of master carpenter Charles A. Powell.

72. Mrs. McGuire's observation about so many weddings is probably the most quoted passage in her diary. Wartime promoted quick romances and quick marriages. Short furloughs, inevitable separations, and the higher possibility of death quickened the pace to the altar.

73. Sir Walter Scott, *The Lay of the Last Minstrel*.

74. These are the concluding lines of Sir Thomas More's *Remember the Time*.

75. Camp Hamilton was the prisoner-of-war release point near Fort Monroe.

76. J. A. Blake commanded Chesapeake Military Prison at Camp Hamilton. *OR*, series 2, vol. 7, 211.

77. On January 15, after a Union naval bombardment and concerted infantry attack, the 1,900-man garrison at Fort Fisher surrendered. Wilmington now ceased to be the last major blockade-running port. The city remained in Confederate hands, but was thenceforth of little importance.

78. For example, see *Richmond Daily Dispatch,* January 6, 12, and 20, 1865.

79. "So Gideon, and the hundred men that were with him . . . blew the trumpets . . . and they cried The sword of the Lord, and of Gideon. . . . And all the host ran, and cried, and fled." *Judges* 7:19–20.

80. After two weeks of preparation, on February 3 Sherman's Union army began its northern advance into South Carolina. A number of skirmishes followed, but Sherman met no strong opposition.

81. Hymen was the Greek god of marriage.

82. In 1860 teenager Mary Garnett was living with druggist John Ludlow and his wife, Maria, in Norfolk. 1860 Virginia Census—Norfolk County.

83. Mrs. McGuire identified her fellow worker in the Dickins Copy as "T. Weever." No such individual appears in the 1860 Virginia census.

84. On February 6, 1865, President Davis finally removed the incompetent and highly unpopular Lucius B. Northrop as commissary general. His successor was Col. Isaac M. St. John. One of the people happiest about this change was General Lee. See Douglas Southall Freeman, *R. E. Lee: A Biography* (New York: Scribner's, 1935), 3:536.

85. Hunter served as Confederate secretary of state, congressman from Virginia, and member of the three-man Hampton Roads peace conference in February 1865. The conference was held aboard the steamer *River Queen* at Hampton Roads. Nothing came of the meeting.

86. Former U.S. senator Mallory of Florida served as Confederate secretary of the navy for the entirety of the war.

87. Sheridan's Union forces controlled the bulk of the Shenandoah Valley by October 1864. Sheridan continued his raiding activities and on March 2, 1865, crushed the remnants of Early's Confederate army at Waynesboro.

88. Back in June 1864, at the urging of Grant, Gen. David Hunter and 15,000 Federals advanced southward up the Valley. Guerrilla attacks on the Union columns triggered retaliatory action by the Federals that included the burning of the Virginia Military Institute at Lexington. Hunter's advance came to a halt at Lynchburg, where Confederates under Early sent the Union commander fleeing westward toward the safety of the mountains.

89. What Mrs. McGuire heard was the almost daily bombardment by Union cannon of Confederate positions on the Richmond-Petersburg line.

90. This was John Thomas Lewis Preston of Lexington. One of the founders of the Virginia Military Institute (VMI), he served brief stints on "Stonewall"

Jackson's staff and in the Ninth Virginia before being ordered back to the institute.

91. Pegram was among the most handsome and admired of Richmond soldiers. He and his bride had honeymooned at Pegram's headquarters near Hatcher's Run. There he was killed in action. Three weeks to the day after the wedding, his bride knelt before his coffin at St. Paul's Episcopal Church.

92. During the 1864–1865 siege of Richmond and Petersburg, Hill had been Lee's most dependable corps commander. That ended just after dawn on April 2, when Hill was shot through the heart while trying to stabilize his lines in front of Grant's massive assaults.

93. Twenty-one-year-old Barksdale Warwick had attended VMI and served intermittently as an aide to Gen. Henry Wise before his March 29, 1865, death near Petersburg.

94. Reference here is to the March 25 daybreak attack launched by Lee against Fort Stedman in the Union lines. The assault lost momentum; Lee had no reserves to commit to the action. While Union casualties were 1,500 men, Confederate losses (mostly prisoners) exceeded 4,000 soldiers.

95. Cooper, the highest-ranking general officer in the Confederacy, served as adjutant and inspector general throughout the four years of war.

96. For their final duty, Lt. William H. Parker and the midshipmen of the C.S. Naval Academy were assigned to accompany the Confederate archives and specie by train to Danville. No person with a first or last name beginning with "J" is listed on the naval school's faculty. J. Thomas Scharf, *History of the Confederate States Navy from Its Organization to the Surrender of the Last Vessel* (New York: Rogers and Sherwood, 1887), 773–77.

97. Camp Jackson was the area around Jackson Hospital, which was immediately northeast of Winder Hospital and Hollywood Cemetery. Today the Downtown Expressway passes through the site.

98. Lee's telegram to Davis was explicit: "I think it is absolutely necessary that we should abandon our position tonight. I have given all the necessary orders on the subject to the troops." Robert E. Lee, *The Wartime Papers of R. E. Lee*, ed. Clifford Dowdey and Louis H. Manarin (Boston: Little, Brown, 1961), 925–26.

99. The greatest resentment of Richmond citizens seemed to be toward acquaintances whose outward allegiance to the Confederacy changed overnight with the fall of Richmond. Nelson Lankford, *Richmond Burning: The Last Days of the Confederate Capital* (New York: Viking, 2002), 124.

100. Out-of-control fires at the Richmond arsenal and laboratory ignited thousands of artillery shells and cartridges that became as deadly as the consuming flames.

101. The new explosions came from three Confederate naval vessels or-

dered destroyed to prevent their capture. Another Richmond diarist likened the noise to "that of a hundred cannon at one time. The very foundations of the city were shaken . . . and the frightened inhabitants imagined that the place was being furiously bombarded." Sallie A. Brock Putnam, *Richmond during the War: Four Years of Personal Observations by a Richmond Lady* (New York: G. W. Carlton, 1867), 365.

102. This word originally was a contraction of the word "Bethlehem." In 1402 a London religious house known as St. Mary of Bethlehem was converted into a hospital for the insane. The word now refers to any lunatic asylum or madhouse.

103. The city powder magazine was a small brick building on a hillside near the poorhouse. Confederates detonated the contents to prevent them falling into Union hands. The *Richmond Whig* later stated that "nothing but a long narrow trench in the ground, looking like the grave of a resurrected giant, marks the spot where the magazine stood." Quoted in Lankford, *Richmond Burning*, 103.

104. Evidence points strongly to this individual being Col. Thomas Green Peyton. A Richmond merchant before and after the war, Peyton was lieutenant colonel and staff officer in the capital for most of the war years.

105. One of Mrs. McGuire's closest friends and a former neighbor in Alexandria, Margaret Randolph Dickins is mentioned often in the diary.

106. Ann Coles Randolph was the wife of prominent businessman John Rutherford.

107. In all likelihood, Mrs. McGuire was referring to Sallie Warwick, whose father was the leading miller in Richmond. Their two-story home on East Grace Street was in the heart of the downtown and the first mansion of the Greek Revival period constructed in the city. Michael D. Gorman to editor, January 15, 2007; Mary Wingfield Scott, *Houses of Old Richmond* (Richmond: Valentine Museum, 1941), 187.

108. Charles Read's United Presbyterian Church was the only house of worship consumed by the fires of Richmond. Read, out of town when the capital was evacuated, walked forty-five miles to protect his church but arrived too late.

109. Abram Warwick and Claiborne R. Barksdale owned what was usually called Gallego Mills, the largest flour mill in the world at the beginning of the Civil War. In many photographs taken of Richmond in mid-April 1865, the hulking ruins of Gallego are conspicuous. Michael D. Gorman, to editor, January 15, 2007.

110. Gen. Edward Otho Cresap Ord had succeeded Gen. Benjamin Butler as commander of the Army of the James. A few days after the capture of Richmond, Ord replaced Gen. Godfrey Weitzel as military commander of the capital.

111. In reworking her diary after the war, Mrs. McGuire got her dates confused and her facts a bit garbled. The Union president, guarded by ten sailors,

arrived in Richmond on the afternoon of April 4 and departed the next day. Mrs. McGuire's account at this point seems based more on hearsay than on personal observations.

112. Secretary of War Edwin M. Stanton did not accompany Lincoln on the trip. One Virginian recalled the Lincoln party being met by "a huge crowd of dirty and jabbering negroes and outcasts." John Esten Cooke, *Mohun* (New York: G. W. Dillingham, 1869), 355.

113. Charles Richardson of Fredericksburg was a lieutenant colonel commanding an artillery battalion when, at the 1864 battle of Spotsylvania, a shell ripped away part of his stomach. After receiving his parole in May 1865, Richardson returned home and operated a pickle factory. Krick, *Lee's Colonels*, 275.

114. In one of the prayers of the Confederate Episcopal *Book of Common Prayer*, the faithful asked God "to behold and bless thy servant The President of the Confederate States, and all others in authority." Union authorities objected to the phrase; Richmond Episcopalians would not return to the original blessing for the "President of the United States and all others in authority." Hence, no reference in the morning prayer service was made to either leader.

115. Thomas Cowper, *The Task*.

116. Johnston and what remained of the Army of Tennessee retreated through North Carolina in the face of Sherman's steady advance. On April 26, Johnston agreed to surrender terms at Bennett Station, near Durham.

117. A North Carolina woman commented at the same period: "Since we heard of our disaster, I seem as tho' in a dream . . . ; I think of it, but I cannot grasp it or its future consequences. I sit benumbed. It is to me like the idea of eternity." Catherine Ann Devereux Edmondston, *Journal of a Secesh Lady: The Diary of Catherine Ann Devereux, 1860–1865 Edmondston* (Raleigh: North Carolina Department of Cultural Resources, Division of Archives and History. 1979), 695.

118. Eliza Davenport, then in her mid-thirties, was the only daughter of prosperous merchant Isaac Davenport. Blanton, *Medicine in Virginia*, 303; 1860 Virginia Census—Henrico County.

119. It is interesting that here Mrs. McGuire attached more importance to the strangulation of the blockade than to Southern defeats on the battlefield.

120. Moses Drury Hoge served as pastor of Richmond's Second Presbyterian Church for more than fifty years.

121. On the night of April 14, John Wilkes Booth assassinated President Lincoln at Ford's Theater in Washington. An accomplice permanently disfigured Secretary of State William H. Seward in an attempt to murder him.

122. Mrs. McGuire had reason to feel that Federals might move against outspoken citizens. Mrs. Lucy Fletcher lost a brother and brother-in-law, killed

in the war. She wrote: "While I could not but experience a thrill of horror on hearing of his [Lincoln's] miserable end . . . it was a just retribution for the thousands of murders which must be heavy on his soul." Quoted in Lankford, *Richmond Burning*, 223.

123. Some accounts state that people began to cheer Lee as he came into sight and that the general acknowledged their praise by repeatedly lifting his hat. However, his chief aide asserted that no "demonstration attended General Lee's return." Walter H. Taylor, *General Lee: His Campaigns in Virginia, 1861–1865* (Norfolk, Va.: Nusbaum Book and News, 1906), 297.

124. "Woe worth the chase, woe worth the day / That costs thy life, my gallant grey." Sir Walter Scott, *The Lady of the Lake.*

125. Emily Simms Forrest was the wife of naval commodore French Forrest. Before the war she reigned over Clermont, the family estate four miles west of Alexandria. George Kundahl, *Alexandria Goes to War* (Knoxville: University of Tennessee Press, 2004), 147.

126. Capt. Jefferson Phelps had served in the Ninth Virginia Cavalry before joining Mosby's Forty-third Virginia Cavalry Battalion. Captured in 1864, Phelps received parole on April 8, 1865, at Mechanicsville. Keen and Mewborn, *43rd Battalion Virginia Cavalry,* 356.

127. Mary McGuire Johns was Mrs. McGuire's stepdaughter.

128. Twenty-two hundred years earlier, the Greek philosopher Euripides wrote in *Medea*: "What greater grief than the loss of one's native land."

129. Andrews, *Women of the South,* 80–81.

130. *Confederate Veteran* 33 (1925): 253.

131. Slaughter, *Settlers, Southerners, Americans,* 110.

132. Interview with De Shields Fisher, Tappahannock, Va., March 9, 2007. Mr. Fisher's mother was a friend of Mrs. McGuire.

Selected Bibliography

Abbott, Martin. *The Freedmen's Bureau in South Carolina, 1865–1872.* Chapel Hill: University of North Carolina Press, 1967.

Abel, E. Lawrence. *Singing the New Nation: How Music Shaped the Confederacy, 1861–1865.* Mechanicsburg, Pa.: Stackpole, 2000.

Alexander, Edward Porter. *Fighting for the Confederacy: The Personal Recollections of General Edward Porter Alexander.* Edited by Gary W. Gallagher. Chapel Hill: University of North Carolina Press, 1989.

Aley, Ginette. "'We are all good scavengers now': The Crisis in Virginia Agriculture during the Civil War." In William C. Davis and James I. Robertson Jr., eds., *Virginia at War, 1864.* Lexington: University Press of Kentucky, 2009.

Allardice, Bruce S. *More Generals in Gray.* Baton Rouge: Louisiana State University Press, 1995.

Ash, Stephen V. *When the Yankees Came: Conflict and Chaos in the Occupied South, 1861–1865.* Chapel Hill: University of North Carolina Press, 1995.

Averill, J. H. "Richmond, Virginia: The Evacuation of the City and the Days Preceding It." *Southern Historical Society Papers* 25 (January–December 1897).

Bailey, James H. *Henrico Home Front, 1861–1865: A Picture of Life in Henrico County, Virginia.* Richmond: n.p., 1963.

Ballard, Michael B. *A Long Shadow: Jefferson Davis and the Final Days of the Confederacy.* Jackson: University Press of Mississippi, 1986.

Bearss, Edwin, and Christopher M. Calkins. *Battle of Five Forks.* Lynchburg, Va.: H. E. Howard, 1985.

Bennett, Lerone, Jr. *Forced into Glory: Abraham Lincoln's White Dream.* Chicago: Johnson, 2000.

Bentley, George R. *A History of the Freedmen's Bureau.* New York: Octagon Books, 1970.

Berlin, Ira. *Slaves without Masters: The Free Negro in the Antebellum South.* New York: New Press, 1974.

Berlin, Ira, Barbara J. Fields, Steven F. Miller, Joseph P. Reidy, and Leslie S. Rowland, eds. *Free at Last: A Documentary History of Slavery, Freedom, and the Civil War.* New York: New Press, 1992.

Berlin, Ira, Joseph P. Reidy, and Leslie S. Rowland, eds. *The Black Military Experience.* Series 2, vol. 1 of *Freedom: A Documentary History of Emancipation, 1861–1867.* New York: Cambridge University Press, 1982.

Bill, Alfred Hoyt. *The Beleaguered City: Richmond, 1861–1865.* New York: Knopf, 1946.

Black, Robert C. *The Railroads of the Confederacy.* Chapel Hill: University of North Carolina Press, 1952.

Blair, William. *Virginia's Private War: Feeding Body and Soul in the Confederacy, 1861–1865.* New York: Oxford University Press, 1998.

Blassingame, John W., ed. *Slave Testimony: Two Centuries of Letters, Speeches, Interviews, and Autobiographies.* Baton Rouge: Louisiana State University Press, 1977.

Bogger, Tommy L. *Free Blacks in Norfolk, Virginia, 1790–1860: The Darker Side of Freedom.* Charlottesville: University of Virginia Press, 1997.

Botkin, B. A., ed. *A Civil War Treasury of Tales, Legends, and Folklore.* Lincoln: University of Nebraska Press, 2000.

Bruce, H. W. "Some Reminiscences of the Second of April, 1865." *Southern Historical Society Papers* 9 (May 1881).

Buck, Samuel D. *With the Old Confeds: Actual Experiences of a Captain in the Line.* Baltimore, Md.: H. E. Houck, 1925.

Burkhardt, George S. *Confederate Rage, Yankee Wrath: No Quarter in the Civil War.* Carbondale: Southern Illinois University Press, 2007.

Calkins, Christopher M. *The Appomattox Campaign.* New York: Da Capo, 2001.

———. *The Battles of Appomattox Station and Appomattox Court House, April 8–9, 1865.* Lynchburg, Va.: H. E. Howard, 1987.

———. *The Final Bivouac: The Surrender Parade at Appomattox and the Disbanding of the Armies, April 10–May 20, 1865.* Lynchburg, Va.: H. E. Howard, 1988.

———. *From Petersburg to Appomattox—A Tour Guide to the Routes of Lee's Withdrawal and Grant's Pursuit, April 2–9, 1865.* Farmville, Va.: Farmville Herald, 1983.

———. *Thirty-six Hours Before Appomattox: The Battles of Sailor's Creek, High Bridge, Farmville and Cumberland Church.* Farmville, Va.: Farmville Herald, 1980.

Campbell, Edward D. C., Jr., and Kym S. Rice, eds. *A Woman's War: Southern Women, Civil War, and the Confederate Legacy.* Charlottesville: University of Virginia Press, 1996.

Campbell, Jacqueline Glass. *When Sherman Marched North from the Sea: Resistance on the Confederate Home Front.* Chapel Hill: University of North Carolina Press, 2003.

Carmichael, Peter S. *The Last Generation: Young Virginians in Peace, War, and Reunion.* Chapel Hill: University of North Carolina Press, 2005.

Carroll, J. Frank. *Confederate Treasure in Danville.* Danville, Va.: Ure, 1996.

Casstevens, Frances H. *George W. Alexander and Castle Thunder: A Confederate Prison and Its Commandant.* Jefferson, N.C.: McFarland, 2004.

Catton, Bruce. *Never Call Retreat.* New York: Doubleday, 1965.

Cauble, Frank P. *The Proceedings Connected with the Surrender of the Army of Northern Virginia, April 1865.* Lynchburg, Va.: H. E. Howard, 1987.

Chamberlayne, Ham. *Ham Chamberlayne—Virginian: Letters and Papers of an Artillery Officer in the War for Southern Independence, 1861–1865.* Edited by C. G. Chamberlayne. 1932. Reprint, Wilmington, N.C.: Broadfoot, 1992.

Chesnut, Mary Boykin Miller. *Mary Chesnut's Civil War.* Edited by C. Vann Woodward. New Haven, Conn.: Yale University Press, 1981.

Chesson, Michael B. *Richmond After the War, 1865–1890.* Richmond: Virginia State Library, 1981.

Chester, Thomas Morris. *Thomas Morris Chester, Black Civil War Correspondent: His Dispatches from the Virginia Front.* Edited by R. J. M. Blackett. Baton Rouge: Louisiana State University Press, 1989.

Cimbala, Paul A. *Under the Guardianship of the Nation: The Freedmen's Bureau and the Reconstruction of Georgia, 1865–1870.* Athens: University of Georgia Press, 1997.

Clark, James C. *Last Train South: The Flight of the Confederate Government from Richmond.* Jefferson, N.C.: McFarland, 1984.

Clark, Malcolm Cameron. *The First Quarter-Century of the Richmond & Danville Railroad, 1847–1871.* Washington, D.C.: n.p., 1959.

Clark, Micajah H. "The Last Days of the Confederate Treasury and What Became of Its Specie." *Southern Historical Society Papers* 9 (October–December 1881).

———. "Retreat of Cabinet from Richmond." *Confederate Veteran,* July 1898.

Culpepper, Marilyn Mayer, ed. *Women of the Civil War South: Personal Accounts from Diaries, Letters and Postwar Reminiscences.* Jefferson, N.C.: McFarland, 2004.

Dabney, Virginius. *Richmond: The Story of a City.* Garden City, N.Y.: Doubleday, 1976.

Dailey, Jane. *Before Jim Crow: The Politics of Race in Postemancipation Virginia.* Chapel Hill: University of North Carolina Press, 2000.

Davis, Burke. *The Long Surrender.* New York: Random House, 1985.

———. *To Appomattox: Nine April Days, 1865.* New York: Rinehart, 1959.

Davis, Jefferson. *The Rise and Fall of the Confederate Government.* 2 vols. New York: Appleton, 1881.

Davis, William C. *Jefferson Davis: The Man and His Hour.* New York: Harper-Collins, 1991.

———. *Look Away! A History of the Confederate States of America.* New York: Free Press, 2002.

Davis, William C., and Bell I. Wiley, eds. *The End of an Era.* Vol. 6 of *The Image of War: 1861–1865.* Garden City, N.Y.: Doubleday, 1984.

Dean, Eric T., Jr. *Shook over Hell: Post-traumatic Stress, Vietnam, and the Civil War.* Cambridge, Mass.: Harvard University Press, 1997.

Delaney, Ted, and Phillip Wayne Rhodes. *Free Blacks of Lynchburg, Virginia, 1805–1865.* Lynchburg, Va.: Warwick House, 2001.

De Leon, Thomas Cooper. *Belles, Beaux, and Brains of the 60's.* New York: Arno, 1974.

———. *Four Years in Rebel Capitals: An Inside View of Life in the Southern Confederacy, from Birth to Death.* Mobile, Ala.: Gossip, 1890.

Dennett, John Richard. *The South as It Is: 1865–1866.* Edited by Henry M. Christman. New York: Viking, 1965.

Dew, Charles B. *Apostles of Disunion: Southern Secession Commissioners and the Causes of the Civil War.* Charlottesville: University of Virginia Press, 2001.

Dooley, John. *John Dooley, Confederate Soldier: His War Journal.* Edited by Joseph T. Durkin. South Bend, Ind.: University of Notre Dame Press, 1963.

Dormon, James H., Jr. *Theater in the Ante Bellum South, 1815–1861.* Chapel Hill: University of North Carolina Press, 1967.

Douglas, Henry Kyd. *I Rode with Stonewall: Being Chiefly the War Experience of the Youngest Member of Jackson's Staff from the John Brown Raid to the Hanging of Mrs. Surrat.* Chapel Hill: University of North Carolina Press, 1940.

Driver, Robert J., Jr. *52nd Virginia Infantry.* Lynchburg, Va.: H. E. Howard, 1986.

———. *Lexington and Rockbridge County in the Civil War.* Lynchburg, Va.: H. E. Howard, 1989.

Du Bois, W. E. B. *Black Reconstruction in America: An Essay toward a History of the Part Which Black Folk Played in the Attempt to Reconstruct Democracy in America, 1860–1880.* New York: Atheneum, 1969.

Duncan, Richard R. *Beleaguered Winchester: A Virginia Community at War, 1861–1865.* Baton Rouge: Louisiana State University Press, 2007.

Durkin, Joseph T. *Confederate Navy Chief: Stephen R. Mallory.* Columbia: University of South Carolina Press, 1987.

Eanes, Greg. *Black Day of the Army, April 6, 1865: The Battles of Sailor's Creek.* Burkeville, Va.: E and H, 2001.

Edmondston, Catherine Ann Devereux. *Journal of a Secesh Lady: The Diary of Catherine Ann Devereux Edmondston, 1860–1865.* Raleigh: North Carolina Department of Cultural Resources, Division of Archives and History, 1979.

Eggleston, George Cary. *A Rebel's Recollections*. 1875. Reprint, Baton Rouge: Louisiana State University Press, 1996.

Engs, Robert F. *Freedom's First Generation: Black Hampton, Virginia, 1861–1890*. 1979. Reprint, New York: Fordham University Press, 2004.

Farmer-Kaiser, Mary. "'With a Weight of Circumstances Like Millstones about Their Necks': Freedwomen, Federal Relief, and the Benevolent Guardianship of the Freedmen's Bureau." *Virginia Magazine of History and Biography* 115 (January 2007).

Faust, Drew Gilpin. *Mothers of Invention: Women of the Slaveholding South in the American Civil War*. Chapel Hill: University of North Carolina Press, 1996.

Faust, Patricia L., ed. *Historical Times Illustrated Encyclopedia of the Civil War*. New York: Harper and Row, 1986.

Foner, Eric. *Reconstruction: America's Unfinished Revolution, 1863–1877*. New York: HarperCollins, 2005.

Freeman, Douglas Southall. *Lee's Lieutenants: A Study in Command*. 3 vols. New York: Scribner's, 1942–1944.

——. *R. E. Lee: A Biography*. 4 vols. New York: Scribner's, 1934.

Friedman, Jean E. *The Enclosed Garden: Women and Community in the Evangelical South, 1830–1900*. Chapel Hill: University of North Carolina Press, 1985.

Furgurson, Ernest B. *Ashes of Glory: Richmond at War*. New York: Knopf, 1996.

Gallagher, Gary W. *The Confederate War*. Cambridge, Mass.: Harvard University Press, 1997.

——, ed. *Struggle for the Shenandoah: Essays on the 1864 Valley Campaign*. Kent, Ohio: Kent State University Press, 1991.

Garidel, Henri. *Exile in Richmond: The Confederate Journal of Henri Garidel*. Edited by Michael Bedout Chesson and Leslie Jean Roberts. Charlottesville: University of Virginia Press, 2001.

Gates, Paul W. *Agriculture and the Civil War*. New York: Knopf, 1965.

Giles, Val C. *Rags and Hope: The Recollections of Val C. Giles; Four Years with Hood's Brigade Fourth Texas Infantry, 1861–1865*. Edited by Mary Lasswell. New York: Coward-McCann, 1961.

Glatthaar, Joseph T. *Forged in Battle: The Civil War Alliance of Black Soldiers and White Officers*. New York: Free Press, 1990.

Gordon, John B. *Reminiscences of the Civil War*. New York: Scribner's, 1903.

Gorgas, Josiah. "Contributions to the History of the Confederate Ordnance Department." *Southern Historical Society Papers* 12 (January–February 1884).

——. *The Journals of Josiah Gorgas, 1857–1878*. Edited by Sarah Woolfolk Wiggins. Tuscaloosa: University of Alabama Press, 1995.

Greene, A. Wilson. *Breaking the Backbone of the Rebellion—The Final Battles of the Petersburg Campaign*. Mason City, Iowa: Savas, 2000.

——. *Civil War Petersburg: Confederate City in the Crucible of War.* Charlottesville: University of Virginia Press, 2006.

Greenough, Mark K. "Aftermath at Appomattox: Federal Military Occupation of Appomattox County, May–November 1865." *Civil War History* 31 (March 1985).

Grimsley, Mark. *The Hard Hand of War: Union Military Policy toward Southern Civilians, 1861–1865.* Cambridge: Cambridge University Press, 1995.

Guild, June Purcell. *Black Laws of Virginia: A Summary of the Legislative Acts of Virginia concerning Negroes from Earliest Times to the Present.* 1936. Reprint, New York: Negro University Press, 1969.

Gutman, Herbert G. *The Black Family in Slavery and Freedom, 1750–1925.* New York: Pantheon Books, 1976.

Hahn, Steven, Steven F. Miller, Susan E. O'Donovan, John C. Rodrigue, and Leslie S. Rowland, eds. *Land and Labor, 1865.* Series 3, vol. 1 of *Freedom: A Documentary History of Emancipation, 1861–1867.* Chapel Hill: University of North Carolina Press, 2008.

Hairston, L. Beatrice W. *A Brief History of Danville, Virginia, 1728–1954.* Richmond: Dietz, 1955.

Hanna, Alfred Jackson. *Flight into Oblivion.* Bloomington: Indiana University Press, 1959.

Harrison, Burton. "Retreat of the Cabinet." *Southern Historical Society Papers* 26 (January–December 1898).

Harrison, Mrs. Burton. *Recollections Grave and Gay.* New York: Scribner's, 1911.

Harwell, Richard Barksdale, ed. *A Confederate Diary of the Retreat from Petersburg, April 3–20, 1865.* Atlanta: Emory University Publications Sources and Reprints, 1953.

Heatwole, John L. *The Burning: Sheridan in the Shenandoah Valley.* Charlottesville, Va.: Howell, 1998.

Heidler, David S., and Jeanne T. Heidler. *Encyclopedia of the American Civil War: A Political, Social, and Military History.* New York: Norton, 2000.

Heinemann, Ronald L., John G. Kolp, Anthony S. Parent Jr., and William G. Shade. *Old Dominion, New Commonwealth: A History of Virginia, 1607–2007.* Charlottesville: University of Virginia Press, 2007.

Hewett, Janet B., et al., eds. *Supplement to the Official Records of the Union and Confederate Armies.* Wilmington, N.C.: Broadfoot, 1994–2001.

Hilliard, Sam Bowers. *Atlas of Antebellum Southern Agriculture.* Baton Rouge: Louisiana State University Press, 1984.

Hodgkins, William H. *Battle of Fort Stedman, March 25, 1865.* Boston: Privately published, 1889.

Holberton, William B. *Homeward Bound: The Demobilization of the Union and Confederate Armies, 1865–1866.* Mechanicsburg, Pa.: Stackpole, 2001.

Horst, Samuel L. *Education for Manhood: The Education of Blacks in Virginia during the Civil War.* Lanham, Md.: University Press of America, 1987.

Hunter, R. M. T. "The Peace Commission of 1865." *Southern Historical Society Papers* 3 (April 1877).

Huston, James L. *Calculating the Value of Union: Slavery, Property Rights, and the Economic Origins of the Civil War.* Chapel Hill: University of North Carolina Press, 2003.

Jackson, Luther Porter. *Free Negro Labor and Property Holding in Virginia, 1830–1860.* New York: Appleton-Century, 1942.

———. *Negro Office-holders in Virginia, 1865–1895.* Norfolk, Va.: Guide Quality Press, 1945.

Jennison, Keith W. *The Humorous Mr. Lincoln.* New York: Bonanza Books, 1965.

Jones, John B. *A Rebel War Clerk's Diary.* 2 vols. Edited by Earl Schenck Miers. 1866. Reprint, Alexandria, Va.: Time-Life, 1982.

Jordan, Ervin L., Jr. *Black Confederates and Afro-Yankees in Civil War Virginia.* Charlottesville: University of Virginia Press, 1995.

Kean, Robert Garlick Hill. *Inside the Confederate Government: The Diary of Robert Garlick Hill Kean.* Edited by Edward Younger. 1957. Reprint, Baton Rouge: Louisiana State University Press, 1993.

Kendall, John Smith. *The Golden Age of the New Orleans Theater.* Baton Rouge: Louisiana State University Press, 1952.

Kenzer, Robert C. "Family, Kinship, and Neighborhood in an Antebellum Southern Community." In William J. Cooper Jr., Michael F. Holt, and John McCardell, eds., *A Master's Due: Essays in Honor of David Herbert Donald.* Baton Rouge: Louisiana State University Press, 1985.

Kimball, Gregg D. *American City, Southern Place: A Cultural History of Antebellum Richmond.* Athens: University of Georgia Press, 2000.

Kmen, Henry A. *Music in New Orleans: The Formative Years, 1791–1841.* Baton Rouge: Louisiana State University Press, 1966.

Krick, Robert K. *Lee's Colonels: A Biographical Register of the Field Officers of the Army of Northern Virginia.* Dayton, Ohio: Morningside Bookshop, 1979.

Lankford, Nelson. *Richmond Burning: The Last Days of the Confederate Capital.* New York: Viking, 2002.

Lebsock, Suzanne. *The Free Women of Petersburg: Status and Culture in a Southern Town, 1784–1860.* New York: Norton, 1984.

Lee, Robert E. *Lee's Dispatches: Unpublished Letters of General Robert E. Lee, C.S.A., to Jefferson Davis and the War Department of the Confederate States of America, 1862–65.* Edited by Douglas Southall Freeman. New York: G. P. Putnam's Sons, 1915.

——. *The Wartime Papers of Robert E. Lee.* Edited by Clifford Dowdey. 1961. Reprint, New York: Da Capo, 1987.

Lee, Susanna Michele. "Reconciliation in Reconstruction Virginia." In Edward L. Ayers, Gary W. Gallagher, and Andrew J. Torget, eds., *Crucible of the Civil War: Virginia from Secession to Commemoration.* Charlottesville: University of Virginia Press, 2006.

Lieber, Francis. *Instructions for the Government of Armies of the United States, in the Field.* New York: D. Van Nostrand, 1863.

Litwack, Leon F. *Been in the Storm So Long: The Aftermath of Slavery.* New York: Knopf, 1979.

Lowe, Richard. *Republicans and Reconstruction in Virginia, 1856–70.* Charlottesville: University of Virginia Press, 1991.

Majewski, John. *A House Dividing: Economic Development in Pennsylvania and Virginia before the Civil War.* New York: Cambridge University Press, 2000.

Mallory, Stephen R. "The Flight from Richmond." *Civil War Times Illustrated,* April 1972.

——. "The Last Days of the Confederate Government." In Peter Cozzens, ed., *Battles and Leaders of the Civil War,* vol. 5. Urbana: University of Illinois Press, 2002.

Manning, Chandra. *What This Cruel War Was Over: Soldiers, Slavery, and the Civil War.* New York: Knopf, 2007.

Marten, James. *The Children's Civil War.* Chapel Hill: University of North Carolina Press, 1998.

Marvel, William. *Lee's Last Retreat: The Flight to Appomattox.* Chapel Hill: University of North Carolina Press, 2002.

Massey, Mary Elizabeth. *Ersatz in the Confederacy: Shortages and Substitutes on the Southern Homefront.* 1952. Reprint, Columbia: University of South Carolina Press, 1993.

——. *Refugee Life in the Confederacy.* 1964. Reprint, Baton Rouge: Louisiana State University Press, 2001.

Mauro, Charles V. *The Civil War in Fairfax County: Civilians and Soldiers.* Charleston, S.C.: History Press, 2006.

McCarthy, Carlton. *Detailed Minutiae of Soldier Life in the Army of Northern Virginia, 1861–1865.* 1882. Reprint, Lincoln: University of Nebraska Press, 1993.

McConnell, John Preston. *Negroes and Their Treatment in Virginia from 1865 to 1867.* Pulaski, Va.: B. D. Smith and Brothers, 1910.

McDonald, Cornelia Peake. *A Woman's Civil War: A Diary, with Reminiscences of the War, from March 1862.* Edited by Minrose C. Gwin. Madison: University of Wisconsin Press, 1992.

McFall, F. Lawrence, Jr. *Danville in the Civil War.* Lynchburg, Va.: H. E. Howard, 2001.

McGuire, Judith White. *Diary of a Southern Refugee during the War, by a Lady of Virginia.* 3rd ed. Richmond: J. W. Randolph and English, 1889.

McMillen, Sally G. *Southern Women: Black and White in the Old South.* Arlington Heights, Ill.: Harlan Davidson, 1992.

Meade, Robert Douthat. *Judah P. Benjamin: Confederate Statesman.* New York: Oxford University Press, 1943.

Moore, Samuel J. T., Jr. *Moore's Complete Civil War Guide to Richmond.* Rev. ed. Richmond: Privately published, 1978.

Mott, Abigail. *Narratives of Colored Americans.* New York: William Wood, 1877.

Netherton, Nan, et al. *Fairfax County, Virginia: A History.* Fairfax, Va.: Fairfax City Board of Supervisors, 1978.

Newhall, F. C. *With General Sheridan in Lee's Last Campaign.* Philadelphia: Lippincott, 1866.

Nolen, Claude H. *African American Southerners in Slavery, Civil War, and Reconstruction.* Jefferson, N.C.: McFarland, 2005.

Owen, William Miller. *In Camp and Battle with the Washington Artillery of New Orleans.* Boston: Ticknor, 1885.

Paskoff, Paul F. "Measures of War: A Quantitative Examination of the Civil War's Destructiveness in the Confederacy." *Civil War History* 54 (March 2008).

Perdue, Charles L., Jr., Thomas E. Barden, and Robert K. Phillips, eds. *Weevils in the Wheat: Interviews with Virginia Ex-Slaves.* Charlottesville: University of Virginia Press, 1976.

Pfanz, Donald C. *The Petersburg Campaign: Abraham Lincoln at City Point, March 20–April 9, 1865.* Lynchburg, Va.: H. E. Howard, 1987.

Phillips, Jason. *Diehard Rebels: The Confederate Culture of Invincibility.* Athens: University of Georgia Press, 2007.

Poague, William Thomas. *Gunner with Stonewall: Reminiscences of William Thomas Poague.* Edited by Monroe F. Cockrell. 1957. Reprint, Lincoln: University of Nebraska Press, 1998.

Pollock, Edward. *Illustrated Sketch Book of Danville, Virginia: Its Manufactures and Commerce.* 1885. Reprint, Danville, Va.: Womack, 1976.

Power, J. Tracy. *Lee's Miserables: Life in the Army of Northern Virginia from the Wilderness to Appomattox.* Chapel Hill: University of North Carolina Press, 1998.

Pryor, Elizabeth Brown. *Reading the Man: A Portrait of Robert E. Lee through His Private Letters.* New York: Viking, 2007.

Pryor, Sara Agnes Rice. *Reminiscences of Peace and War.* New York: Macmillan, 1905.

Putnam, Sallie A. Brock. *Richmond during the War: Four Years of Personal Observations by a Richmond Lady.* New York: G. W. Carlton, 1867.

Quarles, Benjamin. *The Negro in the Civil War.* Boston: Little, Brown, 1953.

Rable, George C. *Civil Wars: Women and the Crisis of Southern Nationalism.* Urbana: University of Illinois Press, 1991.

——. "Despair, Hope, and Delusion: The Collapse of Confederate Morale Reexamined." In Mark Grimsley and Brooks D. Simpson eds., *The Collapse of the Confederacy.* Lincoln: University of Nebraska Press, 2001.

Reidy, Joseph P. "'Coming from the Shadow of the Past': The Transition from Slavery to Freedom at Freedmen's Village, 1863–1900." *Virginia Magazine of History and Biography* 95 (October 1987).

Richardson, Joe M. *Christian Reconstruction: The American Missionary Association and Southern Blacks, 1861–1890.* Athens: University of Georgia Press, 1986.

Ridley, Bromfield Lewis. *Battles and Sketches of the Army of Tennessee.* Mexico: Missouri Printing and Publishing, 1906.

Robertson, James I., Jr. *Civil War Sites in Virginia: A Tour Guide.* Charlottesville: University Press of Virginia, 1982.

——. *Soldiers Blue and Gray.* Columbia: University of South Carolina Press, 1988.

Rubin, Anne Sarah. *A Shattered Nation: The Rise and Fall of the Confederacy, 1861–1868.* Chapel Hill: University of North Carolina Press, 2005.

Sandburg, Carl. *Abraham Lincoln: The Prairie Years and the War Years.* New York: Harcourt, Brace, 1954.

Sefton, James E. *The United States Army and Reconstruction, 1865–1877.* Baton Rouge: Louisiana State University Press, 1967.

Selby, John G. *Virginians at War: The Civil War Experience of Seven Young Confederates.* Wilmington, Del.: Scholarly Resources, 2002.

Sheehan-Dean, Aaron. *Why Confederates Fought: Family and Nation in Civil War Virginia.* Chapel Hill: University of North Carolina Press, 2007.

Shingleton, Royce Gordon. *John Taylor Wood: Sea Ghost of the Confederacy.* Athens: University of Georgia Press, 1979.

Smith, Derek. *Lee's Last Stand: Sailor's Creek Virginia, 1865.* Shippensburg, Pa.: White Mane, 2002.

Spencer, Carrie Esther, Bernard Samuels, and Walter Berry Samuels, eds. *A Civil War Marriage in Virginia: Reminiscences and Letters.* Boyce, Va.: Carr, 1956.

Stephens, Alexander H. *Recollections of Alexander H. Stephens.* Edited by Myrta

Lockett Avary. 1910. Reprint, Baton Rouge: Louisiana State University Press, 1998.

Sterling, Dorothy, ed. *We Are Your Sisters: Black Women in the Nineteenth Century.* New York: Norton, 1984.

Stern, Philip Van Doren. *An End to Valor: The Last Days of the Civil War.* Boston: Houghton Mifflin, 1958.

Stevenson, Brenda E. *Life in Black and White: Family and Community in the Slave South.* New York: Oxford University Press, 1996.

Stoutamire, Albert. *Music of the Old South: Colony to Confederacy.* Rutherford, N.J.: Farleigh Dickinson University Press, 1972.

Sutherland, Daniel E. *Seasons of War: The Ordeal of a Confederate Community, 1861–1865.* New York: Free Press, 1995.

Swint, Henry Lee, ed. *Dear Ones at Home: Letters from Contraband Camps.* Nashville: Vanderbilt University Press, 1966.

Takagi, Midori. *"Rearing Wolves to Our Own Destruction": Slavery in Richmond, Virginia, 1782–1865.* Charlottesville: University of Virginia Press, 1999.

Taylor, Alrutheus Ambush. *The Negro in the Reconstruction of Virginia.* Washington, D.C.: Association for the Study of Negro Life and History, 1926.

Taylor, Walter H. *General Lee: His Campaigns in Virginia, 1861–1865.* Norfolk, Va.: Nusbaum Book and News, 1906.

Thomas, Emory M. *The Confederate State of Richmond: A Biography of the Capital.* Baton Rouge: Louisiana State University Press, 1998.

———. *Robert E. Lee: A Biography.* New York: Norton, 1995.

Torget, Andrew J., and Edward L. Ayers. *Two Communities in the Civil War.* New York: Norton, 2007.

Tremain, Henry Edwin. *Last Hours of Sheridan's Cavalry.* New York: Bonnell, Silvers and Bowers, 1904.

Tripp, Steven Elliott. *Yankee Town, Southern City: Race and Class Relations in Civil War Lynchburg.* New York: New York University Press, 1997.

U.S. Navy, Naval History Division. *Civil War Naval Chronology, 1861–1865.* Washington, D.C.: Government Printing Office, 1971.

U.S. War Department. *War of the Rebellion: A Compilation of the Official Records of the Union and Confederate Armies.* Washington, D.C.: Government Printing Office, 1880–1901.

Vandiver, Frank E. *Ploughshares into Swords: Josiah Gorgas and Confederate Ordnance.* Austin: University of Texas Press, 1952.

Wallenstein, Peter. *Cradle of America: Four Centuries of Virginia History.* Lawrence: University Press of Kansas, 2007.

Warfield, Edgar. *Manassas to Appomattox: The Civil War Memoirs of Pvt. Edgar Warfield, 17th Virginia Infantry.* 1936. Reprint, Mclean, Va.: EPM, 1996.

Waugh, Charles G., and Martin H. Greenberg, eds. *The Women's War in the South: Recollections and Reflections of the American Civil War.* Nashville: Cumberland House, 1999.

Wesley, Charles H., and Patricia W. Romero. *Negro Americans in the Civil War: From Slavery to Citizenship.* New York: Publishers Company, 1967.

West, George Benjamin. *When the Yankees Came: Civil War and Reconstruction on the Virginia Peninsula.* Edited by Parke Rouse Jr. Richmond: Dietz, 1977.

Wheless, John F. "The Confederate Treasure." *Southern Historical Society Papers* 10 (March 1882).

White, Charles W. *The Hidden and the Forgotten: Contributions of Buckingham Blacks to American History.* Marceline, Mo.: Walsworth, 1985.

Wiley, Bell Irvin. *Embattled Confederates: An Illustrated History of Southerners at War.* New York: Bonanza Books, 1964.

———. *Southern Negroes, 1861–1865.* New Haven, Conn.: Yale University Press, 1965.

Williams, Chad L. "Symbols of Freedom and Defeat: African American Soldiers, White Southerners, and the Christmas Insurrection Scare of 1865." In Gregory J. W. Urwin, ed., *Black Flag over Dixie: Racial Atrocities and Reprisals in the Civil War.* Carbondale: Southern Illinois University Press, 2004.

Williams, Edward B., ed. *Rebel Brothers: The Civil War Letters of the Truehearts.* College Station: Texas A&M University Press, 1995.

Wills, Brian Steel. *The War Hits Home: The Civil War in Southeastern Virginia.* Charlottesville: University of Virginia Press, 2001.

Wilson, Keith P. *Campfires of Freedom: The Camp Life of Black Soldiers during the Civil War.* Kent, Ohio: Kent State University Press, 2002.

Winik, Jay. *April 1865: The Month That Saved America.* New York: HarperCollins, 2001.

Wise, John S. *The End of an Era.* Edited by Curtis Carroll Davis. New York: Thomas Yoseloff, 1965.

Work Projects Administration. *The Negro in Virginia.* Winston-Salem, N.C.: John F. Blair, 1994.

Wyatt-Brown, Bertram. *The Shaping of Southern Culture: Honor, Grace, and War, 1760s–1880s.* Chapel Hill: University of North Carolina Press, 2001.

Index